Inside Citrix
The FlexCast Management Architecture

Bas van Kaam

Inside Citrix

Citrix, Citrix Systems, XenApp, XenDesktop, NetScaler, FlexCast Management Architecture, FlexCast, CloudBridge, StoreFront, CloudPortal, ICA, Framehawk, ThinWire and any other products and/or technologies that I might have left out regarding the Citrix portfolio, are all trademarks of Citrix Systems, Inc. and/or one or more of its subsidiaries, and may be registered in the United States Patent and Trademark Office and in other countries.

ISBN-13: 978-1530428526 / ISBN-10: 1530428521

2016 1ˢᵗ edition, version 1.0

Acknowledgements

Writing a book isn't something you do alone. Next to kind people who helped me review hundreds of pages, first and foremost I would like to thank my awesome and sweet girlfriend Tineke.

She thought it was a great idea right from the start and encouraged me to keep going even when I felt like quitting at a certain point (multiple times actually). While writing a book, and doing the research that comes with it is an awesome process all together, it is not something to be taken lightly.

Furthermore, I would like to thank my reviewers Erik Bakker - @Bakker_Erik, Esther Barthel - @virtuEs_IT, Kees Baggerman - @KBaggerman, Tobias Kreidl - @t_kreidl, Marius Sandbu - @msandbu, Geert Braakhekke - @Easi123, Martin Zugec - @MartinZugec and Mick Glover - @XDtipster

Your help is greatly appreciated!

A special thanks goes out to Martin, Erik and Tobias, as they were all very detailed and thorough in their work and took on hundreds of pages each. The result wouldn't be the same without your help.

I would also like to thank the people over at ProofProfessor - @ProofProfessor, for taking care of copy-editing and proofreading my manuscript. They were very professional and a pleasure to work with. Do note that I have made multiple changes and textual additions after I received back my manuscript. Therefore any errors you might stumble upon are not necessarily their fault, I've done the best I can.

And last but most certainly not least, a big thank you to my employer the Detron ICT Group - www.detron.nl - for facilitating me with some of the resources enabling me to successfully write this book.

Interested in purchasing larger (25+) quantities? Contact me directly via basvankaam.com

Contents

Images index

Tables index

A short introduction

About the author

My name is Bas (Sebastiaan, actually) van Kaam, I am 37 years of age and I live in a town called IJm_iiden, which is located in Noord Holland, The Netherlands. I started out in IT as a Helpdesk Support Technician about 16 years ago. From there I worked my way up to engineering and architecting mostly by attending (countless) seminars, webinars, IT-orientated congresses and through self-study courses, all of which I still enjoy and do today.

I started focusing on the Citrix portfolio just over three years ago (although I had been involved in Citrix-related projects before that) and around January 1st 2013 I founded my own personal website/blog over at basvankaam.com where around 75% of my articles are Citrix-related.

I am employed as a Senior Management Consultant working for the Detron ICT Group, one of the leading SBC & VDI consultancy companies in The Netherlands. I am involved in various technical as well as non-technical projects throughout the year, and from a technical point of view I specialise in designing, building, maintaining, troubleshooting and optimising SBC & VDI-oriented infrastructures (mostly Citrix) for mid-sized and larger companies.

As an occasional public speaker I have presented at several national as well as international events throughout 2015, and I will continue to do so going forward. I currently own all major Microsoft and Citrix certifications and I have been recognised as a Citrix Technology Professional (CTP class of 2016), and a Nutanix Technology Champion (NTC), as well as a Subject

Matter Expert (SME) for my contributions to the latest XenDesktop / XenApp 7.6 exams.

I also really like the community and as such I was thrilled to find out that Citrix founded the CUGC platform (@myCUGC on Twitter & https://www.mycugc.org online) not that long ago (May 2015) which has turned out to be a great success. So if you have not done so already, give them a visit and sign up!

On a more personal note I love spending time with my two kids Julia and Sophie, and my girlfriend Tineke. Besides technology I am also passionate about sports, running and CrossFit in particular, and I like to set myself ambitious but realisable goals throughout the year, something at which I succeed (almost) every time.

Follow me on Twitter @BasvanKaam, check me out on Linked-in: https://nl.linkedin.com/in/basvankaam,
and/or read what else I have to say over at basvankaam.com.

Thank you!

Why this book

During the past three years I have written a lot of articles on XenApp, XenDesktop and the IMA (Independent Management Architecture) as well as on the FMA (FlexCast Management Architecture) with the introduction of 7.x platform. Some were high-level, some deep dives, and a few in between.

Most of my articles are based on and written around publicly available information, my own experiences, those of other community members and with a little help from Citrix every now and again, though I never shared any NDA information nor will I do so now.

It goes without saying that I am far from the only one: there are tons of excellent resources out there free for you to read and learn from. In fact, I'll make sure to include a list of community resources near the end of this book.

The only issue with this, although that's probably too big a word, is that most information is scattered over the Internet and you will probably have to visit multiple sites and resources to find what you are looking for. Even when multiple articles covering the same and/or related subject(s) can be found on the same website you will be in for a search.

And while this isn't too big a deal (I mean, most content is written and published during out-of-work hours, meaning someone has sacrificed his or her spare time for this, so who are we to complain?) I just like it when things are organised, so that's what I am trying to achieve here as well. All things FMA and related content bundled into one resource for your convenience, hopefully.

Who is it for?

I have made at least one serious attempt to write a book on Citrix-related technology. Unfortunately I wasn't able to finish it. One of the main reasons for this was the topic I chose, Citrix XenMobile. Seriously, whenever I finished a section or chapter something had already changed or Citrix would have at least announced a new release within the coming weeks.

Of course this all helped (and it still does) in getting XenMobile to where it is today, which is great. However, for me it was very frustrating and counterproductive. In the end I decided to call it a day and use some of the material I had written up until then for some detailed blog posts.

Now, with the FMA it is another story. Although the FMA itself is constantly being improved (especially now that XenApp has been added, see below as well) the basics remain, or most of them anyway. During the last 14 to 16 months I have spent quite some time getting to know certain parts of the FMA. Knowledge I would like to share with you today.

Do note that, **and this is important**, Citrix recently announced a quarterly release cycle regarding both XenDesktop and XenApp. As such I will not be able to provide you with all the latest features and functionalities. In fact, chances are that when this book becomes available there will already be a new edition on the market, 7.9 or perhaps 8.0 even, who knows. But that's the way it is. While unfortunate, I don't foresee any big changes regarding the underlying architecture (FMA). Just keep an eye on basvankaam.com where I will make sure to share any new and relevant information regarding both products and the FMA in particular.

If you are (relatively) new to XenApp / XenDesktop and the FlexCast Management Architecture this book will definitely be helpful. If you have been working with XenApp and/or XenDesktop for some time now but you would like to know a bit more about the ins and outs, this book will probably answer most of your questions as well.

Since I have been writing about the FlexCast Management Architecture for a while now, I have a pretty good understanding of which topics are of interest to my readers, which really helps.

I have also spoken to numerous community folk and readers of my blog who told me that my writing helps them in getting things a bit more organised with regard to troubleshooting, for example. So even if you know all this stuff already and you are a XenApp/XenDesktop/FMA veteran, this book might still come in handy as a reference, or a fun read at the very least. Take your pick.

Scope

Throughout the next 25 chapters I will talk about what the FlexCast Management Architecture is, its foundation, the (main) components and concepts involved, as well as any (closely) related technologies and products that might or might not be optional. I will primarily focus on the main concepts and mechanisms that make up the FMA from an architectural point of view.

As mentioned in the previous 'Why this book?' section, all information shared in this book is based on publicly available information, my own experiences, those of others and a little help from Citrix here and there. However, since I'm not employed by Citrix and don't have any access to company product information, this is all I have. But trust me, I will make sure to include something for everybody. From the basics and beyond to deeper dives where applicable.

Other (closely related) topics will include Citrix printing, the user logon process, resource enumeration & launch (what happens inside the FMA), troubleshooting and more. Topics that you as a Citrix Administrator / Architect have to deal with on a daily basis. Other sub- and/or related components and technologies will vary with regard to the details shared. There is just so much to cover it's nearly impossible to get to the same level of detail on every subject.

I also don't want to steer too far away from the main topic, the FMA. Of course when new (relevant) information becomes available I won't hesitate to share this with you on basvankaam.com, keeping this project a 'work in progress'.

All major, minor and/or optional FMA components will be discussed. However, this book is not meant as an install-and-configure manual, nor will it be a how-to guide. Instead I want to dig deeper into the concepts and technologies that make up and surround the Citrix FlexCast Management Architecture, the true foundation of XenDesktop and XenApp.

As we progress I will also touch on some of the minor or 'less significant' features (although that depends on your point of view of course) along the way. Finally, I will conclude each (technical) section and/or chapter with a list of key takeaways that might be helpful when designing, implementing, troubleshooting or maintaining Citrix XenDesktop / XenApp-based infrastructures.

FMA fact: Also keep an eye out for the FMA fact columns (looking like this one) throughout the book. I have included over 100 of them.

Existing content from basvankaam.com will be included as well. However, all content will be closely reviewed and rewritten where needed. I just felt it would be a waste not to do anything *extra* with all that I have produced up till now.

While I would advice you to read through the first two to three chapters first, after that it doesn't really matter. Each chapter stands on its own and can be treated as such. However, as a result you may find a small overlap between chapters with regard to the information shared, this will be minimal though. You will find references to other sections and/or chapters where applicable.

Is this all still relevant?

Let me explain what I mean by this. Today more and more companies are looking into cloud computing as a potential platform, or alternative to host their company workloads and data, including RDSH and VDI-based architectures. For example, with the Citrix Workspace Cloud (CWC) emerging, IT admins and architects can select and deliver complete Citrix-orientated workspaces (as a service) from any cloud with just a few mouse clicks without having to design, manually install or update anything.

While there might still be some work left on your on-premises or cloud-based VDAs, although Citrix Lifecycle Management can help with this as well, it is getting easier by the day.

So why bother with learning the ins and outs when it comes to XenApp and/or XenDesktop, FMA-based environments? A fair question, and of course CWC is just one example of a so-called PaaS (Platform as a Service) offering: there are multiple.

Next to PaaS we also have IaaS (Infrastructure as a Service) or DaaS (Desktop as a Service) and finally SaaS (Software as a Service): these are all cloud-based services which allow us to get up and running quickly without too much hassle, or at least so it seems.

If you have a look at the overview on the next page you will see a couple, or most, of the cloud options we have today. The darker grey fields indicate what will still need to be managed by our own IT departments.

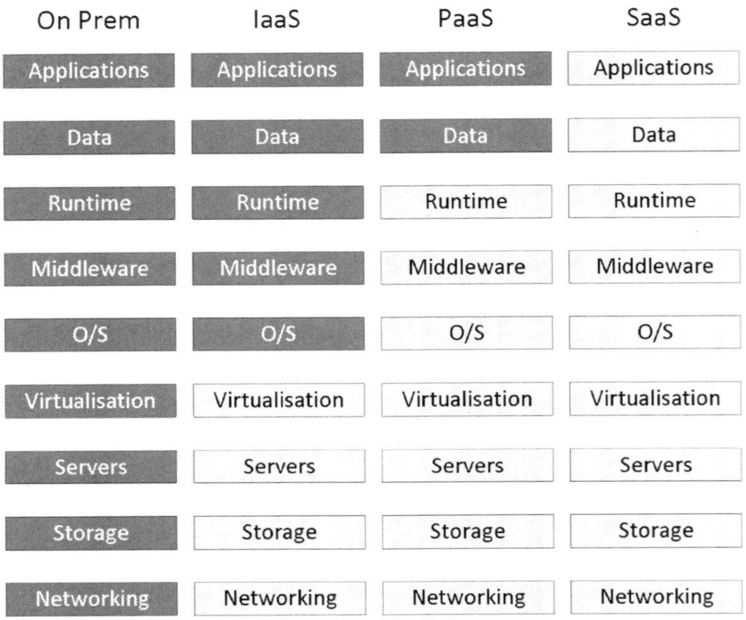

On Prem	IaaS	PaaS	SaaS
Applications	Applications	Applications	Applications
Data	Data	Data	Data
Runtime	Runtime	Runtime	Runtime
Middleware	Middleware	Middleware	Middleware
O/S	O/S	O/S	O/S
Virtualisation	Virtualisation	Virtualisation	Virtualisation
Servers	Servers	Servers	Servers
Storage	Storage	Storage	Storage
Networking	Networking	Networking	Networking

Figure 1: Cloud services overview

While the 'the cloud' is becoming more popular by the day, I don't believe that most companies will have moved their (entire) on-premises datacentres into the cloud within, let's say, five to ten years from now. A lot might and thousands already have, sure, but far from all.

And even if they will there are multiple cloud flavours to choose from. I think most will agree that hybrid solutions and/or architectures will be the way forward, especially when it comes to the virtual desktop / workplace. The reasons for this will of course differ per company and use case, but to give you an idea…

- Company (-sensitive) data will always be an issue. Where is it stored, who has access etc.
- Not all applications function well, or well enough, when physically separated from their data.
- Authentication. A lot of companies do not want user authentication to take place in 'the cloud'. Although this isn't always the case technically, this can be a tough one to get across/explain.
- Trust. Not only with regard to company data as mentioned above, but also regarding uptime, security breaches, SLAs, responsibilities etc. And what about performance and the overall user experience?
- Exit strategy. Companies are often worried that as soon as they have made the leap into 'the cloud' they can't undo it. Or that it will be costly to do so.
- Control. A lot of companies do not want to rely on a third-party handling their infrastructure, data and/or applications. They want to be able to have full control when they want or need it.
- Internet connections. Your Internet connection(s) will become vital. For some it feels like putting all of their eggs into one basket.
- Costs. Hosting your infrastructure/data centre in the cloud isn't cheap (at least not today). Also, making the transitions from on-premises to the cloud takes time, testing and careful planning. It's not something you do overnight.
- Security. The bigger cloud providers are not more secure by default. Sure, on average they invest more when it comes to security, but the bigger you are the more interesting you become. And eventually they will find a way.

- SaaS solutions are great, but they will only get you so far. We're still dealing with tons of legacy (Windows) applications for many more years to come.
- The same applies to DaaS. For a lot of companies DaaS will be a great fit. However, there will also be a bunch of companies for which DaaS will be too restrictive or limited with regard to what they can do or control themselves.
- Besides all this, unless you go with a SaaS or DaaS solution, some monitoring, ongoing management, configuration tasks and troubleshooting will always be needed, even with CWC.
- If supporting and managing your own on-premises virtual desktops / data centre is or becomes easier, cheaper and more flexible than its cloud counterpart, well… You have options.

These are a few reasons why companies might choose to stay with their on-premises datacentres or will only partly leverage cloud resources going forward.

I know I am making this all sound fairly negative, which is not my intention at all. The cloud offers just as many, if not more, advantages, and if we look at recent developments we can see that tens of thousands of companies have already made the transition and many more are on their way. I'm just saying that it is not for everybody, at least not the full package.

And if we fast-forward five to ten years from now I think there will still be plenty of on-premises and cloud-based data centres hosting RDSH and VDI (FMA) architectures for us to manage and maintain.

Another example is IaaS, which also tends to be a popular approach nowadays. Here you will still need to setup, configure and manage your own servers / Operating Systems. XenApp and/or XenDesktop would still need to be installed configured and managed by your local admin crew as well, including any data and applications, and this (configuration and ongoing management) goes for PaaS solutions as well, by the way. And what if something goes wrong? You would still need to troubleshoot. Of course the same rules apply when going hybrid: it certainly helps if you know how all components and services interact.

Even when you are not responsible for managing, upgrading and/or troubleshooting (when needed) your company's infrastructure, all this can still be valuable, fun and useful information.

So that is why I say, **YES** all this is still relevant!

Key takeaways

- When talking about cloud computing remember that there are multiple cloud services to choose from: it is not a one-size-fits-all solution.
- Even when moving your entire on-premises infrastructure (or the biggest part) might be beneficial in the long run, it will still take careful planning and execution to get there.
- Start small and take it from there. Hybrid solutions are the way forward, think CWC, for example.
- A lot of companies benefit by leveraging the cloud for Burst Capacity and backup.
- Don't forget about printing and scanning when hosting your RDSH / VDI-based infrastructure in the cloud (bandwidth limitations).
- True VDI (or DaaS) from the cloud, and with this I mean virtual machines with a desktop Operating System installed, assigned on a one-to-one basis, are still hard to achieve. This is mainly because of Microsoft's licensing restrictions.
- Most DaaS solutions are based on RDSH / XenApp in the back-end, meaning you will share your 'desktop' with multiple users.
- The cloud will no doubt have a major impact on how we configure and manage our future infrastructures going forward. However, on-premises RDSH and VDI infrastructures are here to stay for at least another five to ten years, if not longer (my guess is longer).

The evolution of the FMA

As it stands today, I think most of you know that both XenDesktop and XenApp are built on top of the FlexCast Management Architecture, or FMA in short. And if not, you do now. Of course this didn't happen overnight. XenApp became part of the FMA back in June 2013, the 26th to be exact, when Citrix launched XenDesktop 7.0 (previously known under the code name Excalibur).

It marked the date that Citrix decided XenApp would no longer be sold as a separate product and would from then on be part of XenDesktop. Although this might have come as a surprise to some, the FMA was always known to be the next generation architecture, providing enhanced scalability, robustness and manageability over the IMA. And while in its early days the FMA was a VDI only platform it has slowly but surely evolved to now also support RDSH (hosted shared desktops) as well as hosted / published applications, and tons of other enhancements and features.

This change also meant that any further developments around XenApp 6.5 (and the IMA) would stop as well: no more additional feature packs (with one exception) or other types of enhancements going forward. As a final gesture, together with XenDesktop 7 they also released Feature Pack 2 for XenApp 6.5. Of course this announcement got a LOT of attention and unfortunately for Citrix not in a good way, I'm sure most of you can remember.

On the other hand, it did help in getting the FMA a lot more attention: suddenly Citrix-minded IT folks were aware that there was more than just the IMA, though they probably knew already. And I don't mean this in a bad way. As you might or might not know, the FMA originated with the second big XenDesktop release, which was version 5.0 back in December 2010, the 17th, and stayed with XenDesktop until the 7.0 release – *and forward* – as mentioned. XenDesktop 4.0 (and previous versions) released earlier in 2009 was still primarily based on the IMA.

As a side note, while the Citrix archives do not mention any of this – at least I wasn't able to find any related information – the true birth of XenDesktop actually started with 'Citrix Desktop Server', which back then wasn't considered to be enterprise-worthy by most and only provided some basic VDI features. It was quickly replaced by Citrix XenDesktop 2.0 (IMA-based technology), introducing Citrix's PortICA technology, a huge leap forward. This was around 2008.

At that time (around the release of XenDesktop 7.0) if you were a diehard XenApp administrator who had nothing to do with XenDesktop, the FMA was unknown territory. And now that XenApp was suddenly a part of the FMA as well, some learning had to be done. As you probably know by now, configuring and administering XenApp in 6.5 was, or is, completely different from XenApp as part of XenDesktop in 7.x, and thus FMA.

No matter if XenApp would stay part of XenDesktop or might become available as a separate product in the future, it was now based on the FMA instead of the IMA, period. So you could say that technically, at least for some, there was a challenge no matter what. But the transition from IMA to FMA was just the first hurdle; unfortunately more would follow.

Customers and features

Citrix is known to change its product names from time to time: I'm not telling you anything new here. What is particular hard and annoying about this is explaining these (constant) changes to our customers. The same thing happened here. What? No more XenApp? Why? What do we do now? What about support? I'm sure we can all laugh about it now but that wasn't the case not too long ago.

XenApp is now part of the FMA: great. And if you want to be able to leverage, let's say Windows Server 2012, you will need to upgrade to at least XenDesktop App edition (more on this in a minute) which is fine as well, but what about session Pre-Launch, Lingering, SSO, Power and Capacity Management, Smart Auditor, Zones, Failover policies, Shadowing users and a whole bunch of other features that we (can) currently use in our XenApp deployment?

When compared to XenApp 6.5 there were a ton of features missing, something that Citrix addressed with a phased approach where every new XenDesktop / XenApp edition introduced new features into the FMA, which in some cases were already there in XenApp 6.5. Again, it's ok now, but back then most people weren't too happy about all this.

Having said that, let's not forget that the FMA was basically designed with VDI in mind, period. Technologies and concepts like RDSH (XenApp) and application publishing needed to be built in from scratch. And looking at XenDesktop / XenApp 7.8 today I think they did a really good job.

What about licensing?

With the introduction of XenDesktop 7.0 (and the disappearance of XenApp) Citrix introduced a new type of license under the name XenDesktop App Edition (in addition to the XenDesktop VDI, Enterprise and Platinum licenses). This replaced the 'old' XenApp 6.5 licenses and would offer XenApp features exclusively, or at least that was the general thought behind it. And while this sounds great on paper, in practice it didn't go down very well. In one of their earlier announcements regarding XenDesktop 7.0 licensing, Citrix told us:

> XenApp Enterprise and Platinum customers with active Subscription Advantage can update to this (XenDesktop app) edition at no additional charge and migrate their environments at their own pace.

What they were basically saying was: if you have an active Subscription Advantage but are running XenApp Advanced edition you are out of luck and need to purchase new (XenDesktop Enterprise or Platinum) licenses.

Otherwise these customers would be stuck with IMA, not able to use Windows Server 2012 R2, including some of the other advantages that the FMA brought to the table, a bad marketing move to say the least. Customers, most anyway, couldn't care less about the underlying architecture. All they wanted was, or is, a cost-effective and robust solution that just works.

We love XenApp!

Luckily Citrix paid attention, as they are known to do, and listened. First they assured customers who were running XenApp 6.5 Advanced edition that a separate license Trade-Up Program would be established. Although I never found any specifics on this, soon after I didn't really care because, as if it had never left, they brought back XenApp!

Later that year on March the 26th 2014, Citrix reinstated and officially released XenApp and XenDesktop 7.5 as separate products and downloads, including support for Web Interface! Still based on the FMA and some features missing, but at least now most were happy. To be honest, this was more marketing than anything else: technically nothing changed.

You still download the same bits and bytes, and depending on your license you either install XenApp or XenDesktop, which would then include everything from RDSH to VDI. What about our customers? Now that they finally understood that XenApp was (supposed to be) gone and that its functionality and features were part of XenDesktop, we had to start all over again. At least now we knew this would be the last time. Right, Citrix?

In fact, they even did one better during Citrix Synergy back in May 2015. It was there that they announced extended support for XenApp 6.5. This meant that the end of maintenance for XenApp 6.5 was moved from February 24, 2016, to December 31, 2017, and the actual end of life moved from August 24, 2016, to June 30, 2018. But only for customers who deploy Feature Pack 3 for XenApp 6.5, which was announced as well. A great applause followed.

Dates and differences

Below you will find a recap of some of the most important dates regarding the FMA evolution until now, followed by a brief overview highlighting some of the biggest and main differences that come with the introduction of the FMA compared to the IMA.

- November the 16th 2009. Citrix officially releases XenDesktop 4.0. Still IMA-based.
- December the 17th 2010. Citrix officially releases XenDesktop 5.0. FMA 1.0.
- June the 26th 2013. Citrix officially releases XenDesktop 7.0, including XenApp. FMA 2.0.
- March the 26th 2014. Citrix officially releases XenDesktop and XenApp 7.5 again, as separate products. FMA 2.0.
- September 30th 2015. Citrix officially releases XenDesktop and XenApp 7.6. FMA 3.0.
- December 28th 2015. Citrix officially releases XenDesktop and XenApp 7.7. FMA 3.0.
- February 25th 2016. Citrix officially releases XenDesktop and XenApp 7.8. FMA 3.0.

The FlexCast Management Architecture is a .NET-based services-orientated architecture built upon the WCF (Windows Communication Foundation) framework, which is used for building service-orientated applications consisting of a deployment model built up of controllers (and agents) running multiple highly available stateless services, as you will soon find out. As mentioned, the FMA as we know it today was first introduced with XenDesktop 5; before that, XenDesktop was still primarily based on the IMA. Over time the FMA has evolved from 6 services in its first release back in 2010 to 11 services today (2016) all of which we will have a closer look at throughout the next chapters.

The general idea

Please note. Although I do mention several components and concepts related to the IMA (Independent Management Architecture), I won't go into any further detail. I assume you have at least a basic understanding of the IMA and how it operates. If you are still somewhat unfamiliar with some of the FMA jargon used in the upcoming section and perhaps previous sections, don't worry: during the next chapters I will go over each component, service, technology and concept in more detail.

Next to the earlier mentioned services, the FlexCast Management Architecture is primarily made up of Delivery Controllers and Agents (Virtual Delivery Agents) or VDAs. Delivery Agents are installed on all virtual and/or physical machines managed / provisioned by XenDesktop and/or XenApp 7.x. They directly communicate (and register themselves) with the Delivery Controller(s) and the license server.

The Delivery Controllers in their turn communicate with the Central Site database (Microsoft SQL only), StoreFront, Studio and the underlying Host Connection (your Hypervisor or cloud-based platform of choice, you can configure multiple). With the transition from the IMA to the FMA, the database has become more important.

Next to static information like XenDesktop Site policies, Machine Catalogs, Delivery Groups and published applications and/or (hosted) desktops, it also contains all live dynamic 'runtime' data like: who is connected to which resource, on which server including current server load and connection statistics used to make load-balance decisions.

Although Connection Leasing (which will be discussed in more detail) does a reasonable job in connecting users to their last-used resources (during the last two weeks by default) when the Central Site Database is down, implementing an HA SQL set-up is still recommended.

Without Connection Leasing in place, when the Central Site database becomes unresponsive or unreachable altogether, existing connections will continue to work but new sessions cannot be established/brokered. And like with the IMA, no Site-wide configuration changes are possible.

Architectural changes

Initially when XenApp was released (2013) as part of the FMA, some significant and fundamental changes took place on the underlying architecture: some permanent, some not. To name a few, up to XenDesktop / XenApp 7.6 Zones were no longer optional, in fact, they were gone altogether. All we had were separate (complete) Sites including a mandatory HA SQL set-up per Site: not ideal.

This also meant no more Zone preference (failover) policies, Local Host Cache (LHC) and Load Balance policies were now applied at Site level. Oh, and did I mention that Worker Groups were taken from us as well? Luckily with the release of version 7.7 Zones were reintroduced (no Worker Groups and LHC, though). However, note that these new types of Zones work differently from what we are used to with XenApp 6.5.

Another example would be power management, especially from a XenApp perspective; this is still far from ideal even within 7.8. Other fundamental and permanent changes include no more IMA protocol and service: these are now replaced by the earlier mentioned VDAs (Virtual Delivery Agents), which are installed on Session Hosts' physical and virtual servers and desktops. A much more lightweight approach as opposed to the IMA (where XenApp was basically installed on each system) even when compared to the former 'Session only mode' in XenApp 6.5, more on this as we progress.

The FMA supports multiple Operating Systems like Windows Server 2012 R2 and Windows 8, 8.1 and 10, and the best thing is you can configure multiple Machine Catalogs with different Operating Systems. Which is different from XenApp 6.5 where the whole Farm needed to run the same server OS. Also, the Delivery Controller can run a different OS to the Session Hosts / VDAs it will communicate with.

While most of these changes primarily impacted XenApp, some impacted XenDesktop as well – positively, I might add. The FMA was always designed with VDI in mind so when XenApp was added, as mentioned some fundamental architectural changes were needed.

Today this means that, depending on your license, you will install either XenApp and/or XenDesktop, with XenDesktop giving us the full suite of options including hosted shared desktops, published applications and the ability to auto-provision server machines using MCS and/or PVS, things we couldn't do before. And of course the same applies to Zones, a first for XenDesktop.

No more separate infrastructures for desktops and applications, it is one install, architecture and console (Citrix Studio) to meet all of your delivery needs. It includes several workflows, which simplify and speed up the process of delivering (virtual) desktops, hosted shared desktops and applications to users. Delivery Agents in XenDesktop / XenApp 7.x are configured via policies. Any combination of Active Directory GPOs, the Studio console (HDX Policies) and local GPO settings can be used.

A new VDA

Citrix also had to come up with a new type of VDA, one for server Operating Systems. The one they had now was exclusively designed for desktop machines. The biggest difference between the two VDAs is the underlying ICA protocol stack. For desktop machines, a single-user ICA stack (a.k.a. PortICA) is used which allows only one ICA session at a time. It includes additional HDX features such as USB and Aero redirection, which are only available on a single-user machine. For server machines, Citrix now includes a multi-user ICA stack extending the Windows Remote Desktop Services with the HDX/ICA protocol. This is basically the same ICA protocol stack as developed for Citrix XenApp (6.5 and earlier releases) with some technical adjustments to make it compatible with XenDesktop / XenApp FMA Delivery Controllers. Both will be discussed in more detail at a later stage.

FMA fact: There is also a Linux-based VDA.

While the FMA is under constant development, bringing back XenApp specific features and extending the reach of XenDesktop, this also helps in making the FMA the most flexible and robust platform known today: everybody wins.

FlexCast Delivery technology

FlexCast, a core part of the FMA, offers you several delivery models (methods to deliver an application or desktop to your users). It is designed to support all types of workers (as Citrix likes to call them) out there. For example, Task Workers access a small set of applications, but at the same time they interact with customers, partners and employees. As a result they have access to critical data. A local virtual machine might be the best solution: this is where FlexCast comes in.

Another example, so-called Road Warriors, need access to their desktop from anywhere. Here a hosted VDI or hosted shared desktop might do the trick, again... FlexCast! Of course, it's all up to you: you decide which model best suits the use case at hand! It is more of a strategy for delivering desktop and applications than anything else. FlexCast offers you the following desktop delivery models:

- Hosted shared desktops, non-persistent.
- Hosted VDI, random non-persistent, static non-persistent and static persistent.
- Remote PC (physical PCs only).
- Streamed VHD, PVS.
- Local (existing) virtual machines.
- On-demand (published) applications.

To finalise I'll include an overview (see next page) of all major components available within the IMA vs. the FMA. Be aware that not every component and/or concept delivers the same features and/or functionalities as its counterpart.

Note: To avoid any further confusion, as of now where I say XenDesktop I also mean XenApp and vice versa as part of the same FlexCast Management Architecture.

Table 1: IMA vs. FMA

IMA back then:	FMA as it is today:
IMA – Independent Management Architecture	FMA – FlexCast Management Architecture
Farm	Site
Data Collector	Delivery Controller
Zones	Zones (as of version 7.7)
Local Host Cache	Connection Leasing
Session Host / XenApp server	Virtual Delivery Agent (VDA)
Delivery Services Console / App Center	Citrix Studio and Director
EdgeSight monitoring	Partly built into Director
Application folders	Application folders and Tags
Worker Groups	Machine Catalogs / Delivery Groups
IMA Datastore	Central Site database (SQL only)
Load evaluators	Load-managed policies
IMA protocol and services	Virtual Delivery Agents
Farm Administrators	Delegated Site Administrators

Citrix Receiver	Citrix Receiver X1
Smart Auditor	Session recording
Shadowing	Microsoft Remote Assistance (Director)
USB 2.0 support	USB 3.0 support
Pre-launch and Lingering	Pre-launch and Lingering
Power and Capacity Management	Basic power management from the GUI – advanced via PowerShell
Web Interface / StoreFront	Web Interface / StoreFront
Single Sign-On for all or most applications	For Windows / domain logon only. Configured using a combination of StoreFront, Receiver and policies
Installed Hotfixes inventory	Installed Hotfixes inventory from Studio
Windows Server 2003, 2008 R2	Windows Server 2008 R2, 2012 R2, 2016
Published applications	Published applications
Hosted shared desktops	Hosted shared desktops plus VDI

Key takeaways

- Both XenApp and XenDesktop are built and based on the FlexCast Management Architecture (FMA). And I am pretty sure it will stay like this for many more years to come.
- The FMA was first introduced with XenDesktop version 5.0 back in December 2010. Before that, XenDesktop was also based on the Independent Management Architecture (IMA).
- XenApp became part of the FMA on June 26 2013, which was the official GA date of XenDesktop 7.0.
- The FMA was initially built with VDI in mind.
- This also meant that XenApp was no longer available as a separate product and that they (Citrix) also decided to stop any further development regarding 6.5.
- Luckily, Citrix listened and reintroduced XenApp and XenDesktop as separate products with the release of version 7.5. I don't think they will make a mistake like that again.
- With the addition of XenApp to the FMA, a new (server) VDA was needed.
- The FMA was always meant to be the next generation architecture, providing enhanced scalability, robustness, flexibility and manageability over the IMA.

The FMA, its foundation

The FlexCast Management Architecture is a Microsoft .NET-based architecture built upon the WCF (Windows Communication Foundation) framework. It is a framework used specifically for building service-orientated applications like XenDesktop / FMA, consisting of a deployment model based on Controllers running multiple highly available (stateless) services. WCF is also referred to as a Microsoft software development platform. As per Microsoft:

> WCF is a runtime and a set of APIs (Application Program Interfaces) for creating systems that send messages between services and clients. The same infrastructure and APIs are used to create applications that communicate with other applications on the same computer system or on a system that resides in another company and is accessed over the Internet.

Microsoft's .NET

One of the main reasons why we refer to the FMA as being a .NET-based architecture is because it is built and based on WCF. In fact, the WCF framework itself is built using the Microsoft .NET framework: confusing, right? Let me break it down a little further.

The Microsoft .NET framework is a software framework developed by Microsoft during the late-1990s. The first Beta of .NET was released in late-2000. In simple terms it provides language interoperability across multiple programming languages within a single platform. It does this by including a large Class Library, known as the Framework Class Library (FCL), which holds a collection of reusable classes, interfaces and value types used for writing / programming applications.

Applications which are written for, or use, the Microsoft .NET framework are executed in a software environment known as the Common Language Runtime, or CRL in short. The CRL is the virtual machine component of the .NET Framework and it manages the execution of applications written using the .NET Framework (regardless of the programming language used). Also known as .NET programmes.

When an application is executed a process called just-in-time compilation kicks in and converts the compiled code (used for programming / coding the application) into machine instructions, which will then be executed by the CPU residing in the virtual machine (CRL) mentioned earlier. Next to all this the CRL provides additional services in the form of garbage collection, memory management, type safety and a few more.

In short, the .NET Framework can be used to develop/code .NET-based applications using (at least) the following languages: Visual Basic, Visual C#, Visual F# and Visual C++. These can be either GUI (Graphical User Interface) or command-line-based applications as well as ASP.NET, web forms and XML Web services. And last but not least, we have Microsoft Visual Studio, which is the Graphical User Interface from where all coding and programming can be done.

Virtual Studio + .NET + WCF equals?

But wait, there's more. Visual Studio uses a Microsoft software development platform as its base. In the case of the FMA, we've already established that it is built upon WCF, which is also one of Microsoft's software development platforms.

Let's take one step back and résumé, shall we? First we have the .NET Framework, which can be used to develop or programme .NET-based applications. WCF is built using, and based on, the .NET Framework, while Visual Studio uses WCF as its base development platform from where the FMA or XenDesktop is created. Let's visualise.

Figure 2: Foundation overview

I am aware that this all may sound a bit abstract but hopefully it does give you a basic understanding of how it all fits together and how XenDesktop, or the FMA, was born just a couple of years ago.

Key takeaways

- The FlexCast Management Architecture is a Microsoft dot-net-based architecture built upon the WCF (Windows Communication Foundation) framework.
- The WCF framework itself is built using the Microsoft .NET framework.
- Dot-net-based applications are executed in a software environment known as the Common Language Runtime, or CRL.
- The .NET Framework supports the following programming languages: Visual Basic, Visual C#, Visual F# and Visual C++.
- Citrix offers several SDKs and APIs, plus some additional tools and services to help you build and integrate custom-developed monitoring and management solutions.
- Citrix has its own Citrix Developer Visual Studio Extension free for you to download.
- Google for 'Citrix developer overview' and you are good to go.

FMA main and optional components

The FMA, main components

Whether you are administrating, designing, building, optimising or troubleshooting an existing or new XenDesktop environment/architecture, it's important to know which components and services are involved, how they interact, and what is supposed to happen under normal circumstances.

Only then will you be able to quickly pinpoint any potential issues, or optimise current data flows and keep your users happy. The same applies when designing a completely new XenDesktop and/or XenApp Site; you need to have a good understanding of what is needed under which circumstances.

From a high-level perspective the FMA is built up around nine main components; however, it is within these components that the real magic happens. Take the services that make up the Delivery Controllers and VDAs, for example, but also technologies like Framehawk and ThinWire, Connection Leasing, Zones and concepts like Delivery Groups and Machine Catalogs, your Host Connections and so on.

Although each component and concept will be individually discussed (this will be the biggest chapter by far), as mentioned this book is not meant as an install-and-configure manual and as such I will not cover all aspects and configuration options and/or functionalities available per component / technology. Instead I will focus on the infrastructural side of things and provide you with a more than basic understanding of how all these components and services fit together.

Consider this chapter a warm-up.

The nine main FMA components are:

1. Delivery Controller.
2. Virtual Delivery Agent.
3. StoreFront.
4. Central Site database.
5. Receiver.
6. Studio.
7. Director.
8. License server.
9. Host Connection.

A XenDesktop Site

Before we get into the main FMA components, I would first like to start with a short definition of a XenDesktop / XenApp Site, since this is where all of our main and subcomponents will reside. It encompasses all Delivery Controllers, VDAs, Host Connections and all other components and technologies needed to host and virtualise our desktops and applications, which can then be managed and maintained as a single entity from Citrix Studio. See the image on the next page.

FMA fact: Active Directory is required for the authentication and authorisation of users in a Citrix environment. This includes DNS.

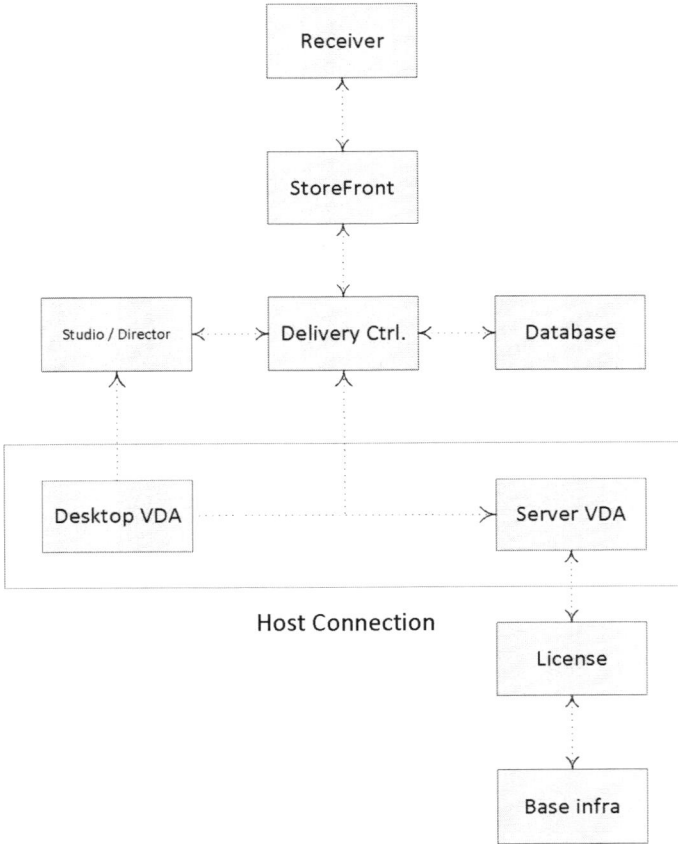

Figure 3: XenDesktop Site main components

Delivery Controller

While this chapter will provide you with a global overview, the chapters 'The FMA Core services' and 'The user login process' will discuss in detail all of the primary FMA services, their individual tasks and responsibilities, including a step-by-step overview of the entire user login and resource enumeration and launch process. Also, the 'Troubleshooting the FMA' chapter will handle troubleshooting using Scout in more detail.

> **FMA fact**: Your Delivery Controllers can be considered as the heart of your FMA deployment.

The Delivery Controller is the real workhorse and centrepiece of the FMA and, as such, it has a lot of responsibilities. To name a few, it brokers (VDA) sessions, verifies user credentials, and plays an important role during user login and resource enumeration as well as launch. It communicates with StoreFront and/or Web Interface, the underlying Host Connection (Hypervisor or cloud-based services), the Central Site database, and it also takes care of load-balancing hosted shared desktop connections. As of version 7.6 it includes and takes care of Connection Leasing as well, which will be discussed in more detail later on.

You could say that the Delivery Controller is in fact the heart of XenDesktop / XenApp. It houses all eleven primary FMA services including the well-known XML service. Here they are:

1. Analytics service.
2. Broker service.
3. Configuration service.
4. AD Identity service.
5. Configuration Logging service.
6. Delegated Administration service.
7. Machine Creation service.
8. Host service.
9. Environment Test service.
10. Monitor service.
11. StoreFront service.

Each service has its own specific responsibility. Note that the XML service isn't mentioned since it is not FMA-specific. As highlighted, during the 'FMA core services' chapter we will have a closer look at each service individually, the XML service included, and how they all interact and communicate within the FMA. This will also include the evolution from an FMA services perspective, as well as FMA service groups and more.

Authentication and enumeration

When a user logs in, either internally through StoreFront or externally through NetScaler, for example, as mentioned the Delivery Controller plays an important role during the user authentication and verification process, as well as with enumerating and launching user resources. This process is also referred to as connection brokering. A Delivery Controller has a direct and live connection with the Central Site database, which holds all static as well as dynamic (real-time) information within the Site. As opposed to the Data Collectors in XenApp 6.5 and earlier, none of this information will be stored locally (no LHC, remember) and all Delivery Controllers will fully depend on the Central Site database to provide this information when needed. Communication between a Delivery Controller and the Central Site database is constant (heartbeat messages are exchanged every 20 seconds with a TTL of 40 seconds).

The Delivery Controller also plays a key role in controlling all registered desktop and server machines (to which your users connect) with regard to availability, load balancing and power management, which includes starting and stopping virtual machines when needed: see also the next chapter on VDAs. It brokers connections between users and their virtual and/or physical desktops and applications while maintaining and optimising these connections wherever and whenever needed using technologies like Session Reliability (Common Gateway Protocol), Auto Client Reconnect, ICA Keep-Alive messages, and workspace control. Note that power management is not available for physical machines, only virtual.

One is none

As an IT specialist you are probably familiar with the saying 'one is none', as this applies to almost all infrastructural components that we 'techies' have to deal with. The same applies to the Delivery Controller. If the server hosting the Delivery Controller role is unavailable, your users will not be able to be authenticated or verified; as a result they will also not be able to access and/or launch any of their virtual desktops or published applications. Therefore at least two Delivery Controller servers per Site should be deployed on different physical hosts (when virtualised) to prevent a single point of failure. All online Delivery Controllers within your Site will actively participate in handling user / session requests at any time (amongst other tasks), if one of the Controllers for whatever reason goes offline, one of the other Controllers will take over its tasks automatically and instantly. All Controllers within a Site have access to the same Central Site database and therefore are equally configured.

FMA fact: Your environment is as strong as its weakest link. Make sure to apply the 'one is none' rule wherever and whenever it makes sense.

A Delivery Controller is different from a Data Collector in many ways. Besides the absence of the Local Host Cache, Delivery Controllers do not communicate with each other, they cannot host any user sessions like a Data Collector can, and as such they also do not have to run the same Operating System as

the VDAs they manage. See the next page for an overview
(table) on some of the most important differences between the
two.

Citrix Studio is the main management tool and console used to
set up and configure XenDesktop and XenApp Sites. It can be
installed on a Delivery Controller or separately on a
management machine, for example. Since the Delivery
Controller plays such an important role, Studio will also have a
direct connection with one or multiple of your Delivery
Controllers.

Table 2: Delivery Controller vs. Data Collector

Delivery Controller	Data Collector
No LHC	LHC
Connection Leasing	No Connection Leasing
Pulls all information, static as well as dynamic from the Central Site database	Has static as well dynamic (run-time) information cached locally
There is no direct communication between Delivery Controllers. No scheduled communication between the VDAs and/or Site database, only when needed	Communicates with the IMA store, peer Data Collectors and its Session Hosts (within its own zone) on a scheduled interval, or when a Farm configuration change has been made
Is responsible for brokering and maintaining new and existing user session only	Often hosts user session, but can be configured as a dedicated Data Collector as well
Can have a different Operating System installed then the server and desktop VDAs	Needs to have the same Operating System as all other Session Hosts and DCs within the same Farm
Core services installed only. The HDX stack is part of the VDA software	Has all the XenApp 6.5 or earlier bits and bytes fully installed
Zones are optional. When configured they do need at least one Delivery	Each Zone has one Data Collector. Having multiple Data Collectors means

Controller present	having multiple Zones
Election does not apply. Deploy multiple, at least two Delivery Controllers per Site / Zone (again, one per Zone is the minimum).	Can, and sometimes need to be elected. Configure at least one other Session Host per Zone that can be elected as a Data Collector when needed
When Central Site DB is down no Site wide configuration changes are possible. By default Connection Leasing will kick in, enabling users to launch assigned resources that have been successfully started at least once during the last two weeks prior to the DB going offline	When IMA DB is down no Farm wide configuration changes are possible. Everything else continues to work as expected due to the LHC present on the Data Collectors and Session Hosts in each Zone
A Delivery Controller can have a direct connection (API) with a Hypervisor or cloud platform of choice	Does not have any direct Hypervisor or cloud platform management capabilities
Almost all communication flows directly through a Delivery Controller to the Central Site Database	Session Hosts as well as Data Collectors directly communicate with the IMA database
VDAs need to successfully register themselves with a Delivery Controller	When a XenApp server boots it needs to have the IMA service running but it does not register itself anywhere

Some of the most important management and configuration activities that take place, either on or though your Delivery Controllers, are:

- Site Creation.
- Manage Delivery Controllers.
- Manage Host Connections.
- Machine provisioning.
- Manage AppDisks.
- Manage Zones.
- Connection Leasing.
- Publish desktops and applications.
- Assign resources to users.
- Configure Site-wide policies.
- Manage user sessions.
- Direct database communication.
- Delegated Administration.
- VDA registration.
- Power management.
- Load balancing.
- Licensing statics.
- Configure App-V infrastructure.
- Troubleshooting (Scout).
- Monitoring.

Most of the above Studio management activities will be discussed in more detail throughout several of the upcoming chapters.

Delivery Controller server sizing

To give you an indication of what might be needed resource-wise, have a look at the following table. Citrix testing has shown that a relatively light virtual machine configuration can handle up to 5000 desktops per Delivery Controller per hour with regard to user authentication, enumeration and resources launch.

Table 3: Delivery Controller server sizing

Component	Specification
Processor	4 vCPUs
Memory	4 GB RAM (minimum)
Network	Bounded virtual NIC
Storage	40 GB
Operating System	Windows Server 2012 R2
XenDesktop edition	7.x

The following Operating Systems are officially supported and tested by Citrix to run the Delivery Controller role:

- Windows Server 2012 R2, Standard and Datacenter Editions.
- Windows Server 2012, Standard and Datacenter Editions.
- Windows Server 2008 R2 SP1, Standard, Enterprise, and Datacenter Editions.

Key takeaways

- As mentioned, your Delivery Controllers have a lot of responsibilities and can therefore be seen as the heart of your FMA deployment.

- Always deploy at least two Delivery Controllers per Site, and if you can per Zone as well. A minimum of one Controller per Zone is needed in the case of a WAN link failure.

- Virtualising your Delivery Controller makes them more flexible, especially in bigger environments. Adding extra DCs or compute resources will be a breeze.

- Almost all Site traffic goes directly through your Delivery Controllers down to the Central Site database and vice versa.

- Try to keep your Delivery Controllers physically close to your database server and any Host Connections you might have set up.

- Delivery Controllers are fundamentally different from Data Collectors: remember that. No LHC, direct database communication, no communication between Delivery Controllers, service- and agent (VDA)-based, and so on.

- StoreFront directly communicates with one of your Delivery Controllers during the user authentication, application enumeration and launch process. You can configure your StoreFront server with a NetScaler load balance VIP address, which will load balance the connections to the Delivery Controllers within the NetScaler VIP.

The Virtual Delivery Agent

VDA in short, is a relatively small piece of software that gets installed on all virtual and physical machines running a Windows server and/or desktop operating system as part of our XenDesktop Site, making their resources remotely available to users.

The VDA communicates directly with the Delivery Controller (it registers itself) as well as with the Receiver software installed on the client end point. It is also referred to as the client-side component of the FMA.

> **FMA fact**: Prior to XenDesktop 7 the VDA was referred to as the Virtual Desktop Agent, while today we know it as the Virtual Delivery Agent, a subtle difference.

During session brokering the VDA is responsible for establishing and managing the connection between the virtual or physical RDSH / VDI machine and the user's end point device. During session initialisation (after a user logs in) it also checks if a valid Citrix license is available and it will apply whatever policies have been configured for that particular session.

The VDA primarily consists of two main services, the Citrix ICA Service (picaSvc2.exe) and the Citrix Desktop Service (BrokerAgent.exe), which communicates directly with the Broker Service on the Delivery Controller.

The VDA Desktop Service consists of multiple plug-ins, like the Director plug-in, a WMI plug-in, the Monitor plug-in, and a few more.

They all communicate with the Delivery Controller through the Desktop Service as mentioned. Both services will be discussed in more detail as we progress.

New (VDA) kid in town

With the introduction of XenApp to the FMA, Citrix had to come up with a server-based Virtual Delivery Agent, since prior to XenDesktop 7.x the FMA was exclusively designed for VDI, meaning VDAs for desktop Operating Systems only.

And so they did. As of XenDesktop 7.x and forward there are now two types of VDAs, or four, depending on your point of view: one for Windows desktop Operating Systems, one for Windows server Operating Systems, and a VDA for Linux as well, which includes options for both desktop as well as server Linux distributions (SUSE Linux Enterprise and Red Hat Enterprise Linux).

As mentioned previously, the biggest difference between the two is the underlying (ICA) protocol stack. For desktop machines a single-user ICA stack (a.k.a. PortICA) is used, which allows only one user session at a time. For server machines, Citrix now includes a multi-user ICA stack extending the Windows Remote Desktop Services with the HDX/ICA protocol.

This is basically the same ICA protocol stack as developed for Citrix XenApp 6.5 and earlier releases with some adjustments to make it compatible with XenDesktop / XenApp FMA Delivery Controllers.

The following server and desktop Operating systems are supported. Server VDA: Windows Server 2008 R2, Windows Server 2012 and R2, and Windows Server 2016 TP4 is supported as well. Not for producton use of course. Desktop VDA: Windows 7 SP1 Professional, Enterprise and Ultimate editions, Windows 8 and 8.1 Professional and Enterprise editions, and as of XenDesktop 7.6 Feature Pack 3 Windows 10 Enterprise edition. Although do make sure to check out the Citrix E-docs since not all features are supported. And as for Linux, desktop and server: SUSE Linux Enterprise and Red Hat Enterprise Linux. These also need Feature Pack 3 installed.

FMA fact: You can configure multiple Machine Catalogs with different desktop and server Operating Systems within the same environment / Site.

As you probably remember, before the 7.x release we basically installed XenApp (full install) onto each server that would serve as a Session Host and/or Data Collector. In comparison, the Server VDA is supposed to be a much more lightweight approach, even when compared to the former 'Session only mode' in XenApp 6.5. It now solely consists of the components needed to host sessions, and, as such, it doesn't share any of the other components and services installed on the Delivery Controllers, which wasn't the case with 6.5 and before.

VDA registration

As soon as a Virtual Delivery Agent starts up, meaning the desktop or server Operating System boots, it will try and register itself with one of the Delivery Controllers known within the Site. To make this happen there needs to be a mechanism in place that tells the VDAs which Delivery Controllers are part of the Site and how they can be reached. For this Citrix introduced the 'auto-update' feature, which is enabled by default. It will keep all VDAs updated when Delivery Controllers are added or removed (go offline) from the Site. Each VDA maintains a persistent storage location to save this (Controller) information. When the auto-update feature is disabled, or does not supply the correct information the VDA will check the following locations (in this order):

- Through configured policies.
- The ListOfDDCs Registry Key.
- OU-based discovery (legacy).
- The Personality.ini file created by MCS.

FMA fact: If a VDA is unable to register itself with a Delivery Controller or communication between the VDA and the Delivery Controller fails for any reason, the machine will stay in an unregsiterred state and won't be directly accesable or manageble through one of your Delivery Controllers.

In addition to the above, when installing the VDA manually you will be prompted for the locations of your Delivery Controllers. One of the options you have is to fill in a Delivery Controller FQDN by hand, or you can let the system do the searching for you. Also, after the Delivery Controller configuration part you have the ability to enable or disable a couple of specific features:

- Optimise performance: This is enabled by default. The optimisation tool is used for VDAs running in a VM on a Hypervisor. VM optimisation includes disabling offline files, disabling background defragmentation, and reducing event log size.

Note: do not enable this option if you will be using Remote PC Access.

- Windows Remote Assistance: This one is also enabled by default. When this feature is enabled, Windows Remote Assistance is used with the user-shadowing feature of Director, and Windows automatically opens TCP port 3389 in the firewall.

- Real-Time Audio Transport for audio: Again, enabled by default. When this feature is enabled, UDP is used for audio packets, which can improve audio performance. Personal vDisk: Disabled by default and only available for desktop Operating Systems. When enabled, Personal vDisks can be used with a master image.

In 'The FMA core services' chapter we will have a closer look at how the registration process takes place and what some of the main differences between the (new) server and desktop VDAs are with regard to the services they host and how they interact.

FMA fact: There is a separate HDX 3D Pro VDA for use with GPU acceleration for example. This type of VDA enables you to make use of hardware acceleration, including 3D professional graphics applications based on OpenGL and DirectX. (The standard VDA supports GPU acceleration of DirectX only.). It can be selected during VDA installation. Resources can either be assigned on a one to one basis (Passtrhough) or shared amongst multiple VMs (vGPU).

VDA in High-Availability mode

Normally all connections run from your installed Agents through your Delivery Controllers. But what if your Controllers are not reachable? So your database is fine but your Controller(s) are not: hmm...

You can configure your Virtual Delivery Agents to operate in something called high-availability mode; this way your users can continue to use their desktops and installed applications. In high-availability mode the VDA will accept direct ICA connections from users instead of connections brokered by a Delivery Controller.

Although it's hard to imagine this ever happening, it's good to know what your options are. When enabled, if the communication with all Delivery Controllers fails high-availability mode is initiated after a preset period of time, which is configurable. By default, it kicks in after 300 seconds.

High-availability mode will be enabled for a maximum of 30 days in total. During this time the VDA will attempt to register itself with one of the Controllers while your users will continue to use their desktop and/or installed applications.

As soon as a Controller becomes available the VDA will try and register itself without any interruptions to the user. From then on all other connections will be 'brokered' as usual. If during these 30 days the VDA is not able to register itself with one of the Controllers the desktop(s) will stop listening for connections and will be no longer available.

As per Citrix: High-availability mode is suitable only for use with dedicated desktops, where the mapping between the user and the VDA is known. You cannot configure high-availability mode for use with pooled desktops.

To enable high-availability mode you need to set / configure the High Availability and HaRegistrarTimeout registry keys. These keys need to be created manually after the Virtual Delivery Agent is installed. With the High Availability key you enable or disable high availability for the VDA. Set it to 1 to enable or 0 to disable. The HaRegistrarTimeout key lets you configure the amount of time the VDA will try and register itself with a Delivery Controller if it loses its connection before initiating high-availability mode on the VDA.

Secondly, you need to provide your users with an ICA launch file that will enable them to make direct ICA connections. You have to create an ICA file for each user who requires this feature: Citrix does not create or distribute ICA files for this purpose.

Limitations

There are, however, a few limitations to using the VDA high-availability feature. These include: user roaming. If a user device is already connected to the desktop, users are unable to connect from a different user device.

Delivery Controller-originated policies. Policies originating on the Controller, such as those governing client drive mapping and access to the clipboard, will not work, as there is no connection to the Controller.

Policies originating from the Domain Controller and Local Group Policy are unaffected. Note that policies from a previous registration persist and are applied, so outdated policies might take effect. Power management. When the desktop powers up, it attempts to register, fails and, after the timeout, enters high-availability mode. NetScaler Gateway and Remote Access cannot be used.

Key takeaways

- VDAs communicate directly with your Delivery Controllers (Desktop service).
- On boot, VDAs register themselves with a Delivery Controller.
- The mechanism used to find a Delivery Controller to register with is referred to as 'auto-update' but can be achieved in other ways as well.
- Registration will be done through port 80 by default; customising your VDA settings through Control Panel can change this.
- VDA registration can be verified by restarting the Citrix Desktop Service on the VDA machine itself. After the restart, look for event 1012 stating it successfully registered with a Delivery Controller.
- A VDA consists of two main services, the Citrix Desktop Service and the Citrix ICA Service. The Desktop Service communicates with the Broker service on the Delivery Controller it registers with.
- The Delivery Controller will also power-manage the VDA, meaning it will (re)boot it when needed (works for desktop VDAs only). It will also tell it to listen for new connections when users login to their VDI environment to ensure a successful connection.
- With the addition of XenApp to the FMA, Citrix created a new Server VDA. This will be discussed in more detail later on.
- Use the VDA in HA mode as a last resort. Hopefully it will never come to this.
- VDAs can be managed through policy.

- Different versions of VDAs can be mixed within the same environment (you can select the VDA used from Studio during configuration and install). Make sure to always check with Citrix to find out which configurations are supported.
- Using mixed versions of VDAs can lead to limited feature support. This includes management and monitoring features through Studio and Director.
- Always try to deinstall the old VDA and install the new VDA.
- Before installing the latest VDA available, make sure to check with Citrix for any known issues that might have surfaced during testing (E-docs).
- Sometimes manually updating to the latest VDA (after reimaging) is recommended.
- For lab set-up purposes you can install the Delivery Controller software, the database, StoreFront, licensing etc. all on one server.

StoreFront

Within a XenDesktop Site you basically have two points of authentication, one of which is StoreFront, and the other the NetScaler Gateway. The StoreFront server communicates with Receiver, the Delivery Controllers and the NetScaler (STA) when users are authenticated externally.

Next to the above StoreFront can be configured to communicate with App Controller as part of a XenMobile deployment, and/or VDI-in-a-Box is also optional. Like the Delivery Controller, StoreFront also plays an important role in the application enumeration and resource launch process and it functions as the main Store (there can be multiple) from where users (can) subscribe to their desktops and applications.

FMA fact: While XenDesktop and XenApp both support Web Interface (EOL June 2018) Citrix recommends using StoreFront for new as well as existing deployments. It is built for the future and as such has a whole bunch of additional features not available in Web Interface.

User authentication

With StoreFront, users are authenticated by the authentication service, which is an integral part of StoreFront. Users can authenticate to StoreFront using different methods: usernames and passwords, Domain pass-through, NetScaler pass-through, using smart cards, or by enabling unauthenticated user access.

As soon as a user logs in by filling in his or her username and password (on the StoreFront web page using the Receiver for website configuration, or using a locally installed Citrix Receiver) the StoreFront authentication service will pick up the user credentials and authenticate them with a domain controller. Here the configurations of Kerberos delegation is also optional.

Once authenticated (1), StoreFront will forward the user credentials, as part of an XML query to one of the configured Delivery Controllers (2), assuming you configured at least two of course. In between, StoreFront will check its local datastore for any existing user subscriptions and stores them in memory.

The Delivery Controller receiving the credentials will again contact a domain controller, this time to validate the user's credentials before responding to the StoreFront server (3). During step (4) the Delivery Controller will check with the Central Site database to see which resources have been assigned to the user and send them over to the StoreFront server (5).

Next, StoreFront will generate a webpage displaying all the resource icons (published applications and desktops) to the user (6). Here I assume that authentication is taking place internally and directly to StoreFront. See the graphical overview on the next page for some more details.

Generate webpage
with icons

6

StoreFront

Authentication

—1——► Active Directory

5

2 XML query

Delivery Controller

Validation

—3—

Assignment

4

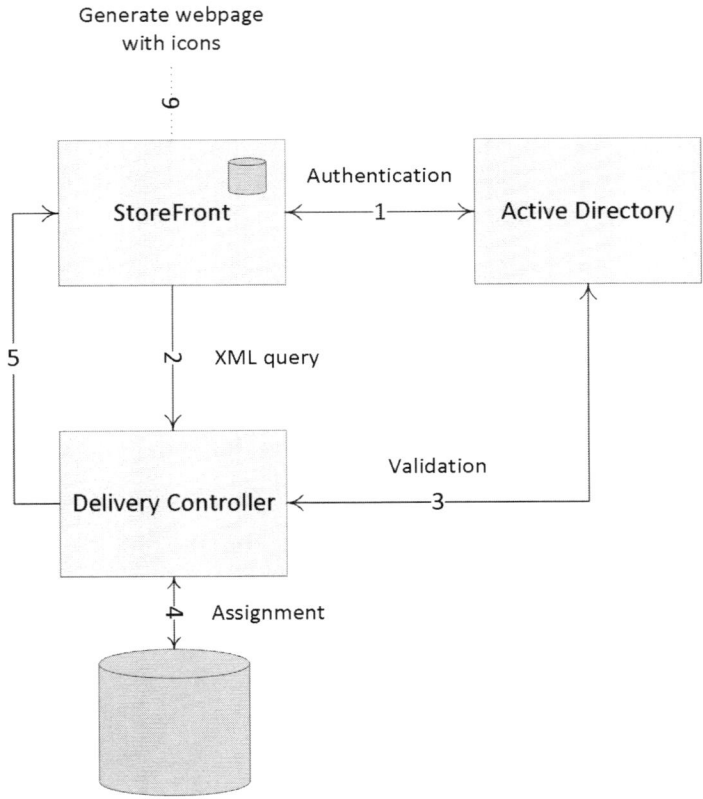

Figure 4: StoreFront traffic flow

FMA fact: Note how I mention user authentication and user validation. There is a difference. Authentication is to make sure that somebody is who he or she claims to be. Verification is done to find out which resources are assigned (permissions) to the user.

Web Interface

If we look at Web Interface, user authentication works a bit differently, it has no internal authentication service. When a user logs in by filling in his or her username and password, Web Interface will immediately forward these credentials, as part of a so-called XML query, to a Delivery Controller where a domain controller will be contacted to authenticate the user before responding to the Web Interface server. As before, Web Interface can also authenticate users to, and enumerate and aggregate resources from, multiple XenApp Farms and XenDesktop Sites, not App Controller, though.

But wait: as of StoreFront 3.0, Citrix reintroduced XML-based authentication. By simply running a few PowerShell scripts user authentication falls back to the XenDesktop / XenApp XML service, like with Web Interface. Useful when StoreFront is not in the same domain as XenDesktop / XenApp or when it is not possible to set up an Active Directory trust. Again, this method will be disabled by default: at least now you have options.

The StoreFront server plays a vital role when it comes to user authentication, resource enumeration and launch. If there is no StoreFront server available your users will be unable to launch any resources (as an exception, although not recommended, a direct ICA connection would work and doesn't need StoreFront). That is why you will always deploy at least two StoreFront servers per Site. By implementing a load-balancing solution, like a NetScaler or Windows NLB, for example your users won't notice a thing when one or multiple StoreFront servers become unavailable.

To be able to provide your users with desktops and applications, StoreFront must be configured with at least one Delivery

Controller (FQDN or IP address). Since 'one is none' as we've learned earlier, we will always make sure to configure at least two Delivery Controllers for HA purposes. In the case of a Delivery Controller failure, StoreFront will automatically fail over to the next Delivery Controller in line; this results in an active/passive configuration.

Within large organisations, where the logon load is higher than average, an active/active approach might be a better fit. This can be accomplished by implementing a load-balancing device like the Citrix NetScaler, or you can choose to let the StoreFront server load balance the connections to the Delivery Controllers instead.

Up to StoreFront 3.5 you will have to manually edit the web.config file for this, locate the following line: <farm name="XenApp" xmlPort="80" transport="HTTP" sslRelayPort="443" loadBalance="on" farmType="XenApp">

Change 'loadBalance' to either "on" or "off".

As of StoreFront 3.5 the above can now be configured by simply placing a checkmark directly from the GUI, you'll find it under 'Manage Delivery Controllers'. As far as I know, the built-in LB mechanism used for this is based on RRDNS technology, or at least the result is similar.

Resource enumeration and subscriptions

When a user logs in for the first time, meaning that there are no active and/or disconnected sessions lingering around somewhere, and right after the user is authenticated the resource enumeration process kicks in and will eventually show the user its assigned resources. That's why the user authentication process and resource enumeration basically go hand-in-hand. When users log in externally, through a NetScaler Gateway, for example, the StoreFront server and the NetScaler will also exchange vital information like user authentication details, the resources a user is allowed to launch and more. Throughout the 'User login process' chapter these steps will be discussed in great detail.

Note that (by default) when using StoreFront, users will first have to subscribe to their resources before they will show up on their main home screen (assuming the Receiver for Web approach with an unconfigured Citrix Receiver is used). Using Keywords, Administrators can pre-subscribe users to certain core applications prepopulating your user's home screens when logging in for the first time. This also works for assigned Desktops. This approach is referred to as 'Self Service Store', which can be disabled from the GUI.

You can use the Keyword: AUTO on a resource of choice so that it will automatically show up in your user's home screen when they log into the Receiver for Web web page.

This is something that can be configured in Studio: simply open up the configuration details of your application and fill in your Keywords of choice. Multiple Keywords can be used at the same time. Other Keywords include: PREFER, FEATURED, PRIMARY, MANDATORY and more. Martijn Hulsman wrote a nice article on the use and the different types of StoreFront Keywords, you will find it here:

http://www.martijnhs.com/2014/05/08/citrix-storefront-keywords-explained/

FMA fact: Note that besides the Receiver for Web approach, where users log into StoreFront by means of a web page, you can also configure your Citrix Receiver in self-service mode. This way your users will be able to subscribe to their resources directly form the local Citrix Receiver interface. See the 'The Citrix Receiver' section for some more detailed information.

StoreFront server

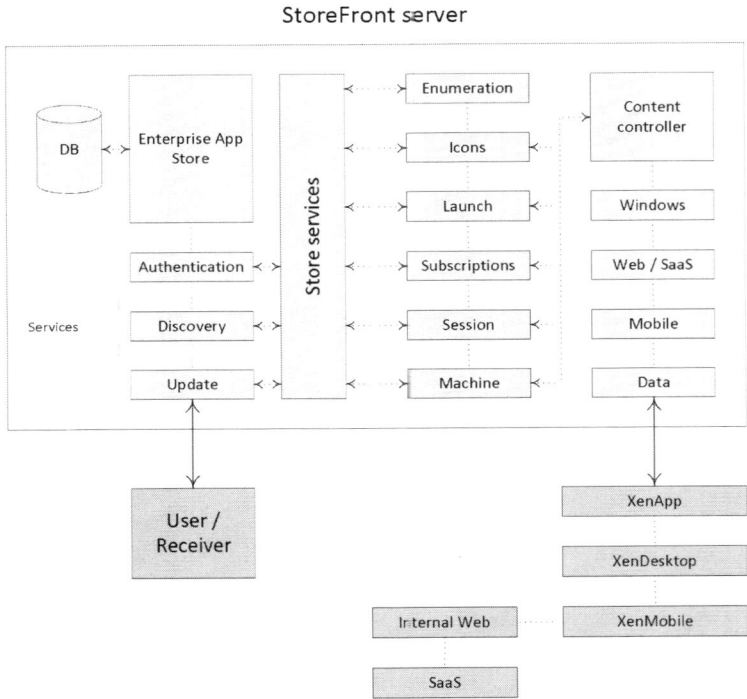

Figure 5: StoreFront internals

When a user subscribes to a resource this information (also referred to as application subscriptions) has to be stored somewhere. Otherwise users would need to subscribe to the same resources over and over again before they would be able to launch it each time they log in. Prior to StoreFront 2.x we needed a separate external database to store all StoreFront-related information: luckily that is no longer the case. StoreFront now uses the Windows Extensible Storage Engine to locally store and index the user subscription information. This is the same technology used by Microsoft Access and Exchange.

> **FMA fact**: Besides using Keywords, as of Citrix Receiver 4.2.100 you can also integrate application and desktop short cuts into your user's Start menus or put them onto their desktops, with no resource subscription needed.

StoreFront servers are grouped together in server groups, and all information stored locally on a StoreFront server, as explained above, will be automatically replicated on a peer-to-peer basis to other StoreFront servers within the same server group. This way, a user resource subscription is made highly available.

Subscription synchronisation

If your users connect to multiple StoreFront servers residing in different StoreFront deployments, or server groups, and they are able to access similar applications and/or desktops within these deployments, then you might want to consider implementing something called subscription synchronisation. This will ensure that all StoreFront servers in both or multiple deployments will exactly know which applications and/or desktops the user is subscribed to, so they won't need to subscribe to an application again when logging onto one of the other deployments.

You can configure periodic synchronisation of users' application subscriptions between stores in different server groups. However, for this to work, all stores need to have the same name and all server groups must reside within the Active

Directory domain containing your users' accounts or within a domain that has a trust relationship with the user accounts' domain.

It is important to note that each store within StoreFront – since you can configure as many as you would like – will have its own datastore where user subscription information will be stored and each subscription datastore is updated independently from each other store.

The same holds true for internal and external access to resources. It is not uncommon to create two separate stores within StoreFront, one for internal and one for external access, since different configurations might be preferred. This also implies that for both stores the users' resource subscriptions would need to be stored twice, once for each store.

This also means that your users will have to subscribe to a resource twice, depending on which store they access, internal or external (remember that each store will have its own datastore where user subscription information will be stored). Luckily we can configure two stores to share a common subscription database. This is done by manually editing the web.config file (this is the StoreFront configuration file). This way it does not matter if the user logs in externally or internally, his or her subscriptions will be the same.

StoreFront Multi-Site configurations

Another great addition to the StoreFront family is the ability to configure multi-Site configurations. As mentioned earlier, with the FMA your central SQL database is probably one of the most important components of your infrastructure: if it's down (without Connection Leasing in place) your Site won't accept any new connections and you won't be able to make any configuration changes (as with the IMA).

Of course there are ways to implement additional SQL high availability, like SQL Clustering, Always-On and mirroring, for example, but what if that particular Site becomes unresponsive for other reasons? It happens. Then an alternative or additional Site would be a good thing to have in place, to say the least. Having multiple Sites, for load balancing as well as HA purposes, is always optional.

FMA fact: Going forward, StoreFront multi-site configurations will be a lot easier to configure and implement. Most functionality will be built into the Graphical User Interface of StoreFront.

You may also want to point or map your users as close to their physical data (centre) or Site as possible, as we can do with the IMA (XenApp) Zone preference policies. Or perhaps you'd like to configure and assign a (non-active) recovery Site, in case of a disaster?

Because of the change in architecture as far as RDSH solutions are concerned, we will need to rethink our designs when it comes to the FMA vs. the IMA and the replacement of Web Interface with StoreFront. But don't worry, it's all (still) there,

even without multiple Web Interface / StoreFronts and/or
NetScaler(s) configured, although this is probably a set-up
which we won't see that often.

By default, StoreFront will enumerate all resources it can find
from all Sites and Farms (remember that with XenApp 6.5 and
earlier, Sites are referred to as Farms) configured. These can
come from XenDesktop, XenApp and/or VDI-in-a-Box
Controllers. So when we add an extra set of Delivery
Controllers from another (load balance, failover or recovery)
Site it will automatically enumerate any resources your users will
have access to. Not a bad thing per se, but this will also mean
that if an application and/or desktop is available from multiple
Sites your users will see an icon for each resource, meaning
double icons assuming you have proper permissions on both
Sites, that is. This is where Multi-Site configurations, and its
aggregation capabilities, come in.

Here I will assume that at least two sites or more are configured.
I'm mentioning this because some of the features discussed can
also be applied on single Site / Farm configurations.

FMA fact: A XenApp Farm (6.5) or XenDesktop /
XenApp Site (7.x) is also referred to as a 'Deployment'
by Citrix. Especially if you spend some time on their E-
docs pages you, will see this term a lot.

Within a StoreFront Multi-Site configuration, when a desktop or
application is available from multiple Sites and/or Farms,
StoreFront can aggregate all instances of that particular resource
and present it as a single icon. For this to work, deployments do
not need to be identical per se, but the desktops and/or
applications do need to have the exact same name and path on

each server: all other configured characteristics need to match as well. Note that XenMobile App Controller applications cannot be aggregated. This comes from the Citrix E-docs website:

> When a user starts an aggregated resource, StoreFront determines the most appropriate instance (Delivery Controller) of that resource for the user on the basis of server availability, whether the user already has an active session, and the ordering you specified in your configuration. Now that's smart, right?

Besides resource aggregation, Multi-Site StoreFront configurations also let us set up highly available deployments. We can configure load balancing, failover or a (non-active) disaster recovery site. You also have the ability to set up something called User Mapping.

This basically means you can set up access to a specific deployment (Site) based on certain user memberships of Microsoft Active Directory groups, like the good old Zone preference policies, if you will. This allows you to create multiple Sites, or deployments, offering different resources, still all aggregated through the same Store, simply by adding multiple Delivery Controllers. However, your users will only be able to see what their permissions allow them to.

Another example would be to create two (it can be more, of course) identical Sites and configure one group of users to always connect to Site A, and another group of users to always connect to Site B. This way Site A can also function as a failover Site for Site B and vice versa. Preferably you'll use at least two separate StoreFront servers, one (or more) per Site. Again, all users will need to have permissions on the same resources, applications and/or desktops at both Sites.

In a multi-site configuration StoreFront will aggregate all instances of a particular resource from all configured Sites / deployments, and will present this to the user in the form of one single icon, so no issues there. Of course this set-up would also work without user mapping configured, although then it would be active / passive instead of active / active, unless you have 2 or more StoreFront servers in combination with a NetScaler configured. Active / passive would also mean you can do with just one StoreFront server if you like.

This same set-up (although configured differently) could also be used to load balance connections between multiple Sites. Instead of contacting one of the 'extra' Controllers for redundancy purposes, connections will be randomly spread across the configured controllers, evenly distributing the load, again using just one StoreFront server, although you could, and probably should, use more, at least two.

Finally we have the option to configure and set up something called recovery sites (deployments). A Recovery Site is basically just another XenDesktop / XenApp Site but it sits idle (passive) until it is called upon. This will happen as soon as all primary Sites, which can be any number from one and upwards, become unreachable.

Location 1 Load Balance   Location 2 Failover   Location 3 DR

Site 1

Site 2

Site 3

Site 1

Site 2

Site 1

StoreFront server group

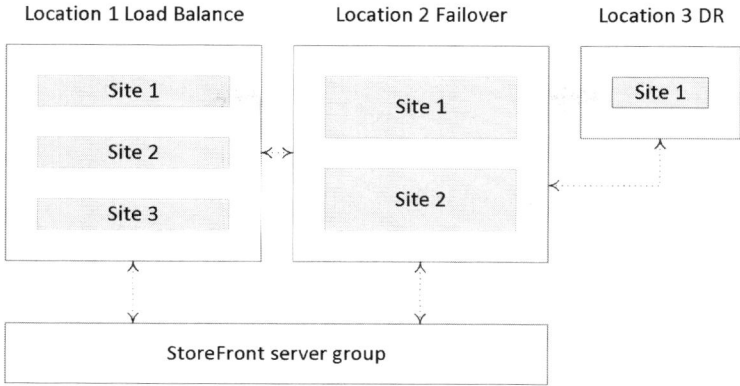

Figure 6: StoreFront multi-site configuration

Prior to StoreFront version 3.5 all of these features needed to be configured manually within the web.config file (the StoreFront configuration file) which isn't all that straightforward. Luckily, Citrix stepped up and with the release of StoreFront 3.5 and onwards some of the abovementioned options are now available right directly from the GUI, like User Mapping and resource aggregation, for example, and more will follow going forward.

The optimal NetScaler Gateway route

If your deployments (Sites) each have a separate NetScaler configured, then StoreFront enables you to define the optimal or preferred NetScaler appliance for users to access each of the deployments.

If you create a store that aggregates resources from two geographically separated locations, each with a NetScaler Gateway appliance configured, then users connecting through a Gateway in one location can start a published resource in the other location.

However, by default, the connection to the resource is then routed through the Gateway to which the user originally connected and must therefore traverse the corporate WAN. With Optimal NetScaler routing we can change this behaviour. Besides the above you can also use NetScaler to load balance the connections made from your StoreFront server to your Delivery Controllers, and the same can be done from your NetScaler to multiple StoreFront servers that you might have: the combinations are endless, so to speak.

FMA fact: We can use the Optimal NetScaler Gateway routing feature to route the user's ICA traffic through the NetScaler most applicable (the one connecting them to their XenDesktop Site in the case of a multi-site deployment) to the user, even if the initial connection was made through another NetScaler.

XenDesktop Site 1

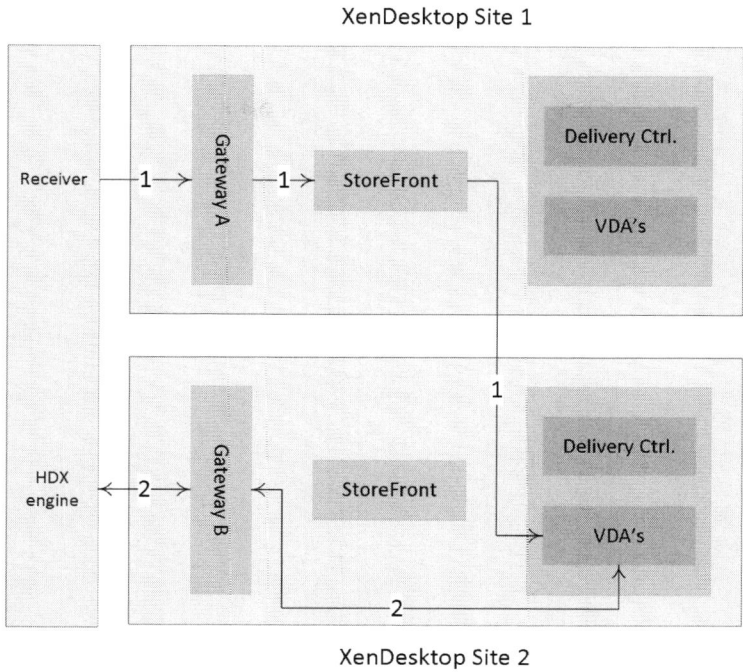

XenDesktop Site 2

Figure 7: Optimal gateway routing

Receiver and StoreFront

To be able to contact Citrix StoreFront and to view, subscribe to and/or launch resources you will need to have access to a Citrix Receiver. By default, when you try to log into a StoreFront web page (Receiver for Web) your local system will be checked to see if a supported version of Citrix Receiver is installed, and if not, you can download and install one directly from the StoreFront web page. See the section titled 'The Citrix Receiver' for some more details on installing and configuring Citrix Receiver. However, installing the Receiver software is not always possible or allowed.

For this reason StoreFront also has an HTML5-based Receiver built-in, so that even when you do not have a Receiver locally installed you will still be able to contact StoreFront, enumerate and launch your personal resources. This is referred to as clientless access, and it can also be used as a fall-back mechanism if for whatever reason your locally installed Receiver does not work properly or fails completely. Basically, we have three ways to get to our resources; however, they all include the Citrix Receiver one way or the other.

1. We can have the Citrix Receiver installed locally. You would then need to fill in your email address (when email-based account discovery is enabled), make use of a pre-configured provisioning file, or manually enter a URL pointing to your StoreFront deployment. Both will need to be provided by your IT department. Note that you will have to use HTTPS for this to work.

2. Secondly we can use the so-called Receiver for Web site approach. Here we create a Store accessible using our Internet browser of choice to log into a StoreFront Store. As mentioned during logon your local system will be checked for a supported Citrix Receiver installation and you have the option to install Citrix Receiver from the StoreFront login page if needed or desired.

3. And third, since installing software, including Receiver is not always possible or allowed; the previous step could be skipped. You would then contact StoreFront using the built-in HTML5-based Receiver. However, this needs to be enabled on the Receiver for Web section within the StoreFront management console; it is not enabled by default. Next to this you will also have to enable and configure ICA WebSockets through Citrix policies using Studio for example. The same applies to

your external users connecting through a NetScaler, a separate HTTP Profile with WebSockets enabled (disabled by default) will need to be created. When using Provisioning Services these policies will need to be applied at vDisk level.

Securing your connections

Internal communication from your web browser or Citrix Receiver to StoreFront will initially contain user credentials, passwords included. When you allow users to log in remotely, to work from home, this same information will need to traverse the unsecure Internet. It is therefore recommended to secure and encrypt all traffic using SSL (Secure Sockets Layer). To enable secure remote access, a NetScaler is the recommended approach. To set up communications using SSL trusted certificates must be installed on all StoreFront servers, as well as the NetScalers. For companies with high security standards the same can be done for traffic sent between your StoreFront servers and Delivery Controllers. You could even take it one step further and also secure traffic sent between and from all installed VDAs. Although this does require some planning and additional work / maintenance, it can certainly be done.

As of version 7.6, SSL has been integrated into the core of the Citrix VDA, making it a lot more straightforward to enable on all machines and connections. This works for XenDesktop as well as XenApp and for persistent as well as non-persistent desktops. There might be a slight performance impact, but it should be negligible.

Beacon-based Receiver connections

Citrix Receiver, combined with StoreFront, uses Beacons to determine if a connection is made internally or externally and routes the connection accordingly. In simple terms, beacons are nothing more than basic URLs used by Receiver to determine its location. When a connection is made, Receiver will try and contact the beacon points (URLs) to determine where the connection originated. It will start with any of the internal-configured Beacons and then move over to external, assuming no match has been found.

Depending on the outcome, the location information will be forwarded to the server providing the actual resources, and the connection will be routed either externally, through the NetScaler Gateway, or internally using StoreFront.

All this makes it much simpler for your users to access their resources. For example, you don't have to configure two separate URLs for your users to remember, one for internal access and for external access: StoreFront and Receiver will figure this out for you. And if you applied the earlier mentioned email-based discovery feature, all they will need to do is download Receiver, fill in their email address and they are good to go.

FMA fact: By default, StoreFront will use your internal services URL as an internal resolvable Beacon point and it will use Citrix.com as the external Beacon point. But you can change them to whatever you like. Just make sure that your internal Beacon is not resolvable externally.

XenApp Services URLs

Users who are unable to upgrade to Citrix Receiver even today can still access StoreFront stores simply by configuring a XenApp Services URL on a per store basis (see the StoreFront documentation for more details on how to configure and enable). If needed, this also works for domain-joined desktop appliances and repurposed PCs running the Citrix Desktop Lock. When you create a new store, the XenApp Services URL for the store is enabled by default.

While XenApp Services URLs are meant to help out users who are unable to upgrade to one of the latest Citrix Receiver versions, they do come with some drawbacks that you need to be aware of. These come from the Citrix E-docs pages:

1. You cannot modify the XenApp Services URL for a store.
2. You cannot modify XenApp Services URL settings by editing the configuration file, config.xml.
3. XenApp Services URLs support explicit, domain pass-through, smart card authentication, and pass-through with smart card authentication. Explicit authentication is enabled by default. Only one authentication method can be configured for each XenApp Services URL and only one URL is available per store. If you need to enable multiple authentication methods, you must create separate stores, each with a XenApp Services URL, for each authentication method. Your users must then connect to the appropriate store for their method of authentication. For more information about configuring user authentication to XenApp Services URLs, see Configure authentication for XenApp Services URLs.
4. Workspace control is enabled by default for XenApp

Services URLs and cannot be configured or disabled.

5. User requests to change their passwords are routed to the domain controller directly through the XenDesktop, XenApp and VDI-in-a-Box servers providing desktops and applications for the store, bypassing the StoreFront authentication service.

Desktop Appliance sites

Users with non-domain-joined desktop machines can access their desktops through something called Desktop Appliance sites. Non-domain-joined in this context means devices that are not joined to a domain within the Microsoft Active Directory forest containing the StoreFront servers. Just as with the XenApp services URL, when you create a new store for a XenDesktop deployment using Citrix Studio, a Desktop Appliance site is created for the store by default.

However, be aware that if you are connecting through a NetScaler Gateway, you will not be able to access a Desktop Appliance site. External connections from outside the network are not supported, period. Also make sure you have the right version of Receiver installed. And, as always, more details can be found on the Citrix E-docs pages.

StoreFront server sizing

The number of simultaneous activities a StoreFront server can handle depends on the number of resources assigned to a user, including the level of overall user activity. The table below is based on a 2-node StoreFront deployment and it can handle around 600 simultaneous activities per second at 80 to 85% CPU usage. The shown configuration is on a per node basis.

Table 4: StoreFront server sizing

Component	Specification
Processor	4 vCPUs
Memory	4 GB RAM (minimum)
Storage	40 GB
Operating System	Windows Server 2012 R2

The following Operating Systems are tested and supported by Citrix to run StoreFront:

- Windows Server 2012 R2 Datacenter and Standard editions
- Windows Server 2012 Datacenter and Standard editions
- Windows Server 2008 R2 Service Pack 1 Datacenter, Enterprise and Standard editions

When running XenDesktop / XenApp 7.8 you need to install at least StoreFront 2.6 or upwards.

Key takeaways

- You basically have two points of authentication within a XenDesktop / XenApp Site: StoreFront and NetScaler.
- When working with Zones always make sure to deploy at least one StoreFront server per Zone. Needed in the case of a WAN link failure.
- Users may need to subscribe themselves to resources they are allowed to start. These user subscriptions are synchronised between all StoreFront servers within the same StoreFront server group.
- The above is also referred to as the 'Self Service Store' setup, which is enabled by default. A bit more on this in the 'The Citrix Receiver' chapter.
- The 'Self Service Store' can be disabled, leaving you with the 'Mandatory Store' configuration. Using this setup all resources for which a user has proper permissions will be displayed by default, no subscriptions needed.
- Combined with the 'Self Service Store' approach you can configure Keywords in Citrix Studio to automatically subscribe your users to certain resources, like a standard desktop, for example. When a user logs in, the resources will be directly displayed on his or her welcome screen.
- If email based discovery is enabled and configured, you have the option to either advertise the Store or to hide the Store. When advertised the Store is presented as an option for your users to add. When you hide it, the user will need configure the Citrix Receiver him or her self using a setup URL or provisioning file, for example.
- When configuring and modifying your StoreFront deployment, especially when editing the web.conf file, make sure you are doing this only using one StoreFront

server at the same time. Preferably the one you installed and configured first.

- You can manually propagate any changes you have made to StoreFront to your other StoreFront servers within the same server group.

- When dealing with multi-site deployments, you can configure specific user groups to be mapped to a preferred site.

- StoreFront multi-site configurations let us configure a Recovery site. This site will sit idle until all other StoreFront deployments stop accepting connections, whatever the reason may be.

- When using a Citrix NetScaler think about using it to load balance all external incoming traffic to your StoreFront servers.

- If you only publish a single desktop to a user, StoreFront will automatically launch it directly after the user successfully logs in to StoreFront. This behaviour can be changed by manually editing web.conf file. Have a look at the following CTX document: CTX139058.

- StoreFront plays an important part in configuring Citrix Receiver pass-through authentication a.k.a. Single Sign-on. Look for the support document CTX200157.

The Central Site database

The XenDesktop Central Site Database holds all Site wide static (policies, configured Catalogs and Delivery Groups, Host Connections, Zones and so on) as well as dynamic (run-time) information (who is logged on to which VDA, what resources are currently in use etc.) needed during the user logon, authentication and resource enumeration process as well as the actual resource launch sequence (load balancing).

Needless to say it is an important part of your infrastructure: when it is down your users won't be able to connect and/or launch resources and IT will not be able to make any configuration changes to the Site itself. Because of this you'll probably want to implement some kind of high-availability mechanism keeping your database up and running at all times, or at least to try and keep downtime to a minimum. Of course, Connection Leasing, which we will discuss in more detail shortly, also helps in keeping certain resources available even when the Central Site database is offline.

First things first

Especially coming from XenApp 6.5 and earlier versions, these types of changes took some time to get used to. Unlike the 6.5 XenApp servers (Data Collectors), the XenDesktop 7.x Virtual Delivery Agents only communicate with the Site Delivery Controller(s) and do not need to access the Site database directly. Having said that, XenApp 6.5 Session Host only servers offer the same sort of benefit. Because they only host user sessions and will (or can) never be 'elected' as a Data Collector for their Zone, hence the 'Session Host only' part, they won't get all the IMA store (database) information pushed into their LHC (Local Host Cache), enhancing overall performance. Also see the 'Local Host Cache' section on page 102.

While Delivery Controllers are comparable to XenApp Data
Collectors, there are some distinct differences. Sure, they both
handle user authentication, are involved during the resource
enumeration process, and are in control of load balancing, for
example, but in very different ways.

Data Collectors are part of Zones with each Zone having its
own (there can be only one per Zone) Data Collector. Having
multiple Data Collectors in your Farm basically means having
multiple Zones. Also, Data Collectors need to be able to
communicate with each other. With Delivery Controllers this
works differently.

Note: Make sure to have a look at the comparison table,
comparing the Delivery Controller to the Data Collector over at
page 60.

Although, as of XenDesktop 7.7, we are able to create Zones
(again), when compared to the Zones in the IMA there are still
some architectural differences between the two. To name a few,
Delivery Controllers do not communicate with each other,
Session Hosts (VDAs) do not communicate directly with the
Central Site database, and of course we now have Connection
Leasing instead of the LHC, although it was never meant as
replacement.

Also, if you look at the characteristics of a XenDesktop 7.8
Zone, at least today, you will notice that you will also have to
place and configure at least one Delivery Controller and
StoreFront server per Zone, but more on this later on. In
addition to the 'Zones' section on page 145, here are some of
the main differences between Zones in the IMA and the FMA,
see next page.

Table 5: IMA Zones vs. FMA Zones

Zones in IMA (6.5)	Zones in FMA (7.x)
Data Collector	Delivery Controller
Keeping resources and users close together, offering load balancing and HA when needed	Simplyfied administration of multiple locations and keeping users close to their rescurces
Max one primary DC per Zone	Unlimited DCs per Zone. Minumum of one is required
Secondary (backup) DCs configured. Election takes place when main Data Collector goes down	All DCs within the same Zone are active
LHC on each DC. Speeds up application enumerations and keeps Farm fully functional when the database is down	Connection Leasing. Enables the launch of certain (assigned) resources when the database is down
DC contacts the IMA database every 30 minutes by default	DC has a direct and continues connection with the FMA database
DC communicates and updates the Session Hosts within its Zone	DC communicates with VDAs in its Zone but primarily for brokering purposes
Load balancing gets applied based on information from the LHC	Load balancing gets applied based on information from DB

DCs exchange (Zone related) information	DCs do not communicate with each other
Zone based policies: Zone Preference and Load Balancing	No specific Zone based policies
No registration	VDAs resgiter themselves
Max of 5 Zones (best practice)	Max of 10 Zones (best practice)
Zones for XenApp only	Zones for both XenApp and XenDesktop

Local Host Cache

In a XenApp 6.5 Farm a Data Collector, including all other XenApp servers with the exception of Session Host only servers, have something called a Local Host Cache (LHC) in which a copy of the central IMA database is cached. And while it primarily functions as a fallback configuration for whenever the IMA database becomes unavailable, it also helps speed up the user authentication and application enumeration process.

Data Collectors also hold and collect dynamic live runtime data used for making load-balance decisions, which it will store in its LHC as well. Delivery Controllers, on the other hand, do not have an LHC, so if they need to authenticate a user or enumerate resources, for example, they will (always) need to contact the Central Site database to get this information. The same goes for load-balancing (dynamic runtime) information: it doesn't get stored locally.

If you have multiple Controllers configured within your Site, but on different physical (geographically separated) locations, keep in mind that they will all need to communicate with the same central database when a user logs in, starts an application or to get load balance information etc., even with one or multiple Zones configured. Consider your bandwidth requirements and make sure to involve the networking team (s) during the design as well as implementation phases.

Also, in a XenApp environment all servers, including the Data Collectors, will contact the IMA database (often referred to as the IMA store) every 30 minutes to update their LHC (except for Session Host only servers, which need to be configured explicitly). In XenDesktop there's no need for this since the Delivery Controllers don't have an LHC and get all their information directly from the Central Site database, live runtime data included. Although the above differences do raise some questions as far as Farm vs. Site designs go, XenDesktop has been doing it this way for a few years and the FMA has proven to be very flexible and robust in many ways.

Minimising downtime

Now that we've established the importance of the Site database and the need to keep it online as close to 100% as possible, let's see what options we have in accomplishing this. To start, it is (highly) recommended to back up your database on a regular (daily) basis so it can be restored if necessary when the database server fails (or the database itself). In addition, there are several high-availability solutions to consider.

When using SQL Server 2012 (Enterprise Edition) or later, Citrix recommends AlwaysOn Availability Groups: a high-availability and disaster recovery solution first introduced in

SQL Server 2012 to enable you to maximise availability for one or more user databases. AlwaysOn Availability Groups require that the SQL Server instances reside on Windows Server Failover Clustering (WSFC) nodes.

The following SQL Server versions are supported:

- SQL Server 2014, Express, Standard, and Enterprise Editions.
- SQL Server 2012 SP1 and SP2, Express, Standard, and Enterprise Editions. By default, SQL Server 2012 SP2 Express is installed when installing the Controller, if an existing supported SQL Server installation is not detected.
- SQL Server 2008 R2 SP2, Express, Standard, Enterprise, and Datacenter Editions.

When SQL AlwaysOn HA isn't possible, or optional Citrix recommends implementing SQL mirroring, with SQL Clustering coming in second. Mirroring the Database ensures that, should you lose the active database server, the automatic failover process happens in a matter of seconds, so that users are generally unaffected. Be aware that full SQL Server licenses are required on each database server, but this goes for some of the other solutions as well. Note that SQL Server Express edition can't be mirrored and clustering isn't supported as well.

Microsoft's SQL Clustering technology can be used to automatically allow one server to take over the tasks and responsibilities of another server that has failed. However, setting up a clustered solution is more complicated, and the automatic failover process is typically slower than with alternatives such as SQL Mirroring.

Again, as mentioned, SQL Server Express doesn't support clustering, at least not out of the box, but with a little creativity, it is possible: Google is your friend (although not recommended for production environments).

Using one of the above methods, in combination with regular (daily) backups, will ensure that your database will (almost) always be online. If anything, it will at least narrow your chances of running into any issues. Make sure to talk to your SQL DBA when needed and spend some time on putting together a SQL Maintenance Plan. SQL Maintenance Plans help you put together various workflows required to make sure that your database is optimized, regularly backed up, and free of inconsistencies.

What about some of the alternatives?

1. VMware HA. Although VMware HA is a great feature in itself, it has no clue with regard to what's running on the VM it's protecting. I mean, your VM will stay online without too much trouble, even if one of the underlying physical hosts goes down, but HA doesn't know when your SQL database goes down or stops responding due to updates gone bad, drives filled up, services stopped or something similar. You could say that VMware HA, and I guess the same goes for Hyper-V or XenServer as well, simply is not application-oriented.

2. VMware App HA. As part of the Enterprise Plus edition, VMware offers Application High Availability. App HA is more intelligent; it can restart failed application components or use the Application Awareness API through VMware HA to reset the VM if needed (no OS reboot). VMware App HA provides

support for SQL, Tomcat, Apache, TC Server and IIS.
For now, no other 'big' applications, like Exchange,
SharePoint, ShareFile and Oracle are supported. But
since it's SQL we're interested in, it could work.
VMware App HA is relatively complex to set up: it
requires multiple VMs and points of management. Also,
as an addition to the applications already mentioned, no
custom or generic applications are supported, and as far
as I could tell it's only supported on vSphere 5.5. On the
other hand, if you are already using VMware combined
with Enterprise Plus licenses you'll have not only App
HA, but also a whole bunch of other cool features and
technologies as well. And if it's SQL you're supporting,
then this is probably the most logical and cost-effective
step to take, especially for smaller and mid-sized
companies. However, when using 'lighter' editions of
VMware or when real enterprise functionality is needed
(more on this in a bit), then this probably won't be your
first choice.

3. VMware Fault Tolerance. One of my favourites. As of
    vCenter Server 6.0 (and vSphere 6.0) a fault-tolerant
    machine can have up to 4 vCPUs (this used to be only
    one). This comes from the VMware website: Fault
    Tolerance (FT) provides continuous availability for
    applications in the event of server failures by creating a
    live shadow instance of a virtual machine that is always
    up to date with the primary virtual machine. In the event
    of a hardware outage, vSphere FT automatically triggers
    failover, ensuring zero downtime and preventing data
    loss. After failover, vSphere FT automatically creates a
    new, secondary virtual machine to deliver continuous
    protection for the application.

4. Symantec ApplicationHA. Although not known by

many, this is probably the most Enterprise product of them all. It supports all major applications, including custom and/or generic applications, over 23 tier 1 applications in total. It's based on Symantec Cluster Server, powered by Veritas agents to monitor and control applications. It can restart failed application components, restart the underlying Operating System, or restart the VM itself. And if all else fails, it can use the last known good backup for restore purposes. The Symantec HA console communicates with VMware through a vCenter plugin providing centralised management for all protected VMs. Of course, Symantec App HA would be a separate purchase, and if you already have VMware running you will probably need a strong business case to get the funds. If it's more than SQL that needs to be supported, if you're going 'Greenfield' or you may have a specific need for one, or multiple, of the Enterprise class features that the Symantec product has to offer, like the number of supported applications or VMs / agents (think big, one of my former colleagues always used to say), then Symantec Application High Availability might just fit the bill.

It is not just the Central Site database

Besides the Central Site database XenDesktop also has a Configuration-Logging database and a Monitoring database. The Configuration-Logging database stores information about all Site configuration changes taking place, including other administrative activities. This database is only used when the Configuration-Logging feature is enabled, which it is by default.

The Monitoring database stores all information used by Director, like session and connection information. Both databases will be discussed in more detail.

Database sizing numbers

When properly sizing your FMA Central Site database you need to keep your eye on two files in particular: the database file itself, which will contain all Site information, the data and objects like stored procedures, tables, views and so on, and the so-called Transaction-Log file. The later contains a record of all transactions, including any database modifications that might have been made by a transaction. If there is a system failure and the current live Site database becomes corrupt and/or unusable in any other way, the Transaction Log can be used (replayed) to re-create the database and bring it back to a consistent state. However this does depend on how you configure the Transaction-Log to handle data. You have the following options:

- Simple Recovery mode: In this mode no log backups are required, meaning that no transaction log data will be saved. If the database fails, all changes made to the database since the last full back up must be redone.
- Full Recovery mode: This mode does require backup logs. If the database fails no work is lost. All data or any specific point in time can be recovered. Full Recovery mode is needed for database mirroring.
- Bulk-Logged Recovery mode: This model is an adjunct of the full recovery model that permits high-performance bulk copy operations. It is typically not used for Citrix databases.

If you back-up your Site database on a daily basis, or at least multiple times per week, simple recovery mode will probably be sufficient. However, it depends. If Site configuration changes are constant, multiple times per week or daily even, then Full Recovery mode might be desirable. Always make sure that high performance storage is used for your SQL infrastructure, SSDs preferably.

Site database

Typically the size of your Central Site database will depend on multiple factors. Since the information stored is both static as well as dynamic, its size can vary during the day. The following factors need to be taken into consideration: the number of configured and registered VDAs, connected and active sessions, the number of transactions taking place during logon and logoff, general logon and logoff behaviour, the physical size of your Site, and a few more. To give you a ballpark indication of its possible size, see the table below. Numbers are in MB.

Table 6: Site database sizing numbers

Users	Apps	Type	Max size
1000	50	RDSH	30
10,000	100	RDSH	60
100,000	200	RDSH	330
1000	N/A	VDI	30
10,000	N/A	VDI	115
40,000	N/A	VDI	390

Note that real-world values may vary. These numbers are for indication purposes only and belong to Citrix Consulting Services.

These same factors also play a role in determining the size of your Transaction Log. Just make sure to regularly back up your Transaction Logs (which will shrink them) by configuring and scheduling SQL maintenance plans on an ongoing basis.

Monitoring database

This one is expected to grow the largest. It contains historical information and, as such, its size depends on multiple factors, which will include but not be limited to: The number of Session Hosts within your Site, including the number of total sessions and connections, and even more specifically, how long data will be stored, which will also depend on the type of license used.

FMA fact: Non-Platinum-licensed customers can keep and store data for up to 7 days, while a Platinum license allows you to store all data for up to a year, with the default being 90 days.

The following table should give you an indication of how the Monitoring database might grow. Again, these numbers are based on Citrix Consulting Services scale testing, assuming a 5-day working week and one connection and 1 session per user. Numbers are in MB. See next page.

Table 7: Monitoring database sizing numbers

Users	Type	1 week	1 month	3 months
1000	RDSH	20	70	230
10,000	RDSH	160	600	1950
100,000	RDSH	1500	5900	19000
1000	VDI	15	55	670
10,000	VDI	120	440	5500
40,000	VDI	464	1700	21500

To help you size your databases Citrix released the Database Sizing Tool for XenDesktop 7.x. After filling in certain information like, the total number of users, sessions, applications, the type of deployment, RDSH and/or VDI etc. it will produce an overview of database sizes at various points in time. This will include day 0, 1, the first week, months, quarter and year. Have a look at the following CTX article for more detailed information: CTX139508.

Configuration Logging database

Overall (without MCS, see below) this one will be relatively small compared to the others. Its size will depend on the number of administrative tasks taking place on a daily basis using tools like Studio, Director and/or PowerShell scripting.

Another important factor impacting the Configuration Logging database size is the use of MCS for provisioning desktops and servers. Without MCS a typical Configuration Logging database tends to be somewhere around 30 to 40 MB in size, while with MCS, depending on the number of machines provisioned, it can easily grow beyond a few hundred MBs.

Connection Leasing

Although assumed by some, Connection Leasing was never meant as a replacement for the Local Host Cache. The Connection Leasing feature (as of XenDesktop 7.6) supplements the SQL Server high-availability best practices highlighted earlier, enabling users to connect and reconnect to some of their most recently used resources, even when the Central Site database is unavailable.

FMA fact: Connection Leasing is meant to supplement SQL High Availability set-ups.

Whenever a user successfully launches a resource, the Delivery Controller will collect information specific to that connection (icons, enumeration and launch information etc.) and will send this to the Central Site database where it will be stored first. Then, in ten-second intervals, this information will be synchronised to all Delivery Controllers known within the same Site where it will be saved on their local hard drives in an XML file format. This is what we refer to as the actual lease information.

Again I would like to highlight that each Controller has a direct connection to the database; Delivery Controllers do not communicate among each other.

Since the number of files can be significant, I'll explain why in a minute, the creation of these files is done in timed batches to distribute the required disk I/O, which will, or might, be needed during creation. By default, each controller will synchronise at a rate of up to 1000 leases every 10 seconds until all leases have been synchronised, although this behaviour can be changed through Registry or GPO.

On average, 2 to 4 GB of additional disk space should be sufficient, depending on the number of users, published resources and/or connections. While for smaller and mid-sized companies the impact of Connection Leasing will probably be minimal, it doesn't hurt to check on the estimated resources needed with regard to CPU and IOPS or disk activity. Citrix has written an extensive article (white paper) on this particular subject, including multiple calculations and examples with regard to the number and total size of lease files generated under certain circumstances, including the expected load on the underlying storage subsystem and Delivery Controllers.

The Connection Leasing white paper can be found here: http://support.citrix.com/content/dam/supportWS/kA460000 000CktXCAS/Connection_Leasing_XenDesktop_7.6.pdf

For each successful lease connection, multiple folders and XML files will be generated and stored within the Central Site database and on each individual Delivery Controller. Lease files are relatively small in size, around 1 KB and, by default, are stored in subdirectories of:

%programdata%\Citrix\Broker\Cache.

- Apps.
- Desktops.
- Icons.
- Leases\Enumeration.
- Leases\Launch.
- Workers.

These folders combined will store various (XML) files whenever a resource is successfully launched.

- The Apps directory will contain a single file per application per Delivery Group.
- The Desktop folder contains an entry for every user-assigned VDA, meaning one for every user assigned to a VDI-based VDA and one for every RDSH-based VDA (not per user). So in the case of a VDI-based architecture, this folder will hold a lot more files when compared to an RDSH deployment, where multiple users share a single VDA.
- The Icons directory holds a file for every unique published resource, one for each application, and one for all desktops to share.
- The Leases\Enumeration folder contains one file per user, which lists all available resources on a per user basis.
- The Leases\Launch directory contains an entry for each successfully launched resource. One for each desktop a user is entitled to launch, and one shared by all applications available to that same user. Here it is assumed that sessions sharing will direct the user to the same host. These launch files contain specific information on the resource launched, including the machine the resource was started on.
- Finally the Worker folder contains an entry per VDA, which does not have to be assigned, so one for every VDI-based VDA and one for every RDSH-based VDA.

All this takes place during normal operations where the Central Site database is up and running and everything behaves as

expected. As soon as a database failure takes place and none of
the active Delivery Controllers is able to communicate with the
Central database, and only then will Connection Leasing
become active. When Connection Leasing kicks in, by default
there will be a two-minute period where no connections will be
brokered; after that, the locally cached leases will become active.
At that same time any registered VDAs will start to deregister,
and again register once the database comes back online and is
reachable.

Once Connection Leasing is active it will use the information
stored within the various XML files to present resources to
users. More specifically, it will use the information available
within the Launch files to actually launch resources. It does this
by contacting the machine where the resource was last
successfully started, as highlighted earlier.

While all this may sound perfect on paper, it is (very) important
to note that all the information stored as part of the Connection
Leasing process (the generated XML files stored locally on each
Delivery Controller) will be valid / usable for a maximum
period of two weeks by default, something which is also
configurable through either the Registry or GPO. When
configured through GPO the configuration details will be stored
in:

HKLM\Software\Policies\Citrix\DesktopServer\ConnectionL
easing

When editing the Registry directly it will need to done at:

HKLM\Software\Citrix\DesktopServer\ConnectionLeasing

This means that, if we go with the default of two weeks at the time Connection Leasing becomes active, resources that have not been successfully launched during those last two weeks will not be available. Also, if a Launch file contains a machine, which might be down for maintenance, shutdown completely, or no longer operational, your users will not be able to launch that particular resource.

Another important point to mention is that Connection Leasing only works for assigned resources; it does not work for pooled desktops. Below is an overview of the limitations while Connection Leasing is active:

- Desktop Studio and Desktop Director operations are unavailable.
- Citrix PowerShell cmdlets requiring database access will not work.
- No VDA load balancing will occur.
- Users can only connect to the last host they connected to when the site database was available.
- There is a small window (2 minutes) during which no sessions will be brokered when the site database becomes unavailable or is restored. This is to allow for environments with SQL HA enabled to fail over.
- Users must have logged onto the resources within the default 14-day period. This can be configured via a registry setting or GPO.
- Connection Leasing does not support anonymous users.

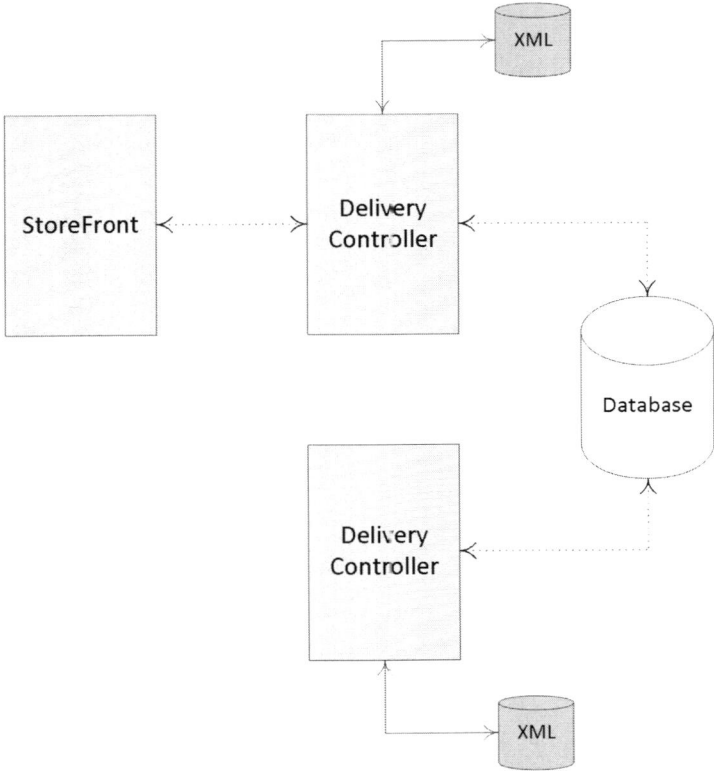

Figure 8: Connection Leasing overview

Key takeaways

- As of XenDesktop 7.x, only Microsoft SQL is supported for the Central Site database.
- It contains all static as well as dynamic Site-wide information.
- Make sure you understand the differences between the IMA and FMA when it comes to your Controllers and the Central Site database.
- If your Site is spread over multiple geographically separated locations, or you have multiple Zones configured, your Central Site database should always be in the Primary Zone, or the main datacentre.
- So even with multiple Zones configured it is still one central database.
- Make sure to implement some form of HA solution for your Site databases, since Connection Leasing is only meant as a supplement.
- Your Delivery Controllers and the Site database are constantly communicating: for this, Windows authentication is required between the Delivery Controller and the database.
- When the database fails (even without Connection Leasing) existing connections will continue to work. New sessions cannot be established and Site-wide configuration changes are also not possible.
- It is not recommended to install SQL on the same machine as a Delivery Controller.
- Try to keep your database server physically close to your Delivery Controllers in the data centre.

- SQL software, server or Express, must be installed and configured before creating a XenDesktop Site after its initial installation.

- While SQL Express is primarily used for PoC and testing purposes it could be used for smaller production environments as well. No HA capabilities though. It's up to you.

- You must be a local administrator and a domain user to create and initialise the databases (or change the database location).

- To be able to create an empty database, to add Delivery Controllers to it, create and apply schema updates and so on, you will need to have the following server and database roles: dbcreator, securityadmin and db_owner.

- When using Citrix Studio to perform these operations, the user account must be a member of the sysadmin server role.

The Citrix Receiver

While first introduced by Citrix at Synergy back in 2009, the Citrix Receiver was formerly known as the 'ICA Client'. As Citrix added more products and capabilities to their portfolio (and thus more clients to install and manage) the name slowly evolved from ICA Client to Citrix Receiver (with a lot of steps in between), as we know it today.

The idea behind Receiver was, and still is, that it functions as a container, or placeholder to hold all other Citrix client software providing administrators with a central point of management. The Receiver itself doesn't really do anything. This way all the various Citrix clients that might be needed on a client device, like the ICA Client software to access online applications and desktops, Password Manager, SSL VPN client software, the Secure Access Gateway client and so on, can all be managed and maintained from a single location.

You might also recall that around the same time Receiver was introduced, Citrix started to rename some of their existing clients. For example, the ICA Client was renamed as the Online Plugin, and the Access Gateway client to Secure Access Plugin; they also introduced an Offline Plugin, Web Plugin etc. The thought behind this was that these clients would 'plug in' to Receiver, which would then take over with regard to management and maintenance. The only thing missing in this approach was a mechanism to deliver (and manage) the various plug-ins to the Receiver software installed on the client device. For this they introduced something called a Merchandising Server together with Citrix Receiver 1.0. The Merchandising Server provides the administrative interface to configure, deliver, and upgrade plug-ins for your users' computers.

From there Receiver has matured from version 1.0 back in 2009 to version 4.4 at the time of writing. The 4.4 client went GA in December 2015, and it was only as of version 3.0 that it was actually referred to as the Citrix Receiver (available as a complete package); before that it was still 'just' a placeholder for all the other plugin clients accompanied by the Merchandising Server mentioned earlier. As of Receiver version 3.2 and newer versions going forward, it slowly moved away from the Merchandising Server for updating and maintaining the plug-ins contained within Receiver, handing this functionality over to Citrix.com. Anyway, let me dig in a bit deeper.

Some history

The Citrix Receiver didn't just appear out of nowhere: it was quite a journey. During the next section I'll try and take you through some of its history and highlight a couple of the most important changes along the way.

- It all started with the first release of the ICA Client software, version 4.0 back in September 1998. Note that I am not referring to the actual ICA protocol and earlier releases like Citrix Multiuser, WinView and WinFrame after that; these were all released (much) earlier.
- It contained the Program Neighborhood, Program Neighborhood Agent (PNAgent) and Web install packages.
- As of version 11.0 it got renamed as the Citrix Plug-in for hosted applications, which was also known as the Web Plug-in. This was over ten years later in June 2008. Although it was renamed, it still contained the same software packages.
- While this didn't directly lead to another name change, around version 11.2 they officially released Citrix

Receiver (version 1.0) together with the Merchandising Server. This was in May 2009 during Citrix Synergy.

- As mentioned, initially Receiver was meant as a placeholder for all other Citrix clients, which as of Receiver 1.0 got renamed one by one (Plug-ins), or most anyway. It stayed this way all through 2010.

- Soon after, when version 12.0 came out (March 2010) it got renamed (again) to the Citrix Online Plug-in. Are you still with me?

- With the release of version 13.0 of the ICA Client software, or Online Plug-in it was now officially renamed as Citrix Receiver, version 3.0 at that time. This happened in August 2011.

- As highlighted earlier, as of version 1.0 Receiver was a self-service orchestrator and an updater, also referred to as the Receiver Infrastructure (Merchandising Server).

- At that time Receiver 3.0 got split into two parts, Receiver Updater and Receiver Inside.

- Receiver Inside was integrated into the Online Plug-in to form a new package, which got named Citrix Receiver Enterprise.*

- It stayed this way up to Receiver Enterprise version 3.4.

- With version 4.0, which got released in June 2013, they changed its name to Citrix Receiver for Windows, the name it holds today.

- The Receiver Updater, as a separate component together with Merchandising Server, stayed with us until August 2015 (EOL). After a user installed Receiver Updater on his or her user device, Receiver Updater installed, updated, and restarted the Citrix Receiver without any user interaction needed.

- In between, from Receiver Enterprise version 3.2 to version 3.4 it still included the original PNAgent software, which was then referred to as Legacy PNA.
- As of version 4.0 the PNAgent functionality was no longer part of Citrix Receiver. This also meant the end of the Desktop Lock feature as it relied on the PNAgent functionality.
- Interestingly enough, Citrix reintroduced the Desktop Lock feature with the launch of Citrix Receiver version 4.2. Only this time they named it Receiver Desktop Lock.
- Citrix Receiver version 4.4 was launched in December 2015, which is the most recent version at this time.
- As of late-2012 they slowly moved away from the Receiver Infrastructure and Merchandising Server, which was EOL in August 2015.
- Today we install and configure Citrix Receiver either manually, using Group Policy (icaclient.adm GPO template), via a (start-up) script of some sort, as part of a base image, using our software distribution software of choice, or… through Receiver for Web sites. When a user accesses a Receiver for Web site from a computer running Windows or Mac OS X, the site will attempt to determine whether Citrix Receiver is installed on the user's device. If Citrix Receiver cannot be detected, the user is prompted to download and install the appropriate Citrix Receiver for their platform.
- When Citrix started to rename their Citrix client software (remember the Plug-ins?) they also introduced a couple of new clients, like the Offline Plug-in, the Desktop Receiver and the Citrix Self-Service Plug-in a.k.a. Dazzle. And I'm sure I left one or two out.

- The Self-Service Plug-in (Dazzle) was integrated with Citrix Receiver and your existing XenDesktop and XenApp infrastructure. It communicated with the Citrix Delivery Services (basically what we now call StoreFront) or Web Interface. Merchandising Server was used to control and manage it.

- The Offline Plug-in, version 5.1, was first introduced in May 2009 and disappeared in July of 2012. Earlier it was also referred to as the Citrix Streaming client, and used, as the name implies, with Citrix-streamed applications. For offline use, I might add. Unfortunately Citrix Streaming never really took off.

- The Desktop Receiver was aimed at launching hosted shared desktops only (full screen), not published applications. Here they added the well-known pull-down menu, making it easier to switch between your hosted desktop session and your local desktop.

* While the standard Receiver for Windows is for general use, Receiver for Windows Enterprise is intended only to support:

- Repurposed PCs and Thin Clients configured with desktop lock
- Applications that require Fast Connect-enabled products
- Applications that require 508 compliance

Don't get confused by the different version numbers. There is a version numbering scheme for the ICA Client software versions (which has been renamed multiple times) and one for the Citrix Receiver versions.

It's not just Windows.

While the previous section primarily focused on the Citrix Receiver for Windows, there is a Citrix Receiver for almost every platform out there; I'll list them here:

- Receiver for Windows.
- Receiver for Mac.
- Receiver for iOS.
- Receiver for Linux.
- Receiver for Android.
- Receiver for Chrome.
- Receiver for HTML5.
- Receiver for Windows 8/RT.
- Receiver for Windows Phone.
- Receiver for BlackBerry 10.

Next to the various types of Receivers there are also multiple Receiver plug-ins like the HDX RealTime Media engine for Microsoft Skype and Lync (multiple versions), Receiver for Desktop lock (multiple versions) and the Offline plug-in.

It is also worth mentioning that Citrix has been working on an X1 release of the Citrix Receiver (X1 stands for eXperience 1st), which, combined with the latest StoreFront release (both are still in tech preview at the time of writing), offers some nice additional features like:

- Enhanced StoreFront management console
- The ability to group resources by organising them under self-managed categories.

- Specific and flexible branding options (no more green bubble theme), including the use of customer logos and different colour schemas.
- Eventually all this will apply to the NetScaler interface (logon page) as well.
- The ability to use one Citrix Receiver for both XenDesktop / XenApp-hosted applications, as well as mobile applications hosted from XenMobile / App Controller (no more Worx Home, it will be part of the Receiver X1).
- A unified look and feel on all devices and different platforms, including connections through the HTML5-based Receiver.

Once the Receiver X1 will be released (GA) there will be no need for any of the other Receiver editions mentioned earlier: the Receiver for Enterprise, for example.

The X1 will be able to offer all the features and functionality you might need, including but not limited to, (legacy) PNA support, the ability to put all published applications in the Start menu or on the desktop, the Store concept where users can subscribe to their own applications, or they can be pre-subscribed using Keywords, the use of Single Sign-on and personal branding (you can get very creative), while the 'old' green bubble theme is still available / optional as well.

FMA fact: The Receiver X1 combined with StoreFront will greatly simplify overall management and improve the user experience on multiple levels.

Citrix Receiver communications

The Citrix Receiver is a client application enabling us to connect up to various Citrix services like XenApp and XenDesktop, but also the XenMobile App Controller, the NetScaler Access Gateway and StoreFront, to name a few more. While Citrix Receiver basically sits idle during the user authentication and application enumeration processes (you don't really need a Citrix Receiver for that), it plays a leading role when it comes to actually launching a published desktop and/or application and establishing a secure connection up to XenApp / XenDesktop. It literally channels the ICA / HDX traffic back and forth between the client and server.

FMA fact: HDX is not a replacement for the ICA protocol. It offers a set of capabilities or technologies that offer a high-definition user experience, which are built on top of the ICA remoting protocol.

Once a resource is launched, after all background communications are done and load-balancing decisions have been made, one of the first things that will take place is something referred to as the ICA handshake.

During this phase the client (Receiver) and the server (VDA) will exchange information on the virtual channels that the client supports: here the client basically tells the server which specific capabilities (virtual channels) it can or should use during the connection. This way the server knows what to expect and what virtual channels it can or should use.

Virtual channels, you say?

I know, virtual channels? Yes. A big part of the communication between the client and the server takes place over and through what Citrix refers to as virtual channels (and not just Citrix by the way). Each virtual channel consists of a client-side virtual driver (part of Receiver) that communicates with a server-side application (part of the VDA).

Virtual channels (there can be 32 channels in total) are mainly used/applied for some of the bigger, well-known features like client drive mapping, smart cards, the clipboard, printing, audio, video and so on. However, the Citrix Receiver also supports a whole bunch of additional features and functionalities that do not involve or need a virtual channel.

And of course, from time to time, new virtual channels are released with a new version or Feature Pack of XenDesktop / XenApp and Receiver products to provide additional functionality. Like Framehawk and ThinWire Plus, for example. Those were released as part of Feature Pack 3 for XenDesktop 7.6, including a new Receiver (4.3) if I am not mistaken) on the client side.

Each virtual channel represents a specific feature or functionality on its own. But don't worry, I will elaborate a bit more on all this during one of the upcoming chapters where we will talk about the ICA protocol and the HDX additions in more detail.

FMA fact: While some think that ThinWire is still a relatively new technique, it is not. ThinWire has always been there. It is a core component of the ICA virtual display channel stack (for over twenty years now). That's why they rebranded their latest addition as ThinWire Plus, although it has had several names along the way.

So you see, most features and functionalities configured at server level (mainly through policies) will need to be supported by the client as well; there is a strong dependency between the two (think about the ICA handshake mentioned earlier). And while most features apply to XenDesktop / XenApp VDAs, some do apply to StoreFront, NetScaler and/or Web Interface as well, most are related to security and communication.

Receiver for web access, which is built into Receiver based on HTML5 technology, or secure remote access via the NetScaler Gateway, NetScaler full VPN capabilities, RSA soft token support, Pass Through authentication, Smart Access policies and filters, IPv6 and more. While these types of features and functionalities mainly apply to components like StoreFront, NetScaler etc. your locally installed Citrix Receiver must be able to support these as well.

As mentioned, some of the bigger and better-known features that get built into XenDesktop come with their own virtual channel; however, the Citrix Receiver also has an extensive and impressive list of features that it is capable of without the need for a virtual channel. Check out the link below to find out more:

https://www.citrix.com/content/dam/citrix/en_us/documents/products-solutions/citrix-receiver-feature-matrix.pdf

Although not mentioned on the Receiver Feature Matrix, the Desktop lock is another example. It is dependent on the type and version of Receiver installed and probably best described as an add-on on top of Receiver. The Desktop Lock feature is often used when thin clients are not optional and you do not want to get rid of your older desktop machines just yet. When installed and configured properly (on a domain-joined machine) it will pass on the user's AD / domain credentials, logging them directly into their VDI session, without the user being able to interact with the local physical desktop.

But there is more. Features like Session Sharing, Session Reliability, Auto Client Reconnect and ICA Keep-Alive etc. are all Receiver-dependent as well, although these have been around for some time now. Again, more details will be discussed in the 'ICA / HDX protocol' chapter.

Connection information

During the StoreFront section earlier I already mentioned a couple of ways how users can connect up to StoreFront using Citrix Receiver. However, this doesn't just happen magically, somehow you will need to tell Receiver how and where to connect to: there are a couple of ways to achieve this.

First, and this is a popular approach, you can configure something called e-mail-based account discovery. This way, all your users will have to do is fill in their email address. After that, once they hit OK, Citrix Receiver will automatically determine the NetScaler Gateway or StoreFront Server associated with the email address. This method is based on Domain Name System (DNS) Service records. The user will then be prompted to log on using their domain credentials.

FMA fact: If you want to make use of e-mail-based discovery you will need to use StoreFront, it does not work with Webinterface.

Using StoreFront you can also create your own provisioning files, which contain connection details needed for your users to connect. Once Receiver is installed all they have to do is double-click the provisioning file and Receiver will be automatically configured. When using Receiver for Web sites, and many do, you can also offer the provisioning file on there. Just like with the Citrix Receiver installation file itself.

As a third option you can provide your users with the information needed to connect up to StoreFront for them to enter manually. Here you can use the XenApp services site if you are still on 6.5, or you can provide your users with the address of your StoreFront server for them to be able to access the Store(s) on there.

After the information has been entered Receiver will first try and verify the connection: once done and successful your users will be prompted to fill in their user credentials.

Self Service Mode

By adding StoreFront to Receiver, as we've just talked about, you can configure something called Self Service Mode (will be enabled by default). It enables the user to subscribe to resources directly from the locally installed Receiver (right-click on the system tray icon) and, just like with the Receiver for Web sites approach, Keywords can also be used to pre-subscribe certain resources to your users.

Another potentially advantage when using this approach (opposed to the more limited Web Access Mode (although preferred by many) where Receiver is not configured and users access a Receiver for Web site) is the ability to (almost) fully manage and customise the application short cut location (or you let your users decide for themselves). This way, published applications can appear in your users' Start menu and/or desktop without them being able to uninstall. Your users will not have to manually subscribe to their resources before being able to launch them. Of course these two modes, Web Access and Self Service, can be configured and used side-by-side.

> **FMA fact**: All, or at least most, of these resource short cut management options were already available with Citrix Receiver Enterprise up to version 3.4, when they killed it. It took up to Citrix Receiver version 4.2 to get this functionality back.

Just be careful and think about when to implement which solution. Not all of your users will be too happy with a preconfigured Start menu or desktop, for example, especially when dozens or more applications are involved. Unfortunately there will always be some pros and cons no matter which route you choose.

You have options

Luckily, when needed you do have some options to play with. Applications can be configured on an individual basis to be placed in the Start menu or on the desktop, or you can let your users decide. Put them all on the desktop or in the Start menu by default or a combination of all options mentioned: it is up to you. This is accomplished by manually configuring the Citrix Receiver. If you want...

- Your users to be able to choose the resources they want in their Start menu, then you configure the Receiver in Self Service Mode.
- Your users to be able to choose the resources they want in their Start menu and you also want to force a few specific resources onto their desktops, then you will need to apply those specific settings on a per application basis.
- By configuring the Receiver with PutShortcutsInStartMenu=False you prevent the Receiver from putting application short cuts into the Start menu automatically.
- PutShortcutsOnDesktop=true will put all application short cuts on the user's desktop.

These are just a few examples to give you an idea of the possibilities: it's very flexible. There are a couple of more options available so make sure to check out the E-docs pages on Citrix Receiver.

FMA fact: By disabling the SelfServiceMode (it is enabled by default) subscribed-to applications can only be accessed through the Start menu and desktop short cuts. This is also referred to as short cut-only mode.

To conclude

Now, of course, there is still a lot more to tell and share when it comes to the Citrix Receiver, but hopefully this section provided you with enough information on some of its inner workings and more specifically why it is such an important piece of the puzzle.

Key takeaways

- No matter how you decide to deploy and configure Citrix Receiver, make sure to instruct your users.
- Don't forget to inform your helpdesk employees when planning configuration changes to Receiver.
- I briefly introduced you to the Web Access and Self Service modes. Remember, it does not have to be one or the other. They can be configured and used side-by-side.
- A couple of years ago the Self Service mode was released as a separate plugin; it is now built into Receiver.
- In fact, some of the most important modules that make up Receiver today are the ICA Client software, the Self Service plugin, and the Single Sign-on module for ICA.
- It all started with the ICA Client software back in 2009. Since then it has gone through a lot of name changes and of course the underlying technology also matured over time.
- The upcoming Receiver X1 is probably a great example of its evolution during the last decade.
- When upgrading to a newer version of Receiver, make sure to follow the step-by-step procedure as outlined by Citrix; have a look this CTX article: CTX135933.
- As it stands today, the Citrix Receiver version 4.4 should be able to upgrade from any of the older Receiver versions that might be installed without any issues.
- When upgrading to a version older than 4.4 and you run into any issues, have a look at CTX137494, the Receiver Clean-Up utility.
- Do not forget about the ICA handshake and the earlier mentioned virtual channels.

- The Citrix Receiver can be managed and configured using various methods, for example: using the command-line, registry settings, StoreFront account settings, or on a per application basis using Studio and Group Policy Objects.
- When viewing the Citrix Receiver Feature Matrix, remember that not all features are on there.
- By default, the HTML5-based and built-in (StoreFront) Receiver is not enabled: this needs to be done manually.

Citrix Studio

Citrix Studio is THE management console that allows us to administrate, configure and manage our XenDesktop and/or XenApp Sites from a single pane of glass. It also provides us with access to real-time data collected through the Broker service running on the Delivery Controller.

FMA fact: By default, Studio communicates with the Controller on TCP port 80.

To give you a better idea of what Studio is all about, have a closer look at the screenshot on the next page. After you have set up your primary Site (something you will always have to do first, assuming there isn't one in place already) you would normally continue with a Machine Catalog closely followed by a Delivery Group and then on to configuring and publishing applications and/or desktops to your users.

But it doesn't stop there. From Studio you have full control over your entire Site and everything in it, including but not limited to Zones, Machine Catalogs, Delivery Groups, Delivery Controllers, XenDesktop and XenApp (Session Hosts) machines and a lot more. Studio also allows us to integrate StoreFront and App-V, and it is also the place where we add and configure our Host Connection (underlying Hypervisor / cloud platform, or multiple), manage and initiate Machine Creation Services, set up delegated administration, and so on. And as you might know, most features are configured through policies, which are also available from Studio.

136

So you see there is quite a lot going on from a management perspective. That's why I thought it might be helpful to go over each object or subject one at a time (as shown in the left-hand side of the Console Root three, see screenshot), starting at the top. Again, this is meant to provide you with an overview of the configuration and management options you have using Citrix Studio, explaining a few concepts along the way. I am not going into all the 'per component' configuration details at this time.

- Citrix Studio (basvankaam)
  - Search
  - Machine Catalogs
  - AppDisks
  - Delivery Groups
  - Applications
  - Policies
  - Logging
  - Configuration
    - Administrators
    - Controllers
    - Hosting
    - Licensing
    - StoreFront
    - App-V Publishing
    - AppDNA
    - Zones
- Citrix StoreFront
  - Stores
  - Server Group

Figure 9: Studio main console

FMA fact: While Studio takes care of most configuration and maintenance tasks, depending on your set-up, it doesn't cover everything. If you are using Provisioning Services, you will still have a second, separate management console. The same applies to Citrix NetScaler.

Basic troubleshooting

Next to configuring and maintaining our Site, Studio also allows us to execute some basic troubleshooting tasks. From Studio you can run several self-diagnostics tests on your Delivery Groups and Machine Catalogs, for example including a Site-wide test. Depending on the size of your Site, the number of machines, Delivery Groups, policies etc. this will take (at least) a couple of minutes. When done, it will let you know about any issues and/or errors that it might have encountered.

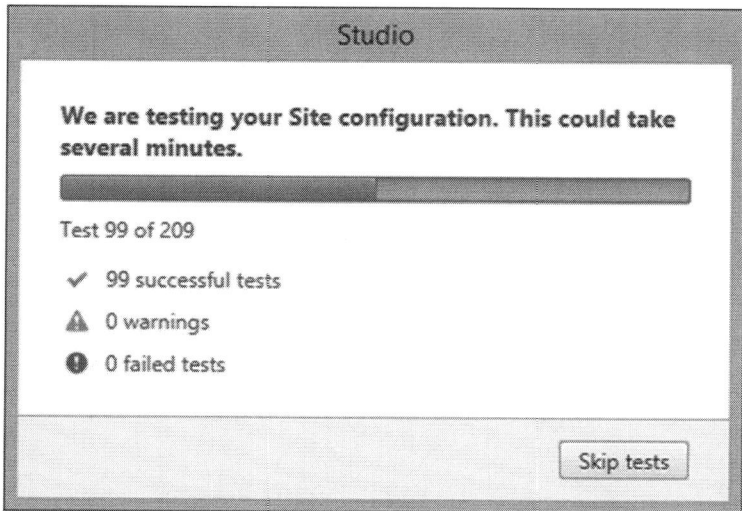

Figure 10: Studio self-test

We also have the option to launch PowerShell directly from Studio, which of course is only helpful if you know your way around PowerShell, potentially helpful none the less. And while this isn't directly related to troubleshooting, you can also use the built-in PowerShell functionality to auto-generate PowerShell scripts on almost everything you can do from Citrix Studio.

As mentioned, Studio is the place from where we configure and manage all, some, or most of our Citrix-related Site-wide policies (something that can also be done using the Group Policy Management Console, or GPMC if installed on your Delivery Controller, or on a separate management server for that matter. Note that for this to work you will also have to install Citrix Studio and the Citrix Group Policy extensions on the same 'management' machine). From Studio we have a couple of options we can use to help in the troubleshooting process, so have a look below:

- An overview of all settings available within all policies combined.
- We can configure filters to apply specific policies to specific objects.
- Policy comparison: by selecting one or multiple configured policies and/or templates you can compare the configured settings within the selected objects.
- Group Policy Modelling allows the user to simulate a policy deployment that would be applied to users and computers before actually applying the policies.
- Citrix Group Policy Modelling, specific to Citrix-related policies only.

Resultant Set Of Policies is only available when using the GPMC approach mentioned above.

We can see the current license usage and overall statistics; how many users are logged onto which machines and Machine Catalogs; we can restart and/or shutdown machines; send out messages to logged in users; and of course we have the ability to log off users if needed. Studio is also used to put machines, or Machine Catalogs, in maintenance mode.

Now that you have a basic understanding of what Studio is about, including some troubleshooting 'first steps', let's continue with the one-by-one feature and concept explanation, following Studio's console root from top to bottom.

Search

Here we can search for machines, Catalogs, applications, sessions, plug-in versions, Operating Systems, Agents, Delivery Groups, users, IP addresses and so on; the list is almost endless. Searches can also be saved for later (re)use – a very handy feature to have.

Machine Catalogs

Catalogs are collections of virtual or physical machines from where we publish our applications and/or desktops. Catalogs allow us to manage groups of machines as a single entity. We can configure different Operating Systems per Catalog; however, only a single Operating System per Catalog is allowed. During the creation of a Machine Catalog, when adding machines, we also select the mechanism used to manage / provision our machines, which can be either by hand or by using MCS and/or PVS.

AppDisks

Citrix AppDisks are based on application-layering technology and available as of XenDesktop version 7.8. See the 'Application

Delivery' chapter for more detailed information around application layering in general. AppDisks are created, managed and assigned directly from Citrix Studio; hence no separate management console is needed.

Delivery Groups

Delivery Groups allow us to assign resources to our users (also see Machine Catalogs two paragraphs back). To be able to create a Delivery Group you must first create one or more Machine Catalogs and at least one machine must be unassigned and free for use. When creating a Delivery Group we add one or multiple machines from a Machine Catalog (note that a machine can only be assigned to a single Delivery Group), we select the resources that we want to publish to our users, AppDisks and App-V-based applications included, and finally we add in the users who will have access to these resources. As with the Machine Catalogs and AppDisks, all management is done from Studio.

Applications

From here we can manage all of our published applications. We can add new ones or change and maintain existing ones. We can delete them, have a look at their properties, manage tags, do a search, move applications, rename or disable them and arrange them in folders to further simplify overall management. We can also see which applications are actually being used, if they are enabled or disabled, their source, installation paths, the groups they belong to, and by whom they can be administered.

Policies

A great deal of what happens within our XenDesktop / XenApp Site is configured through Citrix policies; the Policy node in Studio is where you will find everything needed to configure and manage your Citrix policies. As highlighted earlier, besides Studio, Citrix policies can also be configured and maintained from a central management server or Domain Controller using the GPMC. Within Studio you will also find seven predefined and configured policy templates; you can create your own template or simply configure policies on an individual basis. Policies and templates can be compared and policy Modelling is also optional from Studio. If you want to be able to do an RSOP you will have to use GPMC-based GPOs instead. Policies can also be exported if and when needed.

Logging

The configuration-logging feature enables us to track administrative activities within Studio, including the ability to create custom reports in CSV, HTML or both. It will track everything from image updates to Delivery Group creation and all that is in between. During the initial Site configuration you can select where the database will be created.

Configuration

While it will provide you with a Site overview when selected, and the ability to start or stop with the Citrix Customer Experience Improvement Programme, the configuration node is nothing more than a placeholder for some of the more advanced configuration options you have within Studio, which will be covered in the next few sections. By clicking on the Configuration node, new options and features will present themselves.

Administrators

This is where we configure delegated administration within our Site. Delegated administration is based on three pillars: (1) Scopes, a collection of objects a user is allowed administer like connections, Catalogs, Delivery Groups etc.; (2) an

Administrator, the person responsible for executing the actual administrative tasks; and (3) Roles, a set of permissions which are granted to an administrator. These can be based on the built-in Studio roles or they can be custom-made.

Controllers

Here we can see all of our active and non-active Delivery Controllers within our Site. Under the 'Last Updated' section it will state '0 minutes ago' if everything is ok. This is because your Delivery Controllers will have a continuous connection with the Central Site database through a heartbeat mechanism where a heartbeat message is sent every 20 seconds, which has a default timeout of 40 seconds.

Hosting

This is where we add, configure and manage our so-called Host Connection, or multiple. A Host Connection is nothing more than your underlying Hypervisor or cloud platform of choice. As you might have noticed at the beginning of the 'The FMA, main components' section, the Host Connection is also one of the nine main components that make up the FlexCast Management Architecture as a whole. In fact, it completes the list; needless to say, I will be covering Host Connections in the 'Hosting' section in more detail later on.

Licensing

Citrix Licensing and the Citrix License Server are covered in detail in the 'Citrix Licensing' chapter. In Studio it will show us all of our active XenDesktop and/or XenApp licenses, when they will expire, the type of license (Evaluation, for example) and the model used: user/device, or concurrent, plus the Subscription Advantage date and if SA is supported (for example, it will show not supported when in Evaluation mode).

You will also find the license server name, the port number used, how many licenses are actually in use and who is allowed to administer the licenses from within Studio. And last but not least, you have the ability to allocate and add licenses, change the license server and edit the product edition.

StoreFront

Here you can add an existing StoreFront deployment. This will allow you to configure the Citrix Receiver installed as part of the machines in your Delivery Groups, when publishing hosted shared desktops. Do note that this will not enable StoreFront management from Studio, for this your StoreFront deployment will have to be added in sperately.

App-V Publishing

Used for adding/removing Microsoft App-V Management and Publishing servers. Once done, you will be able to publish virtualised App-V applications. These applications will then be 'streamed' over the network using your App-V set-up of choice. Check out the chapter 'Application delivery' for some more detailed information on this. As of XenDesktop version 7.8 we now also have the ability to manually add App-V packages directly from Studio. In fact, all you have to do is fill in the accompanying UNC path and you are good to go, no further infrastructural App-V components needed. Ctxappvlauncher.exe will take care of everything.

AppDNA

Before XenDesktop 7.8 AppDNA was only available as a separate product (and it still is). It is now integrated into Studio, although it will still need to be installed as a separate product, in fact, it can be selected when installing or upgrading to XenDesktop 7.8. Citrix describes AppDNA as follows:

AppDNA software simplifies the four key areas of application management: Discover application issues with sophisticated testing. Model application outcomes to determine the best plan of action. Automate application remediation and packaging processes. And finally, manage ongoing application evolution after launch of the migration or virtualisation project.

In short, it will tell you if your application is compatible with other applications and/or software you might already be using and the Operating System you would like to install it on. This includes locally installed applications, App-V packages, AppDisk packages, web applications etc. Eventually it will tell you if any issues are to be expected and what you can do to remedy them. It also offers features like patch impact analyses, which works in sort of the same way. It can also automatically create MSI packages to be used in production environments instantly, a very handy and welcome tool to have in your tool belt: Platinum licenses only, though.

Zones

This is a feature that a lot of people have been waiting for. Zones are back! However, you need to be aware that these are not the Zones that we were, or are, used to with XenApp 6.5, or at least not yet anyway. Citrix already announced a phased approach when it comes to reintroducing Zones back into XenApp, which of course now also apply to XenDesktop – something we didn't have before.

Zones originated in the IMA and worked quite well because of a feature / mechanism named Local Host Cache (LHC), which is available on every machine with the XenApp 6.5 bits and bytes installed (also see 'Local Host Cache' on page 101). It basically caches all static IMA (Farm-wide) database information as well as any dynamic live runtime data with regard to server load, apps running, users connected, and so on. It will check in periodically with the central IMA database and update its cache when needed. Also, whenever a major configuration change on Farm level is made, all Session Hosts and Data Collectors will be notified so that their LHC can be updated right away.

Now as soon as the central IMA database becomes unavailable or unreachable for whatever reason, all machines would continue to function based on the contents stored in their LHC. Existing essions will continue without any interruption and new sessions can be established as well. However, configuration changes to the Farm itself are not possible as long as the IMA database is down / unreachable. I am not saying it is perfect (the LHC can get corrupted), but it certainly offers some advantages when compared to the first few releases of the FMA, especially with regard to geographically separated locations.

FMA fact: Do not compare FMA-based Zones (7.x) with IMA-based Zones (6.5). There are some distinct differences between the two. Make sure to check out the table on page 101.

While the FlexCast Management Architecture offers multiple advantages over the Independent Management Architecture, it comes with a few challenges as well. For example, with the FMA the Central Site database still plays a key role, especially when dealing with multiple locations spread throughout the country, or globe even (remember that there is no LHC within the FMA). Of course Connection Leasing helps but only up to a certain point. And while deploying and configuring multiple separate Sites, including an HA SQL set-up do help, it also makes managing these deployments much more complex.

This is where Zones can help. Normally when we deploy multiple Sites these will need to be managed and maintained on an individual basis, meaning that for each Site you will have a separate HA SQL set-up holding all Site-wide configurations' information, static as well as dynamic, as mentioned earlier.

Imagine having to manage and equally configure up to 5 separate Sites or more, setting up and configuring your Delivery Controllers, Host Connections, HDX policies, Delivery Groups, Machine Catalogs, SQL HA and so on; of course this is not impossible but most certainly not desirable.

Zones give us the ability to configure up to ten satellite Zones under our primary Zone (which is also where our HA SQL set-up would live). From here we are then able to manage, maintain and configure all Zones, including our primary Zone as a single entity, or Site from Citrix Studio, requiring a single SQL HA set-up. Since all Zone-related static and dynamic data will also be stored in the same Central Site database there are a couple of prerequisites to consider before thinking about implementing and configuring Zones.

XenDesktop Site

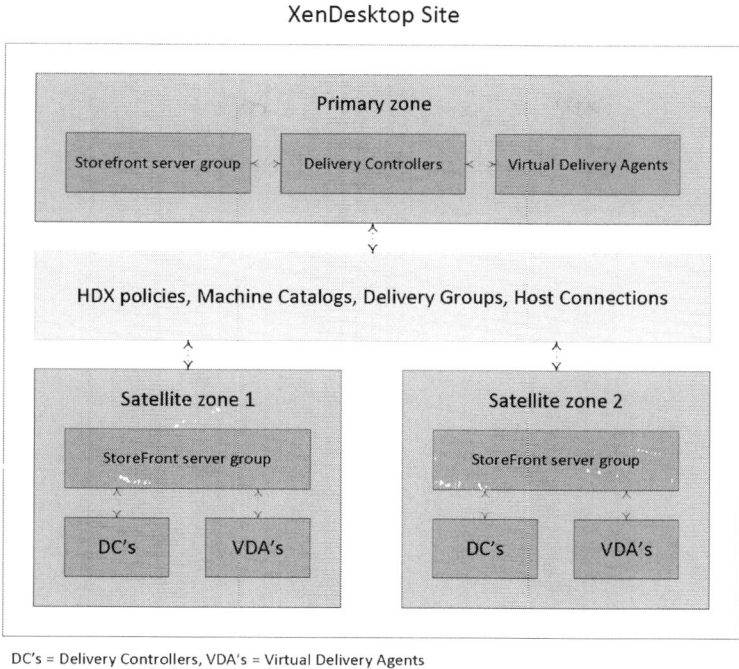

DC's = Delivery Controllers, VDA's = Virtual Delivery Agents

Figure 11: XenDesktop Zones

FMA fact: If the RRT to and from a satellite Zone is near or above 250 ms, a separate Site deployment, including an SQL HA set-up, is advised.

Also see Citrix's blog posts on the new Zoning feature:

https://www.citrix.com/blogs/2016/01/12/deep-dive-xenapp-and-xendesktop-7-7-Zones/

When the FMA was first introduced, setting up and configuring separate XenDesktop Sites was basically the only way we had to service geographically separated locations.

This was mainly due to potential latency and congestion issues with regard to the Central Site database, since all Delivery Controllers should be able to constantly read and write to and from the database. And while some changes have been made to minimise this SQL interaction, this also imposes some limits on the quality of the link between the satellite Zone and the primary Zone containing the database.

To back this up, Citrix released a detailed overview of the currently recommended connection quality limits regarding the connections between the locations that should be taken into account when setting up remote satellite Zones. The number of VDAs and user sessions in and from a satellite Zone also play an important role in determining the minimal bandwidth and RTT needed.

FMA fact: If you want to limit the number of brokering requests originating from a satellite Zone there is a Registry Key, which can be configured for this.

The above-mentioned Key can be found here: HKLM\Software\Citrix\DesktopServer\ThrottledRequestAddressMaxConcurrentTransactions. It is set per Delivery Controller. If the key does not exist, then no limit on brokering requests will be enforced.

As highlighted earlier, when thinking about implementing satellite Zones there are a couple of prerequisites, pros and cons that need to be thought through, I will list most here. Note that these will probably change over time: remember the phased approach mentioned earlier:

- If the RRT is near or above 250 ms, a separate Site is still advised.
- With (satellite) Zones, each Zone is basically a sub Site but without the need for highly available SQL Central Site database.
- You will (always) have one primary Zone/Site (it's named primary by default but this can easily be changed) and optionally multiple satellite Zones.
- You can name the Zones anything you like, though the name must be unique within the Site itself. Just note that, while spaces in a Zone name won't be a problem, you cannot use special characters.
- You can set up delegated administration specific to managing and maintaining Zones.
- Citrix Studio is configured only in the primary Zone and from there you will be able to manage each Zone independently from each other, policies included.
- When needed, you can publish Citrix Studio from the primary Zone to other Zones.
- This also applies to Citrix Director.
- Each Zone will have (at least) its own Delivery Controller, StoreFront server, NetScaler (optional) and of course one or multiple VDAs, desktop or server machines.
- Zones enable us to connect users to resources, which are closest to them, keeping traffic 'local'.
- Traffic flows as usual (resource enumeration and launch) with the Delivery Controllers in the Zones directly communicating with the Central Site database and the license server in the primary Zone.
- So while you don't need an HA SQL set-up within each Zone, as we would have with separate Sites, we still need

to have at least one additional Delivery Controller and StoreFront server. Yes, one is enough, though this is not recommended.

- This set-up also means we still depend on Connection Leasing once the Central Site database becomes unresponsive or unavailable altogether. And, although Connection Leasing might be a 'nice to have' feature up to this point, something tells me this will soon change.

- Delivery Controllers in the primary Zone will store leasing information for all Zones including the primary Zone while Delivery Controllers in the satellite Zones will only store leasing information for the primary Zone and their own Zone, not for any additional Zones.

- New features and functionality will first find their way into CWC (which includes both XenApp and XenDesktop as part of the Applications and Desktop service) before they become available in the on-premises products. The same applies to Zones: long before they became available within XenDesktop and XenApp they were first reintroduced and extensively tested within CWC.

- VDAs within a Zone automatically register with a Delivery Controller in their own Zone (preferred Controller). If none are available, they will attempt to register with a Controller in the primary Zone. When successful they will stay registered even if a Controller in the Zone it originated from becomes available again. There is no fallback mechanism, at least not today. When a Machine Catalog is moved from one Zone to another, all the registered VDAs will reregister with the 'new' Delivery Controller of that Zone.

- VDAs in the primary Zone can and will only register with a Controller in the Primary Zone.

- When a Zone Delivery Controller fails, another one in the same Zone will take over. If none are available, it will auto failover to a Controller in the primary Zone, which makes sense since a Zone's VDAs will also register themselves in the primary Zone when no local (preferred) controllers are available.
- Make sure to keep your Machine Catalogs close to any host connection they might be using. You can add one or multiple host connections per Zone if needed / desired.
- Provisioning services is not 'Zone aware'. Configure the Machine Catalogs by hand using Citrix Studio. If you let PVS handle this, the Catalog(s) will be created in the primary Zone by default.
- While Zones might not be the Zones we had, or have with XenApp 6.5, we now have Zones for XenDesktop as well, which we didn't have before!

Table 8: Zone quality connection limits

# Of supported sessions	# Of session launches	Minimum acceptable bandwidth	Max Round Trip Time allowed
< 50	20	1 Mbps	250 ms
50 – 500	25	1.5 Mbps	100 ms
500 – 1000	30	2 Mbps	50 ms
1000 – 3000	60	8 Mbps	10 ms
> 3000	60	8 Mbps	5 ms

Key takeaways

- Citrix Studio is THE management console that allows us to administrate, configure and manage our XenDesktop and/or XenApp Sites from a single pane of glass. It also provides us with access to real-time data collected through the Broker service running on the Delivery Controller.
- Studio also provides us with a range of basic troubleshooting tools and options.
- While Zones are not a new concept, you need to be aware that Zones within a 7.x deployment are not the same as with XenApp 6.5 – not yet anyway. There are some distinct differences between the two, as we have clearly seen in this chapter.
- Citrix is working on a phased approach with regard to the reintroduction of Zones; needless to say, this is phase one.
- Zones in the FMA still depend on the Central Site database: there is no LHC.
- The main focus of this first releases is to simplify overall management and keep traffic local.
- Make sure to keep an eye on the RTT between Zones; it needs to be below 250 milliseconds; less is more in this case. Consult the table for recommended values.

Citrix Director

Director is a real-time web-based tool (can be installed as a website on your Delivery Controllers) that allows administrators to monitor, troubleshoot (real-time as well as historical) and perform support tasks for their end-users. It is Citrix's first line of defence and it is, by default, included with all editions of XenDesktop and/or XenApp, although higer editions do offer some additional functionality. As of XenDesktop 7.x it has some of the former EdgeSight functionality built in (historical reporting mainly) and if you own the proper licenses (Platinum) for both XenDesktop and NetScaler you can monitor your NetScalers (HDX Insight) using the same console as well.

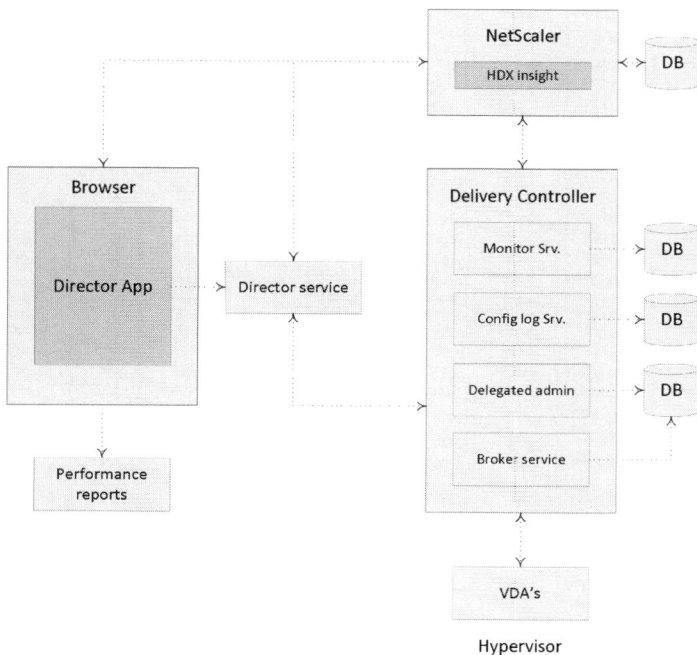

Figure 12: The Director service

Performance and monitoring data

By default, Director has access to:

- Real-time data from the Broker Agent using a unified console integrated with EdgeSight features, Performance Manager, and Network Inspector.
  - EdgeSight features include performance management for health and capacity assurance, and historical trending and network analysis, powered by NetScaler HDX Insight, to identify bottlenecks due to the network in your XenApp or XenDesktop environment.
- Historical data stored in the Monitor database to access the Configuration Logging database.
- ICA data from the NetScaler Gateway using HDX Insight.
  - Gain visibility into end-user experience for virtual applications, desktops, and users for XenApp or XenDesktop.
  - Correlate network data with application data and real-time metrics for effective troubleshooting.
  - Integrate with XenDesktop 7 Director monitoring tool.
- Personal vDisk data that allows for runtime monitoring showing base allocation and gives helpdesk IT the ability to reset the Personal vDisk (to be used only as a last resort).
- The command-line tool CtxPvdDiag.exe is used to gather the user log information into one file for troubleshooting.

Source: Citrix E-docs website

> **FMA fact**: Make sure to check out CTX139382 for a whole bunch of best practices around Director.

Citrix EdgeSight (reporting)

As already briefly highlighted, Director makes use of Citrix's EdgeSight technology, which is now an integral part of Director. However, not that long ago, it was still available as a separate product offering the ability to monitor applications, devices, sessions, license usage, and the network in real time, allowing users to quickly analyse, resolve, and proactively prevent problems. The latest version that was released was 5.4.

While EdgeSight (reporting) was very powerful it was also quite complex to operate and work with. Today Director probably covers up to 80 – 90% of all tasks needed by first as well as second line support engineers and at the same time it is very easy and straightforward to navigate. As you might recall Citrix Director started out as a fairly simple monitoring and troubleshooting tool only capable of offering real-time support.

As time progressed people started asking for historical reporting features as well as trend analysis capabilities, and rightfully so. This is where the earlier mentioned EdgeSight functionality comes in. They reused and re-written part of the original code and primarily focussed on the reporting functionality now available in Director, as we know it today.

> **FMA fact**: As it stands today, the EOL for EdgeSight has been set to 30-June-18, or 24-Aug-2016, depending on if you have a valid software maintenance and/or Subscription Advantage. In that case, the EOM is set to 31-Dec-17 or 24-Feb-2016.

While Director will be shipped with every XenDesktop / XenApp version, offering real-time assessment and troubleshooting capabilities, the additional reporting and trends analysis functionality does require a Platinum license for both the XenDesktop and/or XenApp, depending on which product you are using. The same applies to the network analysis functionality; you will need at least a NetScaler Enterprise or Platinum license for this. With an Enterprise license you will be able to store historical data for 60 minutes, while with a Platinum license there is no limit.

Historical data

The ability to view historical data / reports, including trend analysis can be very helpful when troubleshooting your XenDesktop / XenApp deployment. Since the data storage restrictions for XenDesktop / XenApp are slightly different per platform license, I'll summarise them below:

- All editions: Will have free use of Director troubleshooting and real-time monitoring with data storage for up to 7 days (data will be groomed after 7 days).
- XenDesktop 7.x Platinum: In addition to the above the Platinum license offers the performance management feature including historical monitoring of data for up to a full year, which will be stored in the Configuration Logging database. By default data will be groomed at 90-day intervals. This can be changed up to 367 days by means of a PowerShell applet. Run: Set-MonitorConfiguration to change the default grooming settings.
- XenDesktop 7.x Platinum plus NetScaler Enterprise: In addition to the above, the NetScaler Enterprise license

offers networking analysis plus 60 minutes of data storage max.

- XenDesktop 7.x Platinum plus NetScaler Platinum: Offers the exact same functionality as above but with the added advantage of unlimited data storage. Note that this is tested, and thus officially supported by Citrix up to three years.

Using the standard Director reporting feature you will have direct access to information like: the peak number of sessions during the last month, the average user logon duration time (current and historical), device registrations failures during the last couple of days, weeks, months and more.

While using Director gives us access to a ton of information, it is impossible to include everything. Another option you have is the so-called Monitor Service OData API. This can be used to create custom reports for analysing purposes. It is all about getting the information out of your database and converting it to a, for us humans, readably format. And while this may sound complex, it doesn't have to be. In fact, all you need is Microsoft Excel. Using the Open Data (OData) protocol you basically let Excel directly communicate with your Delivery Controller. Have a look at the following Citrix blogpost for some more detailed information on how to set this up:

https://www.citrix.com/blogs/2015/02/12/citrix-director-analyzing-the-monitoring-data-by-means-of-custom-reports/

Views and delegated administration

Director offers different interface views, which are or can be tailored to the various administrative roles and responsibilities available within Director. This way you can limit the amount of information and data available to Helpdesk Support Technicians, while Site Administrators might have full access to all that Director has to offer. Director also has various built-in administrator roles for this purpose, ranging from full administrator to host or Machine Catalog administrator, for example, and a few in between. You also have the ability to configure your own custom admin roles, Studio Delegated Administration is based on three concepts: administrators, roles, and scopes.

Monitoring

When it comes to monitoring your XenDesktop / XenApp Sites Director has a lot to offer. Take the default Dashboard view, shown when you first log into Director. Depending on your license type it will show you the following information:

- Any connection failures that may have taken place.
- Failed desktop OS machines and/or any failed server OS machines.
- The actual license status.
- The number of currently connected sessions.
- The average user logon duration.
- Infrastructure health. Here it will keep an eye on your Delivery Controllers, including any Hypervisor hosts that might be used as well.

From here you can easily drill down further by simply clicking one of the highlighted failures, if any. You can also click one of the statistics numbers shown on the Dashboard or select a predefined filter from the Filters menu; the Filter view will then open to display all data based on the selected machine or failure type. The Trends view will access historical information on sessions, connection failures, machine failures, logon performance, and load evaluation for each site. When further inspection is needed here are some of the options you have using the Trends view:

- You can export all graphical data to a .PDF, Excel or .CSV file.
- View trends for sessions.
- View trends for connection failures.
- View trends for machine failures.
- View trends for logon performance.
- View trends for load evaluation.
- Hosted application usage.
- Desktop and server usage.
- Virtual machine usage.
- Network analysis data using HDX Insight.
- And more.

To further troubleshoot and/or manage any potential issues, you can control the state of a machine in various ways. These include:

- Start, restart and forced restart.
- Shutdown and forced shutdown.
- Suspend and résumé.

If you further drill down into the machine details (using the machine details view) Director can also show you any hotfixes that might have been installed on the VDA, physical and/or virtual. Another option would be to put a machine in maintenance mode so that no further connections are possible.

FMA fact: As of version 7.7 Director can be configured to make use of integrated Windows authentication so that domain-joined users gain direct access to Director without re-entering their credentials on the Director logon page.

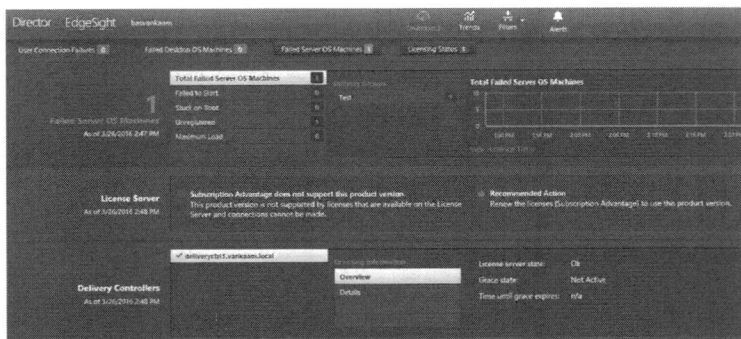

Figure 13: Director main dashboard

Alerts and notifications

Director offers us various ways in which alerts can be viewed and displayed. For example, on the main dashboard Director shows us critical alerts and warnings, which are updated every minute by default. An overview of all alerts can be viewed by selecting 'Alerts' at the top of the Director page, more granular information on a per alert basis can be viewed by selecting one of the alerts shown on the main dashboard directly or by selecting 'Go to Alerts' at the bottom of the Director page when viewing current alerts and warnings. An orange triangle tells us that a minimum threshold of a condition has been reached, and a red circle tells us that the maximum value of the threshold has been reached.

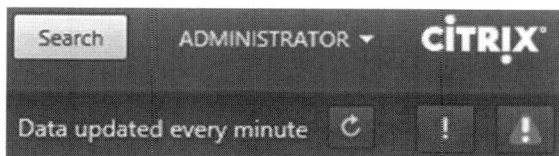

Figure 14: Alerts section in Director

Director allows you to manually configure multiple Citrix Alerts policies. When defining the various thresholds you can also configure notifications to be sent by email to individuals and groups when alerts meet and exceed the thresholds you have set up. You have over ten policy conditions to choose from.

SCOM integration

As of XenDesktop / XenApp version / Director 7.7 you can integrate SCOM alerts directly into your Director interface. Note that at the time of writing the integration will only support SCOM 2012 R2. Any alerts generated by SCOM will be directly visible within Director at the same locations as with the configurable Citrix alerts mentioned earlier. The SCOM alerts will include the severity, time raised, name and source. To find out any details regarding a specific alert all you have to do is click on it and more detailed information will be displayed. If you go to the 'Alerts' section directly, you will find a separate tab dedicated to SCOM alerts as well, here you will be able to filter all SCOM alerts based on the management pack used, machine source, severity and a preconfigured time period. As a final note, all alerts information can also be exported to .PDF, .CSV and/or Excel files if needed.

FMA fact: The actual SCOM web interface can be launched from within Director as well. You will find it on the 'Alerts' page.

Comtrade SCOM management pack

In addition to the above, I am (pretty) sure you guys have heard about the Comtrade SCOM management pack acquisition by Citrix not too long ago. The following (SCOM) packs will be available exclusively from Citrix: XenApp, XenDesktop, NetScaler, XenMobile, ShareFile, XenServer, StoreFront, Web Interface, Provisioning Services, License Server and CloudBridge. Note that, as it stands today, the abovementioned management packs will only be available for Platinum XenDesktop and XenApp customers.

This comes from one of the Citrix blogs over at Citrix.com/blogs covering the Comtrade acquisition:

The SCOM packs integrate Director's helpdesk capabilities and add detail for admins to monitor their infrastructure and workloads, all from a single pane of glass. And the latest version of Director can also aggregate SCOM alerts into the helpdesk dashboard for enhanced troubleshooting. Additional value using SCOM packs with Director include:

- End-to-end Citrix infrastructure monitoring, including XenApp, XenDesktop, StoreFront, Web Interface, Provisioning Services, License Server, XenServer, NetScaler and CloudBridge.
- Aggregate health overviews across multiple sites and versions with SLA dashboards.
- Advanced monitoring of applications, delivery groups

and sites.

- Advanced user experience monitoring, with expanded alerts, for logon and session performance.
- Launch Director within the management pack GUI to drill into user sessions from SCOM alerts.
- Topology views with detailed relational information.

Insight services integration

As of XenDesktop / XenApp version 7.8 you can now access Citrix Insight Services from a drop-down menu in Director, providing you access to additional diagnostics information. Insight Services (check: cis.citrix.com) collects data from multiple sources, which include Citrix Scout and Call Home services.

Citrix Call Home performs periodic collections of your systems and product configuration, plus performance, error, and other information. This information is then sent over to Citrix Insight Services for proactive analysis and resolution. This is where the FMA analytics service plays a key role.

FMA fact: Director can also be used to monitor and troubleshoot IMA-based architectures in the form of XenApp 6.5. Features include, but are not limited to: Shadow sessions, Machine details pane, HDX panel, Delegated Administration support, and Activity Manager for 6.5.

Conclusion

Citrix Director is another example of one of Citrix's products which is under constant development: it is being improved faster than I can write, but hopefully this chapter will at least give you an indication of its added value. It continuous to grow and gets better and better with each new version.

Key takeaways

- Director is a real-time monitoring and troubleshooting web-based tool.

- Citrix EdgeSight technology has been built into Director (primarily used for historical data reporting, trends and analyses). The EdgeSight software will no longer be available as a separate product. The latest version of EdgeSight was 5.4, which is still supported until 31-Dec-17 if you have a valid software maintenance and/or Subscription Advantage.

- To be able to make use of the built-in historical reporting fucntionality Platinum XenDesktop / XenApp licenses will be needed.

- To make use of the network analysis functionality you will need to have at least a NetScaler Enterprise or Platinum license.

- Depending on your XenDesktop / XenApp / NetScaler licenses, you will be able to store historical data for a certain period of time. See the overview.

- Director offers different views for administration and troubleshooting purposes, including the ability to configure delegated administration on a per role basis.

- Alerts and notifications are directly visible and accessible from the main dashboard.

- The main XenDesktop / XenApp infrastructural services are also being monitored by Director, these are visible from the main dashboard view. It uses PowerShell for this.

- SCOM alerts and notification can be configured and viewed from Director as well. Just recently, Citrix acquired the SCOM Comtrade management packs for Citrix environments.

- Insight Services can now be accessed directly from Director. It is fuelled with analytics data from Scout, as well as Citrix Call Home.
- Insight services can also be accessed directly by going to www.cis.citrix.com.
- Director can also be used with IMA, XenApp 6.5 based environments. It supports 'older' VDAs.

Citrix Licensing

Licensing can be complicated, not only do we need to consider XenApp and/or XenDesktop licenses; we also have to deal with Microsoft licensing, if we like or not. Throughout this chapter I will focus on the different types of Citrix licenses available, how they get applied from a XenApp/XenDesktop perspective and what other types of (Microsoft) licenses we need to take into consideration, like: RDS, VDA (no, this is not the Citrix VDA), CDL etc.

FlexNet

Citrix relies on Flexera software to take care of licensing, FlexNet licensing software to be a bit more specific (also formerly known under the names FlexNet Publisher and FLEXlm). Here is a quote from their website:

> FlexNet Licensing empowers application producers to combat software piracy and increase revenues by easily enabling new pricing, packaging and software licensing and activation models. It supports the full software-licensing spectrum, from strict enforcement to usage-based trust but verifies, and enables software protection, monetization and compliance of on-premises, SaaS, cloud, virtualized and embedded applications.

Citrix Licensing technical overview

Before you will be able to upload any type of license you will first have to install and configure Citrix Licensing. Citrix Licensing consists of the following components:

- License server – A system that allows licenses to be shared across the network.
- License files – The files that you need to license your product. These files are stored on the License Server.
- License Administration Console – The interface you use to manage your license files and your License Server.
- Web Services for Licensing – Enables Studio, Director, and the Licensing Administration PowerShell Snap-in to communicate with the License Server and manage users, allocate and install licenses, display License Server health, license usage, and other alert messages.
- Simple License Service – Enables allocation and installation of license files on a License Server using a web page interface.
- Product-side settings in your Citrix products that are associated with the License Server.

At least one license server needs to be present within a Citrix environment. Since the license server role is a relatively light one, you may choose to co-host it on a machine, which performs other tasks as well. Or, and this is not an uncommon approach, the Citrix License Server role can be shared with other license servers: like Microsoft Licensing.

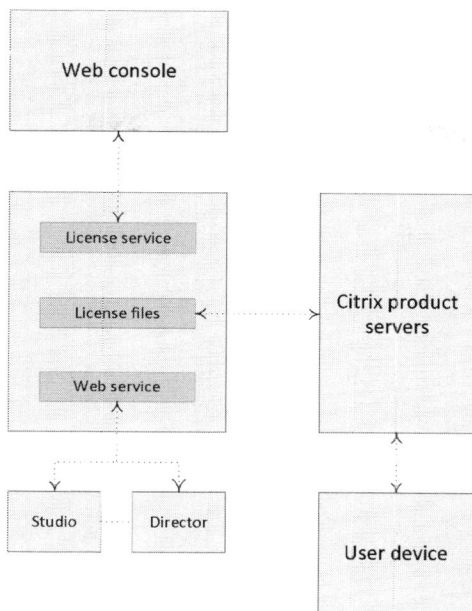

Figure 15: License infrastructure

User, device and concurrent

Licenses come in various forms and shapes: licenses can be user-/device-based or concurrent. A user license allows a single user access from an unlimited number of devices, while a device license allows an unlimited number of users' access from a single device. Concurrent licenses live somewhere in between; they are not tied to a specific user or machine.

Here it is important to note that the user/device license type is not about choosing between a user or device license type, no, the license server will decide that for you, I'll elaborate a bit more on this in a minute. Again, you either buy user/device licenses, or concurrent. Microsoft licenses will be discussed in more detail as we progress.

FMA fact: By default, you can only use one type of license within your XenDesktop Site. You either purchase / upload user/device or concurrent: they cannot be mixed. If you require both, you must set up and configure separate Sites, license servers included.

XenApp and XenDesktop license types

To start, the XenDesktop license model offers user/device as well as concurrent licenses. These are available as perpetual, which basically means you buy them once and then pay an annual fee on a per license basis. Of course this does not include Subscription Advantage (SA) or Software Maintenance (SM), but we'll get to those in just a bit. XenApp licenses, when purchased separate from XenDesktop are a bit different in that they are only available as concurrent licenses. These can be purchased as perpetual as well and do also not include SA / SM. Note that I said 'separate from XenDesktop' because when you buy XenDesktop Enterprise or Platinum licenses this will also include the use rights to XenApp. Meaning that user/device licenses can be used with XenApp just as easy, in fact Citrix won't even know the difference.

A bit more detail

When making use of concurrent licenses, as soon as a user logs in a license will be assigned to that user for the duration of the session, and as soon as the user logs off that same license will become available for use again. Be aware that there is no direct communication between license servers. If you configure multiple license servers they will not be aware of each other and multiple licenses could be checked out. Make sure to point all of your production machines to the same license server. The types of licenses that can be used also depend on the product you are using. XenApp only supports concurrent licenses, while XenDesktop supports user, device as well as concurrent licenses. With a concurrent license, a number of sessions to different products that are controlled by the license server will be available using just that single license allocated to the user. If, however, some services are made available from a server that taps into a different license server to gain access, the user will have consumed multiple licenses.

As mentioned, when using user/device licenses, the license server will decide the type of license that will be applied, and at the same time it will always allocate the smallest amount of licenses needed. Let me explain how this works. When user 1 logs in for the first time, on PC 1, the license server will assign a user license to user 1. However, when user 1 logs off and user 2 logs on to PC 1, the license server will notice that multiple users are now logging on and using PC 1. Because of this it will reassign the earlier user license, which was assigned to user 1 to PC 1, turning it into a device license.

Now if user 1 logs onto PC 2 the license server will pick up that user 1 logs on to multiple machines and thus it will assign a user license to user 1. Unless multiple users previously used PC 2 as well, then it will continue to use a device license for PC 2 and user 1 will still be without an assigned license. This is controlled by the MAC address of the device, which the license server keeps track of.

FMA fact: The license server uses tables to track user\device license (asignment) information (as described above).

172

The thing to note here is that once a user and/or device license is assigned to either a user or device, it will stay assigned for a minimum of 90 days before it will be checked in again. This is in contrast to concurrent licenses, which will be checked out for the duration of the session and checked in again once the session is ended. Licenses can be revoked, when an employer leaves the company, for example, and still has a license in use (90 days). Citrix created a licensing management command line utility named UDADMIN for this, which allows Administrator to manually revoke licenses.

License usage data will be updated every 15 minutes by default, while rebooting the license server will force an update as well. Bram Wolfs created a GUI around the ADADMIN tool: one of the added advantages of using this tool is the ability to manually revoke one or multiple licenses at once, but of course it does more than 'just' that. You will find it here:

http://bramwolfs.com/2013/08/06/udadmin-gui-a-free-tool-to-manage-xendesktop-userdevice-licenses/

How many licenses are needed

To give you an indication on how many licenses you might need you can use the following formula: A - C + B = # user/device licenses. A is the total number of users, B would be the total number of shared devices and finally C, the number of users that will exclusively be using those shared devices. Let's say we have 800 users (A), 300 shared devices (B) and a total of 400 users who will only be using the shared devices (C), this makes 800 - 400 + 300 = 700 licenses. Using this formula you can also calculate at which point it makes more sense to purchase concurrent licenses. These are about twice the price of a user/device license.

FMA fact: The process of assigning licenses to users and/or devices, whether concurrent or not, is also referred to as the checking in and checking out of license tokens.

Each time a certain Citrix product starts, it will open up a connection to the license server by checking out a so-called startup license (1). This startup license file enables Citrix products to maintain a continuous connection to the License Server. When users connect to a Citrix product (2), it draws licenses from the License Server. That is, the Citrix product requests to check out a license from the License Server on behalf of the user or client device (3). When the license is successfully checked out, the user can actually use the product.

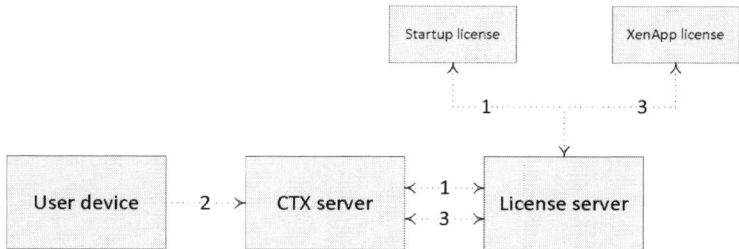

Figure 16: License checkout

FMA fact: Both XenDesktop and XenApp product licenses must be purchased with Subscription Advantage or Software Maintenance for a minimum of one year from delivery.

License programmes

Citrix offers different licensing programmes aimed at supporting any commercial enterprise, educational institution or government agency worldwide. If you would like to know more about these programmes I would suggest contacting one of your Citrix sales representatives, as they should be able to help you. Just be aware that, at any time, you may only have one active commercial licensing programme and one active public sector licensing programme. The link below will provide you with additional information as well:

www.citrix.com/buy/licensing/programs.html

Grace periods

If, for whatever reason, the Citrix License Server cannot be contacted, the users and products are protected by a grace period without any interruption or loss of functionality. To make this possible, XenDesktop stores a replica of the licensing information from the License Server, including the number and type of licenses. As soon as the connection to the license server is lost it will enter its grace period and use the licensing information stored locally. The maximum time allowed for a grace period is usually 30 days, although this might differ slightly per product.

Citrix infrastructural components and the license server exchange heartbeat messages every five minutes to indicate to each other that they are still up and running. When the heartbeat fails for whatever reason, the mentioned grace period will kick in using the locally cached license information as mentioned above.

High availability

While it is not a necessity to make your license server highly available, it's always optional. By default it will rely on the grace period to kick in, as mentione above. However, if you already have a NetScaler in use it is a relatively simple process to set up load balancing between two license servers in an active\passive setup.

Supplemental

As of version 7.6, Citrix has introduced a supplemental grace period. It will allow your users to connect to XenDesktop and/or XenApp, but other products as well, while all licenses are in use. The default supplemental grace period is 15 days and during this period there is no limit on connections. Just be aware that after this period expires the 'normal' connection limits will be enforced and new connections will no longer be accepted. A quote from Citrix on this:

> Supplemental grace periods are granted per product and edition and per Subscription Advantage Eligibility date (per product) and only for Retail licenses. For example, if you have two clients requesting XenDesktop Enterprise Concurrent, with different Subscription Advantage Eligibility dates, two supplemental grace periods are granted.

Note that the old licensing model involved granting a certain percentage (approximately 10%) of overdrafts above the current license count. This has been changed in the current version of XenDesktop/XenApp and now goes by a grace period instead of an unlimited time for overdrafts.

> **FMA fact**: As soon as a Citrix product enters a grace
> period, one or several event messages (Windows Event
> Viewer) might appear. Here you can also see the
> remaining time left within the grace period.

While we focus on XenDesktop and/or XenApp for now, be
aware that there are more Citrix products out there, such as
paid-for versions of XenServer, which also require a license of
some sort. Also, with XD & XA the licenses reside on the
license server, as we've just discussed, but with a NetScaler the
license file will need to be uploaded to the actual device itself.

> **FMA fact**: All Session Hosts as part of the IMA are
> responsible for the checkout and handling of licenses,
> and thus need to be able to communicate with the
> license server. Within the FMA this is handled by your
> Delivery Controller (s).

Getting your licenses

Getting your hands on your Citrix licenses is a simple, three-step
process. If you are a new Citrix customer you will first need to
register for a license programme (also see 'License Programs' a
few paragraphs back) before you will be able to purchase any
licenses.

In all other cases, if you want to renew or update your licenses it
will be a matter of activating (your order confirmation email
contains instructions for activating licenses).

Then allocate (when asked, enter the license you wish to
allocate. Select the specific number of users you wish to deploy,
and generate your license file). And finally download (save your

license file and copy it to your license server using the License Management Console. The server will then read and initiate the license file).

FMA fact: When licenses are allocated they are 'bound' to your license server, which is identified by its local hostname and is CaseSensitive.

You might also want to visit:

https://www.citrix.com/buy/licensing/management.html for some more detailed information regarding Citrix Licensing. Here you will also find information with regard to edition updates, and as always contact your Citrix representative when in doubt.

FMA fact: You can also visit the Citrix Trial Center where you can get limited trial licenses to try out certain products. However, note that some licenses will only be available for registered Citrix partners.

Editions

Both XenDesktop and XenApp are available in different editions. Depending on the edition you purchase, more or less specific features and functionalities will become available for you to use and configure. XenDesktop is available in VDI, Enterprise and Platinum, while XenApp is available in Advanced, Enterprise and Platinum. Visit Citrix.com for more detailed information about the differences between the platform editions mentioned above.

Subscription Advantage, Software Maintenance

As mentioned, each edition of XenDesktop / XenApp must be purchased with at least one year of Subscription Advantage and/or Software Maintenance. Subscription Advantage entitles you to, among other benefits, any product updates, including major and minor releases, released during your membership period.

After your initial one-year membership period expires, you may choose to renew your Subscription Advantage membership. A Subscription Advantage membership and its associated license are distinct from your license to run the product. All licenses for retail products are permanent. If you do not renew your Subscription Advantage membership, your Citrix products will continue to work. However, while you are still entitled to software updates, you are not allowed to use, or upgrade to newer software releases (next versions).

Citrix Software Maintenance combines world-class 24x7 unlimited technical support (worldwide) with product version updates to keep your Citrix environment running optimally (meaning it also includes Subscription Advantage). You will be able to log an unlimited number of incidents and get access to a specific set of support tools and other knowledge resources. As a bonus this includes a discount for Citrix Synergy tickets. Citrix now has a total of six support centres around the world offering true 'follow the sun' support in eight different languages!

Next to their 'Standard' product life cycle support policy, which consists of Mainstream Maintenance, Extended Maintenance and End of life, Citrix also introduced two new forms of product maintenance not too long ago; the Long Term Service

Release (LTSR) and the Current Release (CR). To start with LTSR, and I will quote Citrix on this, the benefits include:

- Extended Lifecycle: For each Long Term Service Release, the clock restarts, giving you 5 years of mainstream support and 5 years of extended support (separate contract required).
- Predictable Maintenance: On a regular schedule, Citrix will release cumulative updates for each Long Term Service Release. These updates will typically contain just the fixes for that release void of new features to simplify ongoing maintenance.
- Reduced IT Costs: By opting to implement a Long Term Service Release, you will have access to the highest quality releases with the most predictable maintenance schedule to streamline your management efforts, which can lower your total cost of ownership.

While the benefits of the Current Release software maintenance offer:

- Rapid innovation: The IT world changes quickly and Current Releases will provide access to the latest security, productivity and collaboration features to help keep your workforce competitive.
- Address new business challenges: Current Releases will extend the flexibility of the XenApp and XenDesktop architecture to address more use cases, giving you more value out of your current investment.
- Faster delivery of enhancements: Citrix welcomes your enhancement requests to further improve our app and desktop delivery technology, and the faster release cycles

of Current Releases will help expedite your enhancement request.

While the CR might seem new, it really isn't. CR is basically the way it has always been before the LTSR was introduced. They just had to come up with a second name to make a clear distinction between the two.

See this blogpost over at basvankaam.com for more detailed information:

http://www.basvankaam.com/2016/04/06/the-citrix-long-term-service-release-vs-the-current-release-whats-really-new/

FMA fact: Citrix also offers Appliance Maintenance, which provides technical support to diagnose and resolve issues encountered with appliance hardware with the latest upgrades for the software elements of hardware products. Malfunctioning appliances are also replaced under this agreement to minimise customer downtime. Note that all licenses within a programme must be either on call-in support or not – they cannot be mixed! If one desires different support levels, different licensing subscriptions must be used to separate these, as well as separate license servers!

Monitoring license usage

Now that we have covers some of Citrix's basics with regard to licensing, let's have a look at how we can view and monitor our licenses using Citrix Studio.

On the Licensing node in Studio you have a direct overview of the types of licenses you are using and how many licenses are actually being used at any given time. It will tell you the license model (per user, device or concurrent), which port number is used for communicating with the license server, general Site information, an expiration date, if Subscription Advantage is supported, and more.

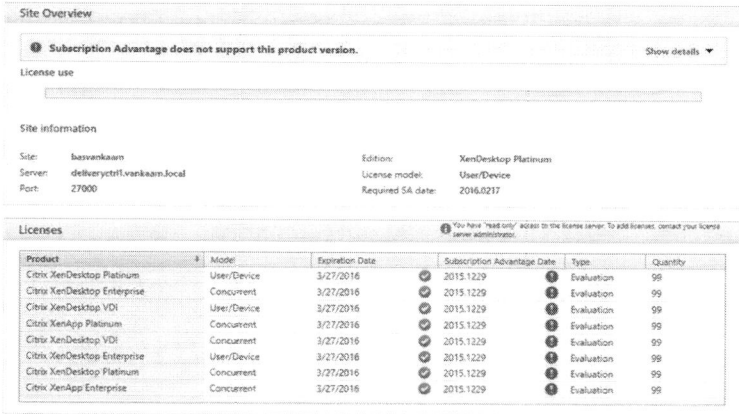

Figure 17: Studio licensing

What about Microsoft?

We cannot run Citrix without Microsoft, I am not telling you anything new here. Using Microsoft software also means it will need to be licensed from a Microsoft perspective, unfortunately this is often where the confusion starts. Let's see if I can help you understand what is needed from a licensing perspective when Citrix and Microsoft products are used together. I will start by explaining some of the different types of Microsoft licenses involved when dealing with VDI and/or RDSH based deployments.

Microsoft VDA licenses and Software Assurance

VDA stands for Virtual Desktop Access. Each Windows and non-Windows device that will access a Windows desktop Operating System (OS) based virtual machine (which applies to VDI only) needs to be licensed with a Microsoft VDA license. If your corporate Windows PC's are licensed as part of Microsoft's Software Assurance program or Windows Intune, these VDA licenses will automatically be included.

This entitles you to use a Windows based PC as a VDI endpoint (to access a Windows desktop OS based VM) without having to purchase separate VDA licenses, which is always optional as well. Especially for smaller companies who cannot afford the SA program. There is, however one exception, if you are using non-Windows machines, like a (Linux based) thin client, you will still need to purchase separate VDA licenses for those machines. And by the way, a VDA license goes for a $100 per year, per device. But wait there's more.

> **FMA fact**: Technically speaking, Software Assurance is an upgrade of existing licenses (usually OEM). That's why you cannot have SA on thin clients (there is no existing license to upgrade) and you have to buy VDA license instead.

When a user has a corporate VDA licensed device (at the office), he or she is also entitled to use his or her home PC to access a corporate Windows desktop OS based VM as part of that same VDA license. However, if the user would bring that same personally owned, non-corporate device into the office, then a separate VDA license will again be needed. To use a Microsoft quote on this one: **Roaming rights** are only applicable while roaming outside of the corporate domain, hence any device accessing a Windows virtual desktop within the corporate domain needs to be licensed with either Windows Client SA or Windows VDA.

Makes sense?

> **FMA fact**: If you are not accessing a Windows desktop OS VM on a server, but from a physical PC, you do not need a Windows VDA license. This also means that VDA licenses do not apply to Citrix XenApp.

CDL licenses

Next to the VDA license Microsoft also introduced a so-called CDL license, which stand for Companion Desktop License. It comes at an additional charge and is not included as part of the Microsoft SA program. This allows a user to access a Windows desktop OS based VM (on the corporate network) from up to four different devices, including iOS and Android tablets etc. (BYOD). For this to (legally) work the earlier discussed VDA license will somehow need to be taken care of as well.

Software Assurance, a bit more detail

Software Assurance and VDA licenses can be user or device based. With device based being the more restrictive of the two. With a device based SA or VDA license you are restricted to the earlier mentioned roaming rights, and additional CDLs might be needed to enable access to your VDI environment from multiple devices, iOS and Android tablets included. With a per user SA or VDA license subscription these limitations do not apply. Windows can be locally installed on any device running Windows 7/8/8.1/10 Pro or Enterprise or Windows tablet up to 10.1 inches in diagonal screen size. And your users will have access to your VDI environment from all of their devices, no additional CDLs needed. Also, while with per device SA or VDA licenses you are restricted to non-corporate devices while away from the office to access your VDI, as explained previously, with per user SA or VDA licenses you will have access externally as well as internal from any device without needing to purchase any additional VDA licenses.

FMA fact: Software Assurance benefits (either per use or device) allow you to have up to four virtual machines (VDI), or one physical machine running a Windows desktop Operating System.

RDS licenses

When Microsoft RDS, Remote Desktop Services technology is used to delivery applications and or virtual Desktops (VDI and/or RDSH based) to your users these will also need to be licensed accordingly.

From a XenApp perspective this is nothing new, for most of you anyway. XenApp runs on top of Microsoft RDS technology (former Terminal Services) and thus needs to be licensed with RDS CALs (per user or device) as well. While this does not apply to XenDesktop Virtual Desktop Infrastructures, RDS technology can also be used to offer desktop OS based VMs leveraging Windows Server 2012 / 2016 as the base infrastructure (a.k.a. Microsoft VDI, note that I am not referring to Server VDI). In this case both VDA and RDS licenses will be needed. But that's beyond the scope of this chapter.

FMA fact: Microsoft RDS licenses are needed in combination with Citrix XenApp, not XenDesktop. And Microsoft VDA licenses are needed in combination with Citrix XenDesktop, not XenApp.

Windows server and desktop OS licensing

Besides the mentioned licensing requirements your base server and/or desktop Operating Systems will also need to be licensed. Besides a server license, which allows you to install a Windows server Operating System on a single machine, you will also need to purchase server client access licenses on a per user basis. This gives a single user the right to make use of the server services, like file sharing, printing etc. These types of licenses are often covered by one Microsoft's Volume Licensing programs, which are of course different from the 'boxed' retail licenses. Do note that different programs are available primarily depending on the size of your organization.

Desktop Operating System licenses work in sort of the same way with regard to Volume licensing. However, desktop OS licenses do not need any additional client access licenses as with the server variant. Some of the Volume License solutions (can) also include the earlier mentioned Software Assurance (again, per user or per device, make sure to understand the differences between the two) program offering additional benefits, as with their latest Windows 10 offering, for example. However, as per Microsoft: For devices or users that do not qualify for Windows Software Assurance, you can license Windows VDA for access to the benefits of Windows Software Assurance.

Application virtualization

Amongst other things, the Microsoft Desktop Optimization Pack, or MDOP offers us various virtualization technologies including Microsoft App-V, which is often used in combination with both Citrix XenApp as well as XenDesktop. Unfortunately it doesn't come for free; it is available as a separate subscription to Microsoft Software Assurance customers. If you would like to combine App-V streaming technology with VDI virtual desktops then you would need an MDOP license for each client device accessing the VM. If it's streaming to XenApp (RDSH) servers that you are interested in then no additional licenses will be needed (this will already be covered by your RDS CAL).

As a side note, when using XenApp to only stream packaged applications down to a virtual or physical desktop, no RDS CAL licenses will be needed since no actual resources will be utilized on the RDSH server.

Service Providers

For Service Providers and independent software vendors Microsoft has the Services Provider License Agreement program (SPLA). This is what Microsoft has to say about it: With the SPLA, service providers and ISVs can license eligible Microsoft products on a monthly basis, during a three-year agreement term, to host software services and applications for their customers.

The SPLA supports a variety of hosting scenarios to help you provide highly customized and robust solutions to a wide set of customers.

And while the above is very true and helpful, when it comes to VDI it is also very, very restrictive. Unfortunately there is no

SPLA agreement for multi-tenant / cloud environments when VDI is thrown into the mix. Well, there is, but you will have to use dedicated hardware on a per customer basis. This includes everything from your servers to the underlying storage platform and all that is in between. Even when virtualization is applied, the physical hosts that your VMs run on need to be dedicated per customer (also referred to as a tenant). This is the reason why true DaaS, meaning a desktop based Windows Operating System from the cloud is not possible.

Technically it is, but the 'dedicated hardware per customer' statement doesn't make for an interesting business case, at all. Of course DaaS is still a (relatively) popular approach, but because of the desktop OS licensing restriction highlighted earlier, in 99% of all cases XenApp, or RDSH technology will be used insetad.

There are exceptions, in some cases a server OS (Windows Server 2008 R2 mostly) is used in a one to one relationship, which is also referred to as Server VDI, a niche use-case though.

FMA fact: Another thing to keep in mind when trying to achieve 'true' cloud based VDI, is that customers will have to provide their own (Windows desktop OS) licenses. A Service Provider is not allowed to sell these.

Citrix Service Providers

To complete this chapter I have also included some information regarding the CSP licensing program since it offers some very attractive benefits. Instead of re-inventing the wheel, so to speak, I will quote Citrix on this one. The following comes from the Citrix Service Provider Program FAQ document:

The Citrix Service Provider Program is a Citrix partner program designed specifically for service providers who provide and/or resell hosted software services to end-user customers. The Citrix Service Provider Program helps partners build high-value hosted workspace businesses through extensive guidance, support and tools to plan, build, market and sell.

The Citrix Service Provider Program addresses the service provider market for offsite, multi-tenant hosting, and augmented with on-premises equipment if needed to satisfy service level agreements. In this setup, the end-user customer is not the licensee and does not manage nor access the management infrastructure of the Citrix Service Provider.

The Citrix Service Provider program extends to service providers the "right to use" Citrix products as the underpinning of their delivery infrastructure and gives Citrix Service Providers (where applicable) the flexibility of a monthly "active subscriber" pricing and licensing model. Service providers always have access to the most current versions of Citrix products available in the program and only pay for actual end-user usage recorded or accounts active during the previous calendar month.

Benefits

These include the following:

- Flexibility to host complete mobile workspaces – hosted desktops, applications, mobile device management and file sharing with monthly service provider licensing.
- Ability to host Citrix enabled services on a worldwide basis.

- Fast entry into the quickly growing Desktops-as-a-Service market.
- Extremely compelling and flexible monthly pricing
- Active subscriber pricing, which can drive greater profitability.
- Volume discounts.
- No membership fee to join the program.
- No upfront commitments or minimum purchase requirements.
- Pricing stability.
- Streamlined reporting process in sync with the Microsoft SPLA program.
- Flexibility to choose between two levels of service.
- Ability to offer IaaS on a monthly basis.
- Accurate and rapid reporting using Citrix tools (Premium level privilege).
- Right to offer free of charge 30-day end-user evaluations of hosted services.
- Lower total cost of ownership (TCO) with greater server and user density in the data center.
- High end-user satisfaction with any device, any time access and a high definition experience.
- Access to design for best practices with Citrix Service Provider Reference Architecture.
- Access to the Citrix Service Provider Center of Excellence, an end-to-end business, sales, marketing and technical resource for growing a service provider business.
- Complete sales training resources including training decks, reference cards and technical sales insights.
- Turnkey marketing resources, including campaigns, datasheets and marketing tools.

- Access to Citrix Marketing Concierge, a full-scale marketing system for managing email campaigns, webinars and roadshows with pre-set customizable campaigns.
- Opportunity for design review with Citrix Service Provider Solution Architects.
- Ability to use Citrix corporate logo and partner program logo.
- Access to Citrix Partner Central portal.
- Access to Citrix partner events such as Citrix Summit

In addition to the Microsoft SPLA program

Microsoft has been extremely supportive of the Citrix Service Provider program. The two companies have been working together for more than 26 years; the Citrix Service Provider program is modeled in large part after the Microsoft SPLA program. The Citrix Service Provider program helps Microsoft drive additional service provider business and increases the numbers of monthly subscribers using Microsoft technologies. Additionally, the Citrix Service Provider program allows ISVs to offer applications as SaaS-based solutions via Citrix Service Providers or on their own.

A big thank you to the community (that also means you) for helping me out on this chapter.

To summarize

XenDesktop:

Table 9: XenDesktop license overview

License type	Description
Citrix XenDesktop	Yes. Either concurrent or per user/device
Microsoft RDS CALs	No
Client Operating System	Yes. But can be part of your Software Assurance / VDA licenses
Microsoft SA / VDA	Yes. Either per device or user, can be part of SA subscription as well
Microsoft CDL	Optional. When SA / VDA is licensed per device and multiple (up to 4) devices are needed (BYOD)
MDOP	Optional. But only in combination with SA. Streamed to VDI VM is one MDOP license per client device
Citrix XenDesktop	Yes. Either concurrent or per user/device

XenApp:

Table 10: XenApp license overview

License type	Description
XenApp	Yes. Concurrent when it is XenApp only. Or per user/device when part of XenDesktop Enterprise / Platinum license
Microsoft RDS CALs	Yes. Either per user or device
Server Operating System	Yes. Volume License / Retail licenses. Also needs server client access licenses
Microsoft SA / VDA	Optional. VDA only when SA is not possible on a per user or device basis
Microsoft CDL	No
MDOP	Optional. But only in combination with SA
XenApp	Yes. Concurrent when it is XenApp only. Or per user/device when part of XenDesktop Enterprise / Platinum license

Key takeaways

- Citrix Licensing relies on Flexera software, as do many other product vendors, by the way.
- The license server is a relatively light role and can easily be shared with other roles on a single virtual of physical server. A single license server is able to handle over 10,000 continuous connections.
- XenDesktop and XenApp licenses come in different forms. There are per user, per device and concurrent licenses available. The license server will decide which one to apply / check-out.
- A user license gives a single user the right to start sessions on an unlimited number of devices. The license is bound to the user and is device-independent.
- A device license works the other way around. A session can be started from a single device, but it does not matter by whom. It is user-independent.
- If a user/device license is issued, it is applied to a license token for both a XenDesktop and a XenApp license token, even if you only connect to just one or the other. They are always issued in pairs.
- Concurrent licenses are not bound to a user or device: you can use them for both. However, these are more expensive to purchase.
- If the license server becomes unavailable for some reason it will make use of a built-in grace period of 30 days. Everything will continue to function as before. This basically means you will have 30 days to get the license server up and running again.
- While products like XenDesktop and XenApp are both licensed through a central license server, a product like

NetScaler, will need its license installed directly on the device itself.

- Citrix offers various forms of support and maintenance. Subscription Advantage allows you to upgrade to the latest versions, Feature Packs and so on. Software Maintenance, on the other hand, offers you 24x7x365 support. When purchasing either XenDesktop and/or XenApp you will need to also purchase at least one year of Subscription Advantage and/or Software Maintenance, which isn't that uncommon.

- Recently they released their Current Release (CR) and Long Term Service Release (LTSR) product support options. For each Long Term Service Release, the clock restarts, giving you 5 years of mainstream support and 5 years of extended support, plus more. Current Releases will provide access to the latest security, productivity and collaboration features to help keep your workforce competitive, plus extras.

- The 'new' CR release isn't really new; it is basically the way it has always been before they introduced the LTSR option.

Host Connection

When you install XenDesktop and start Studio, you will first need to create a new Site or join an existing one, no other options are there. If you don't join an existing Site but create a new one, and let's call this step one, then step two and three will walk you through the Machine Catalog and Delivery Group creation processes. If your XenDesktop / XenApp Session Hosts will include virtual machines, and you would like to be able to auto-provision and manage new virtual machines, then you will also have to configure a Host Connection.

Your Host Connection is basically nothing more than a bridge to your underlying Hypervisor and/or cloud platform of choice where your VMs (will) reside. From a Hypervisor's perspective this can be either: Microsoft's Hyper-V, VMware's vSphere or Citrix's XenServer. Since you will need to be able to start, stop, create, delete and monitor your VMs from Studio, some sort of management software will be needed, meaning SCVMM in the case of Hyper-V, Virtual Center if you go with VMware, or XenCenter if XenServer is used. Although with XenServer, technically you do not necessarily need a separate management infrastructure (advisable though), a stand-alone XenServer, or Poolmaster would be sufficient to connect to.

At least one of these needs to be in place for this to work; Studio will then use the Hypervisor's APIs to communicate and manage the virtual machines. It goes without saying that it will do the same for Azure or AWS, for example.

FMA fact: You might have heard about the Nutanix Acropolis Hypervisor. It will soon be available as a Host Connection within XenDesktop as well.

No MCS and/or PVS VMs

As I already mentioned, you don't need to configure a Host Connection, it is optional. Although this is very true, it will also limit your options when it comes to VM provisioning. If you decide not to configure a Host Connection, then you won't be able to leverage XenDesktop MCS to automatically create tens, hundreds or thousands of VMs based on the same master / golden base image (single image management). So no MCS-based pooled and/or dedicated desktop Catalogs.

When there's no Host Infrastructure configured, some options will be missing from the Machine Catalog creation wizard. On the Machine Management page (when configuring a Machine Catalog) only physical hardware will be enabled by default, and virtual hardware will be unavailable since there's no underlying Hypervisor or cloud platform configured. Also, on the same page, you'll see some options with regard to image management where MCS will be completely greyed out while PVS and 'Another service or technology' are both selectable. It is also possible to import and manage other types of virtual (or physical) machines using Catalogs, without enabling and using PVS and/or MCS.

You also cannot use the 'XenDesktop set-up wizard' from Provisioning Services, you'll need a Host Connection for that as well, which makes sense. When available, we then could also choose 'virtual hardware' in combination with PVS image management and import one or more device collections from PVS into our Catalogs with just a few clicks. The type of vDisk used (on a device collection) is managed from the PVS management console, just as pooled and dedicated desktops are managed from the XenDesktop (MCS) Studio console.

Do note that by using the PVS management console instead of Studio you will be able to provision virtual machines, even without a Host Connetion configured. PVS is able to directly communicate with vCenter and/or the vSphere Host.

Host Connections can be configured during the initial Site set-up or at a later stage by selecting 'Hosting' at the left-hand side of the Citrix Studio console; it is located under 'Configuration'. You have the following options:

- VMware's vSphere.
- Microsoft's Hyper-V.
- Citrix's XenServer.
- Amazon Web Services.
- Microsoft Azure.
- Citrix CloudPlatform.

And as mentioned earlier in one of the FMA fact remarks, the Nutanix Acropolis Hypervisor will be added to the list shortly.

Inside Citrix

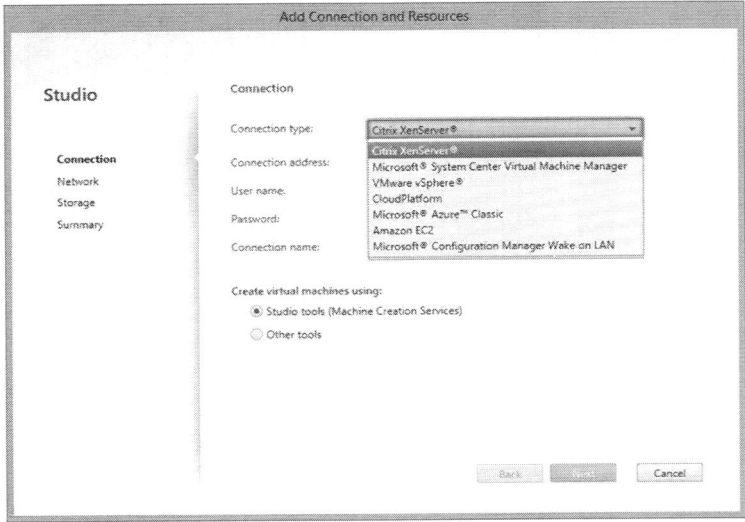

Figure 18: Host connection in Studio

Key takeaways

- While in earlier releases of XenDesktop / XenApp 7.x Host Connections were limited to Hypervisor platforms, cloud environments are now supported as well.
- As it stands today, MCS can be used in combination with Azure, AWS and/or the Citrix CloudPlatform. However, PVS is not supported: it simply does not work. It also works for, or with all Hypervisors mentioned. The Nutanix Acropolis Hypervisor will be added to the list shortly.
- MCS only works with virtual machines.
- You can add multiple Host Connections if you want, also combining cloud and on-premises Hypervisors.
- When adding Hypervisor Host Connections you will have to use the addresses of your System Center Virtual Machine Manager, Virtual Center or XenCenter.
- When using Zones make sure that the Host Connection configured for a Zone is close to, or actually physically located within, that Zone.

The NetScaler Gateway and ADC

Although considered as an optional component to the FMA, you rarely see a full-blown Citrix environment without one. It is often referred to as Citrix's personal Swiss Army knife because of its flexibility and numerous capabilities when it comes to handling inbound and outbound network traffic. The Citrix NetScaler Gateway is by far the best-known 'edition' of the NetScaler. But what most people do not realise is that the Gateway functionality built into the NetScaler is only about 5% (well, maybe 10) of what it is capable of. In fact, the Citrix NetScaler is often used for very large-scale deployments, which do not even include Citrix XenDesktop and/or XenApp. Let me elaborate a bit more on this.

The NetScaler ADC and Gateway

Most of the confusion starts with the terms Citrix NetScaler and Citrix NetScaler Gateway. Although they sound very similar, and they do have an overlap, there are multiple differences depending on the licenses used.

Citrix NetScaler refers to their Application Delivery Controller, or ADC, line of products, while the NetScaler Gateway, formerly know as the Citrix Access Gateway, or CAG, is primarily used for secure remote access to XenDesktop and/or XenApp environments.

You basically buy a 'normal' NetScaler but with limited functionality due to the NetScaler Gateway License you upload. NetScaler ADCs are capable of doing much more than 'just' remote access: they can be used for load balancing and HA, content switching, application offloading, application firewalling, cloud connectivity, hybrid cloud solutions, and much more.

Multiple books have been written on each of these subjects independently. In fact, you might want to give Marius Sandbu a Google, or look him up on Amazon: he has written some very exciting stuff around NetScaler.

Physical and virtual appliances

A NetScaler (ADC or Gateway) appliance can either be physical or virtual. If you decide to go virtual, be aware that the underlying Hypervisor, or virtual machine, that it runs on needs to have sufficient resources to handle your external connections, SSL offload and whatnot. As far as the physical appliances are concerned, Citrix offers a whole range to choose from. Depending on the physical model you choose, your network throughput will increase (this goes for the virtual platforms as well), as does the amount of RAM and/or dedicated SSL chip capabilities.

FMA fact: Just recently, Citrix introduced the CPX model, which is Citrix's containerised version of NetScaler; mainly used for testing and development use cases. It is still in tech preview at the time of writing.

A NetScaler VPX is a virtual appliance which runs on your Hypervisor of choice; a NetScaler MPX is a physical appliance; and last but not least, a NetScaler SDX is a physical appliance (running a customised edition XenServer) which is capable of running multiple VPX appliances, up to 80 in total, depending on your underlying physical resources. It comes with a (branded) XenServer pre-installed. Check out the main Citrix NetScaler products page over at Citrix.com: it will provide you with an overview of all physical as well as virtual models available.

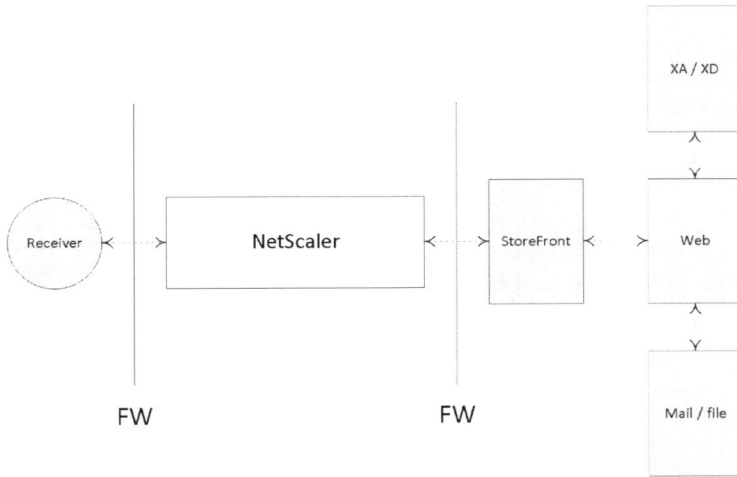

Figure 19: Typical NetScaler Gateway setup

ADC Edition licenses

No matter which type or model of ADC NetScaler you pick, you have three different edition licenses to choose from (a.k.a. as platform licenses): Standard, Enterprise or Platinum. Depending on the edition you purchase, different functionality becomes available after you upload your license file. NetScalers are upgraded using the so-called pay-as-you-grow model.

FMA fact: While there is a separate NetScaler Gateway license available, also know that each 'normal' ADC NetScaler (Standard, Enterprise or Platinum license) includes the Gateway functionality by default: no additional licenses needed.

Let's say you start out with a Standard NetScaler license, never mind the physical or virtual underlying platform, and after a while it turns out you need certain functionality not available within the Standard license portfolio. Next you simply buy an Enterprise license providing you with the feature(s), you need (like Dynamic content caching, for example) and all you have to do is upload the license file and you are good to go.

A bit more on licensing

Other NetScaler licenses include: Internal, Partner use, Demo, Evaluation, Express, Developer and/or VPX. Licenses are assigned to physical and virtual appliances. NetScaler SDX appliances require licenses for each physical appliance and each virtual instance. Although NetScaler VPX edition licenses are handled and purchased separately, they work in the same way as the ADC MPX and SDX licenses as far as feature enablement goes; the same applies to 'Burst Packs', by the way, read on...

Burst packs

Citrix also offers 'Burst Pack' licenses. When applied these will temporarily increase the network throughput capabilities of your NetScaler appliance (physical and virtual). This way you can handle sudden, and perhaps unforeseen, traffic spikes without having to heavily invest in new hardware.

Make sure you check out the Citrix NetScaler data sheet: it will show you all the different features available per edition. It's a lot to take in, so take your time and if you're not sure about what you're reading, it's probably best to contact one of your Citrix sales representatives.

From a high-level perspective, when purchasing a Citrix NetScaler follow these steps:

- First you need to decide which physical or virtual model to go with: think about the amount of network throughput you may need, SSL offloading capabilities, that sort of thing.

- Next, depending on specific features or functions you would like to use, you choose your edition (platform) license. So if it is the Gateway functionality you are looking for, go with the Gateway license.
- Finally you may want to purchase a maintenance contract with Citrix: they come in gold, silver or bronze, representing three, two or one year (s) of support. Contact your Citrix representative for more information.

FMA fact: The virtual NetScaler (VPX) can handle up to 1500 concurrent ICA connections (supported by Citrix, theoretically it can handle more). If you need more, then you'll have to upgrade and purchase a physical MPX appliance, which, depending on the model, can handle anything ranging from 10,000 to 35,000 concurrent ICA connections at a time.

Universal

Next to the Access Gateway Edition, or platform license, you might also need an Access Gateway universal license, a.k.a. a Concurrent User license (CCU). This license enables the Access Gateway Enterprise edition appliance to support a specific number of concurrent users to make use of features like full SSL VPNs, Smart Access Endpoint Analysis, Clientless Access to the websites or Micro VPNs in the case of Citrix XenMobile. Note that the total number of concurrent user sessions logged onto a NetScaler Gateway virtual server cannot exceed the license count defined in the NetScaler Gateway universal license.

> **FMA fact**: There's a lot of overlap between the two (ADC and Gateway): it basically all comes down to the license you purchase and upload, with the NetScaler Gateway license being the most 'basic' one.

Note that these licenses also apply to the ADC NetScaler family highlighted earlier, and that they are optional: you don't necessarily need them. The NetScaler Gateway is available as a virtual appliance as well as physical and upgrading, if it's more than standard Gateway functionality that you need; also works by uploading a Standard, Enterprise or Platinum (ADC) license.

Basic NetScaler terminology

NetScalers can be hard to get: if it is not the licensing that will get your head spinning, then it will be the terminology used within NetScaler configurations to get things up and running. Here I will provide you with the basics that you will need to know to get started.

Virtual servers

The NetScaler uses vServers (virtual servers) to deliver different kinds of services and they come in several different tastes; for example, you can have a virtual server for secure gateway purposes, handling secure remote access for your users. You can have a virtual server to load balance traffic, one to handle content switching or VPN access etc. Needless to say, you can, and probably will have, multiple virtual servers on your NetScaler at any given time. A vServer is what they call a logical object.

However, it doesn't really matter what kind or type of virtual server we want to implement: there are a few basic steps, which will (almost) always need to be taken care of.

Think of the NetScaler virtual server as the first point of contact (though a firewall will probably sit in front) from an external user perspective when trying to access resources from your internal network: it is where the external connection terminates and the NetScaler takes over. A virtual server will have a VIP, or virtual IP address, which will be 'known' on the outside. Besides a VIP, it will also have a name (primarily used for administration purposes), including a definition of the protocol and port it will support.

Service and server objects

Once a virtual server has been configured, one of the next steps will include the set-up and configuration of a so-called service object. A service object basically represents an application running on one of your back-end systems, like HTTP, when dealing with web server requests. This is how it would work. First we create a service object and give it a name, again primarily for administration purposes; then within the service object we tell it to what type of protocol and port number it should apply its magic and last but not least, to which physical or virtual back-end server it should forward the actual requests, HTTP in this case. Once done, the service object and the virtual server will be bound together, a process referred to as binding.

To help the service object in actually finding the physical or virtual back-end system, as mentioned above, we will also need to create and configure a server object (don't get confused, yes, we have server and service objects) which we will then need to bind to the earlier created service object. The server object will also have a name within the NetScaler configuration, just like the virtual server and service object, and it will point to the IP address or FQDN of the actual back-end system handling the HTTP requests, one server object per back-end web server.

A quick résumé

We have our virtual server, which has a VIP or virtual IP address, a name, protocol and port number. The virtual server is then bound to a service object, while the service object is bound to a server object, which points to the actual physical or virtual back-end server handling the HTTP requests. Are you still with me?

Time to monitor

Load balancing, when implemented / configured, will take place at a virtual server / service object level. Obviously there will need to be a way for the virtual server to monitor the service objects on the back-end system it is load balancing to. Also see the image on the next page.

Otherwise, if one or multiple of those services become unavailable (down), because the accompanying back-end system has crashed, and the virtual server doesn't know about it, it will keep load-balancing requests to those service objects resulting in 404 errors, the requested resource is not available. Enter monitors...

A monitor is another logical object that sits in between the service and the server object (note that it is bound to the service object) and constantly monitors the overall health and availability of the physical or virtual back-end systems (the services on it) handling the actual HTTP requests. As soon as a monitor notices that a back-end system, or the services on it, becomes unresponsive it will show the accompanying service, that it has been bound to, as down within the NetScaler management console, and it will stop sending traffic its way.

Netscaler

```
   +------------------------------------------------------------------+
   |                                                                  |
   |   +--------+     +----------------+     +---------+     +---------------+   |
<--+-->|  VIP   |<--->| Service object |<--->| Monitor |<--->| Server object |<--+-->
   |   +--------+     +----------------+     +---------+     +---------------+   |
   |                                                                  |
   +------------------------------------------------------------------+
```

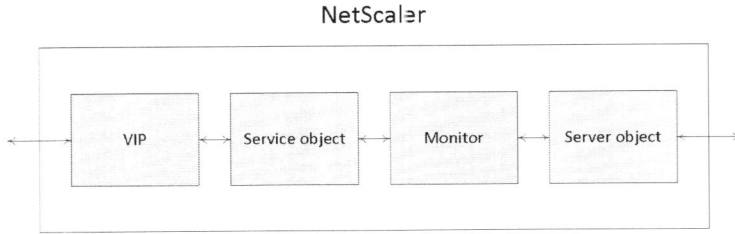

Figure 20: NetScaler objects

NetScaler IP Address

The NSIP address (NetScaler IP Address) is the IP address which is used by the Administrator to manage and configure the NetScaler; it is also referred to as the Management IP Address. It is mandatory when setting up and configuring the NetScaler for the first time: there can only be one NSIP address, it cannot be removed and when it's changed you will have to reboot the NetScaler.

Subnet IP Address

A SNIP (Subnet IP Address) is used for server side connections, meaning that this address will be used to route traffic from or through the NetScaler to a subnet directly connected to the NetScaler. The NetScaler has a mode named USNIP (Use SNIP), which is enabled by default, this causes the SNIP address to be used as the source address when sending packets from the NetScaler to the internal network.

When a SNIP address is configured, a corresponding route is added to the NetScaler's routing table, which is used to determine the optimal route from the NetScaler to the internal network. If it detects the SNIP address to be part of the route it will use it to pass through the network traffic using the SNIP address as its source. A SNIP address is not mandatory. In a multiple subnet scenario you will have to configure a SNIP (or MIP: I'll discuss this in a minute) address for each subnet separately. Also, when multiple SNIP addresses are configured on the same subnet, they will be used in a round robin fashion. By default, a SNIP address is not bound to a NetScaler interface; all network traffic is transmitted on all interfaces. So you could say that it's closer to a network hub than anything else. Fortunately, you have a few options in binding SNIP addresses to a NetScaler interface, or multiple, when needed.

FMA fact: A NetScaler SNIP address is probably best compared to a layer 3 routing table entry. Not only does it tell the NetScaler that it has a connection to a specific network, so it is 'known', it also tells it how and where to reach it so that it is able to route network traffic its way.

Mapped IP Address

The NetScaler has a feature referred to as USNIP, use Subnet IP, which is enabled by default. If this 'mode' is disabled, then no SNIP addresses can or will be used. Ok, so what then, you ask? Or what if you have a subnet connected to the NetScaler without a SNIP address configured? This is where the Mapped IP Address comes into play.

If a MIP (Mapped IP) address is configured it would be used as the source IP address if the abovementioned USNIP mode is set to disabled or when no SNIP addresses are available. Also, when used in conjunction with a SNIP address, if they both reside on the same subnet, for example, a MIP address might also be used as a source IP address when routing traffic from the NetScaler. However, only if the MIP address is the first address on the subnet will a route be added to the NetScaler routing table.

NetScaler

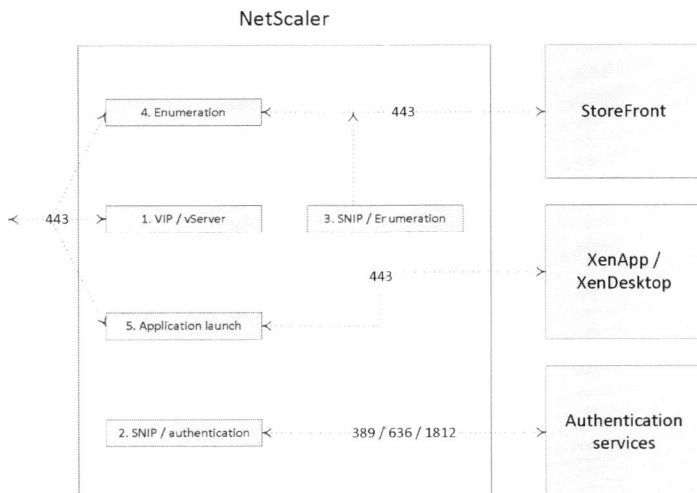

Figure 21: NetScaler internals

NetScaler Default route

When configuring a NetScaler from scratch it will also ask you for a default route, which will function as the default gateway for the NetScaler. Without any internal routes known to the NetScaler, in the form of a SNIP or MIP address, it wouldn't know what to do with the received traffic or where to send it. It will then send out all traffic over its default route, back onto the Internet where it probably came from to begin with.

FMA fact: You can also configure a SNIP address as a management IP, instead of, or better said, alongside the NSIP address used to manage your NetScaler.

Note that internal network traffic can also be sent through the NetScaler: this is not uncommon when load-balancing traffic destined for StoreFront and/or Delivery Controllers using a load balance virtual server.

When traffic is routed using one of the NetScaler's SNIP addresses, the source address of the IP packets changes into that of the SNIP address, which makes sense since it will route traffic to subnets directly connected to the NetScaler. When multiple SNIP addresses have access to the same subnet, the SNIP which sits closest to the actual target will be used.

A SNIP address is not mandatory when setting up and configuring your NetScaler. The use of so-called net profiles is also optional; they can be used to predefine which SNIP should be used for back-end communication. When firewalls are in place this also helps in simplifying the creation of ACL rules, since only one address will need to be defined.

Static routes

Let me give you an example to try and explain what a static route might look like. Let's say you need access to a resource which is located on network D, but you will have to go through, or contact, network A to get there. Well, that's basically it. You give the NetScaler a specific path to follow when a certain network or resource needs to be addressed. It will be listed as a static route.

Let's say you have a SNIP configured on your NetScaler connecting you to subnet A. On your internal network you also have a subnet D, but it isn't directly reachable from the NetScaler. Traffic will have to travel over, or through, subnet A, which is connected to a routing device connecting it to subnet

D. SNIP addresses only work with directly reachable subnets / networks, so adding an additional SNIP for subnet D won't work.

Instead you need to configure a static route (add route) telling the NetScaler to route network traffic destined for subnet D over, or through, subnet A, including the IP address of the routing device connected to subnet D. Here the same rules apply as before, if no 'known' route to subnet D is configured, the NetScaler will forward all traffic to its default route highlighted earlier.

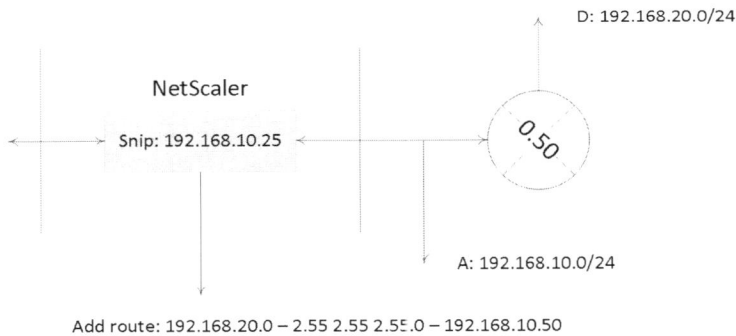

D: 192.168.20.0/24

NetScaler

Snip: 192.168.10.25   0.50

A: 192.168.10.0/24

Add route: 192.168.20.0 – 2.55 2.55 2.55.0 – 192.168.10.50

Figure 22: Static route

The NetScaler Unified Gateway

Not too long ago, as part of the NetScaler 11.0 release Citrix, announced the NetScaler Unified Gateway. In simple terms it comes down to a single vServer receiving all inbound traffic, which will then be routed to the appropriate virtual servers that are bound to the Unified Gateway virtual server, making it possible to access multiple services (as configured on the internal virtual servers) by using just a single IP address / URL. And while the technologies behind it aren't really new (they basically made use of existing technologies like Content

Switching, Client Access and Bookmarks) it does offer some additional benefits. The Universal Gateway virtual server can be paired with a NetScaler Gateway virtual server, to secure remote access where and when needed, including one or multiple load-balancing virtual servers. Some of the added advantages include:

- A single IP address / URL to access multiple back-end services like: XenDesktop / XenApp applications and desktops, mobile and web applications hosted by XenMobile and access to cloud resources. Freeing up the need for additional IP addresses.
- All known features of the NetScaler and XenDesktop platform can now be applied on one single platform while offering multiple back-end services, like: Single Sign-on, HDX and NetScaler Insight Services, End Point Analyses, RDP proxy, Content Switching, Smart Access Control etc.
- Triple A (AAA) support, which allows integration with cloud services Office 365 and SSO against existing NetScaler Load Balance servers.

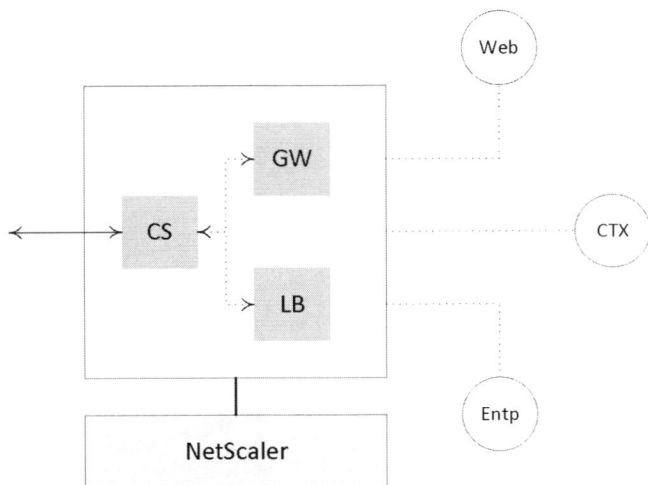

Figure 23: NetScaler Unified Gateway

> **FMA fact**: You can configure as many Unified Gateway
> virtual servers as you like or need.

Securing NetScaler connections

When connecting from a remote location we want to make sure
that we are connecting to the trusted company network and that
it isn't being spoofed in any way.

In our case we would set up the Citrix NetScaler to function as a
remote secure gateway (virtual server) as the first point of
access, authenticating and authorising our users. However, the
question remains, how does the user know, after filling in the
external facing URL of the NetScaler, that it is connecting to the
actual (trusted) company network and that the machine
answering the request is who it says it is? This is where
certificates come into play.

SSL certificates

The NetScaler will have an SSL certificate installed, which it uses to identify itself to the remote user / machine, convincing them that it is who it says it is, the certificate is (or should be) proof of that. Now I know, anyone can forge or counterfeit a digital certificate, so there needs to be a mechanism in place which tells the end-user / machine that it can trust the certificate presented by the NetScaler during the set-up and negotiation of the remote connection. Enter the Certificate Authorities (CA).

Certificates can be acquired, generated or purchased in multiple ways. You can set up your own internal domain-based PKI, Public Key Infrastructure, and start handing out certificates. This way you create your own internal Certificate Authority.

This can also be done on the NetScaler, by the way. You can also generate self-signed certificates, which are issued by the machine itself. This basically means that the machine generating and signing the certificate trusts itself. This can be done on the NetScaler as well. Or, last but not least, you can purchase a certificate from a well-known, respected and, most importantly, trusted external third-party Certificate Authority.

Let's resume, shall we? A certificate is always issued and signed by a Certificate Authority of some sort. This can be a private CA when you set up and configure your own internal PKI, for example, a self-signed certificate as mentioned above, where the machine issuing the certificate is basically its own CA (it can't assign certificates to other machines), or the CA can be external, a third party as I also highlighted.

It is all about trust

When a user / machine connects to an external resource like a
NetScaler (Gateway), the external resource will present a
certificate to try and prove that it is who it says it is. As
mentioned, certificates are issued and signed by so-called CAs.
And here it comes, the CA who originally issued (and signed)
the certificate to the external resource needs to be trusted by the
user / machine (or client) connecting to that resource. If the CA
is trusted all is fine and you will end up on the web page you
requested. If the CA who issued the certificate of the external
resource is not trusted by the client you will end up with a
security warning where you need to decide to continue or not.
These may differ slightly, depending on the browser type and
version used.

Another example would be when the NetScaler communicates
with one of your StoreFront servers (or vice versa): here SSL
encryption can be applied as well. In this case the NetScaler will
connect up to the StoreFront server requesting a secure
connection to exchange information. The StoreFront server will
show the NetScaler its SSL Certificate to prove that it is who it
says it is. In this case the NetScaler will need to trust the CA
which issued and signed the StoreFront certificate. The same
rules apply.

The advantage of purchasing certificates from a well-known
third-party CA is that all major web browsers, by default, already
trust these companies / CAs. So when you connect to a website
/ resource showing you a certificate issued and signed by a well-
known third-party CA, you will not have any issues getting onto
the actual web page you requested.

Internal Certificate Authority

If you don't use a trusted third-party CA, you will need to come up with a way to make all of your users / devices trust your internal CA. Of course this is doable, but it involves some extra effort which, depending on the number and types of external users / clients, can be a daunting task. The same applies to self-signed certificates: you will need to make sure that your users / clients trust the machine (CA) that issued the self-signed certificate.

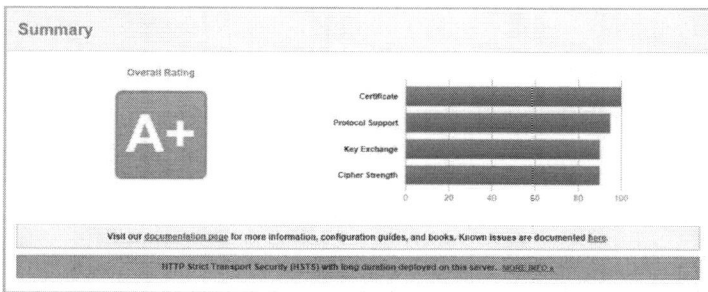

Figure 24: SSL Labs online security check

External CAs have a very extensive and intensive authentication and verification programme you will need to go through before they give out one of their certificates. This is one of the main reasons why these CAs are trusted within most major web browsers, as mentioned earlier. The cost per certificate can greatly vary per vendor, as well as the type of certificate you want to purchase. Also, the time a certificate will be valid will have an influence on the overall costs as well. Some well-known CAs are: GoDaddy, Verisign, GlobalSign and DigiCert. If you give it a Google you'll come up with a few more, I'm sure.

Different types of certificates

When creating or requesting a digital SSL certificate you have a few options. Of course you can decide on the lifespan of the certificate, 2 years, five years and so on and so forth, the number of bits used for encryption etc., but there are some other variables you may want to consider, two in particular.

Wild card certificates

We could make use of a wild card certificate. A wild card certificate can be used on multiple devices / machines without having to purchase or generate multiple separate certificates. So instead of generating or purchasing two separate certificates for your NetScaler and your StoreFront server, like, external.vankaam.local and internal.vankaam.local, we could do with just one in the form of *.vankaam.local. It supports an unlimited number of subdomains.

SAN certificates

Another one I'd like to highlight is the SAN, or Subject Alternative Name, certificate. A SAN certificate can be used to secure multiple domains like vankaam.com, basvankaam.org, mydomain.com etc. I think you get the point.

DMZ considerations

The device responsible for offloading all SSL traffic, the Citrix NetScaler in our case, can live within our DMZ. And the web server(s) for which SSL traffic is being offloaded can be safely placed on our (more secure) internal network (although this doesn't apply to all use cases of course) without having to worry about unsafe connections since, next to user authentication (when applicable) which can be handled by the NetScaler as well, all traffic can be checked, inspected, decrypted and possible re-encrypted by the NetScaler before finally ending up on the web server. Next to SSL offloading, the NetScaler is also capable of SSL and TCP multiplexing and supports features like HTTP caching and compression or front-end optimisations to optimise various web applications for a much more responsive website.

Key takeaways

- The NetScaler can do more than 'just' provide secure remote access to XenDesktop and/or XenApp environments.

- All NetScalers are (almost) equal with regard to the functionality and features that they can deliver. Depending on the type of license you upload, certain functionalities and/or features will become available. Pay as you Grow.

- The main differences between the physical appliances can be found in the compute resources and the type of Cavium SSL accelerator card that they hold. This card is used to decrypt and encrypt SSL traffic. The more powerful the card, the more SSL transactions it will be able to handle.

- NetScalers can be physical (MPX and SDX), virtual (VPX), virtual on physical (VPX on SDX) and containerised (CPX).

- While not mentioned earlier (except for the license type) there is also a NetScaler Express edtion. It is free of charge and a potential great resource for smaller deployments, PoC's and test environments. The VPX Express edition offers the same features as the VPX standard edition. However, there are a few limitations to keep in mind like: no SSL Offload capabilities, max 5 Mbps throughput, licensed per year. Other than that it is definitely worth having a look at.

- There are three main ADC platform licenses available: Standard, Enterprise and Platinum. There is also a separate NetScaler Gateway license and a universal license.

- If you need to temporarily increase your network bandwidth think about purchasing and applying a Burst Pack.

- Remember the one is none rule? Well, it applies to NetScalers as well.

- NetScaler HA (2 nodes) is always set up as active-passive, with one NetScaler being the primary node of the two, and thus the active one. The secondary node(s) will send a continuous stream of heartbeat messages (interval is configurable), checking to see if the primary device is active and accepting connections. If it fails to respond, and after multiple retries, a secondary node will take over, which is referred to as a failover. NetScaler clustering, which is Active / Active using ECMO, can grow up to 32 nodes in total.

- When applying NetScaler HA be aware that different NetScaler models cannot be paired: the model and make of both NetScaler appliances must be equal and both NetScalers must run the same software version, licenses included.

- The NetScaler can also provide secure remote access to XenMobile web, SaaS and mobile applications. The latter is referred to as Micro VPNs. In fact, you need a NetScaler for this.

- Always start small and contact your Citrix sales representative when in doubt. Remember the Pay as you Grow model: you can't go wrong.

- When dealing with larger and more complex environments, consider having a look at the NetScaler Unified Gateway set-up.

- Make sure to apply SSL certificates to secure your in- and outbound connections.

- It is thought of as a best practice to use third-party certificates when dealing with external, inbound connections, and to use internal CA certificates for all internal SSL traffic, from your StoreFront Server to your Delivery Controllers, for example.
- When setting up a test lab or PoC environment, self-signed certificates can be helpful.
- NetScaler can secure remote access for both StoreFront as well as Web Interface.
- When implementing a Citrix NetScaler certain firewall ports will need to be opened. Always check the Citrix product documentation before implementing.

Provisioning Services

When it comes to delivering the base Operating System within Citrix-orientated environments we have a couple of options to choose from. For one, we can decide to install and manage everything manually, like we are used to doing on our home PCs. Second, you can use an automation tool of some sort (or script it yourself) to install and update your XenApp servers and/or XenDesktop VDI machines, which isn't that uncommon. However, ongoing maintenece will always be a challenge.

And third, we can leveredge single image management in the form of either Citrix Machine Creation Services (MCS) and/or Citrix Provisioning Services (PVS). MCS will be discussed in the next chapter, for now I would to spend a minute or two talking about PVS: what it is, how it works, and what some of the advantages are, or can be. Note that this chapter is primarily meant to give you a high-level overview of Citrix Provisioning Services, as I'm not going to cover all the ins and outs that come with setting up, managing and maintaining a PVS Farm; some details will be included, though.

An overview

Provisioning services is based on software streaming technology. Simply put, a single read-only (hence the single image management remark earlier) vDisk or virtual disk will be streamed over the network to multiple so-called target devices, which can be XenApp servers or XenDesktop VDI-based VMs. You will always have at least two provisioning servers for HA purposes, or more depending on the size of your deployment and the number of target devices that need to be serviced.

You could easily provision several hundreds or thousands perhaps of physical and/or virtual machines from 'just' two provisioning servers, although more would be preferred.

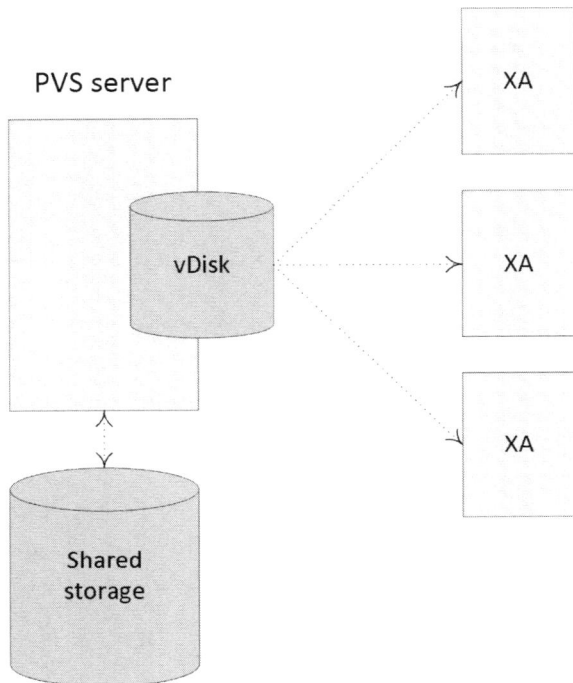

Figure 25: PVS overview

Virtual Disk (vDisk)

It all starts with the actual vDisk, or the creation of it. This is the process of configuring and installing all desired software (including applications) and additional components onto a physical and/or virtual machine of choice, like we would normally do when creating a master image; in fact it is not uncommon to use Microsoft SCCM, or a similar solution for this. This machine will be referred to as the Master Target Device.

Next, using specific PVS client software, which will need to be installed on the Master Target Device as well, a vDisk will be created (exported) from the device's local hard drive. vDisks can be stored locally on the provisioning server, on a network file share, or on a shared storage platform accessible by all provisioning servers. Although a great deal of reads will probably be read from cache once the first few machines have booted (read-only vDisk, remember) when dealing with potentially hundreds of machines all trying to access the same vDisk, some consideration regarding the type of storage used to store the vDisk will be needed.

As mentioned vDisks can be assigned to multiple target devices in read-only mode, also referred to as Standard Image mode, meaning that the vDisk will be shared by multiple physical and/virtual devices at the same time. Each machine will have a Write Cache location assigned to it where all the writes to the (read-only) vDisk will be stored, more on these in a minute. However, vDisks can also be assigned in a one-to-one fashion, which is referred to as Private Image Mode, allowing the user to read and write to the vDisk. All changes made will be saved.

vDisk's life cycle, Versioning

The life cycle of a vDisk is pretty basic, at least in theory. After creating a vDisk and assigning it to multiple target devices, which is basically step one, it will need to be maintained and updated from time to time. Finally, when no longer in use, a vDisk might need to be retired and taken out of production. While each of these phases have their own specific steps to consider, I would like to briefly highlight the built-in Provisioning Services Versioning technology used for updating and maintenance purposes.

When updating and maintaining a vDisk (in read-only standard mode) using PVS versioning, it will involve creating a new version of the current vDisk, also known as a differencing disk, which will then be linked to the original vDisk. When Versioning is used, this process can be automated, but it can be done manually as well. Next the newly provisioned (differencing) vDisk needs to be assigned to the Master Target Device mentioned earlier and booted in maintenance mode, something which is also easily done from the Versioning console. Once booted, you are free to make your changes and shut down the Master Target Device after you are done.

FMA fact: vDisk updates can be automated and scheduled. This feature supports updates detected and delivered from WSUS and SCCM Electronic Software Delivery servers.

As a final step, the updated vDisk will need to be promoted to either Test or Production. This step can also be automated and scheduled when needed. Beware that when you create multiple 'new' versions, these will all be differencing disks pointing back to the original vDisk. Citrix advises merging the differencing disks back into the base image whenever you have created 3 to a maximum of 5 differencing disks a.k.a as a chain of differencing disks. This will not only save you some disk space, but will also positively impact performance. Again, you will use the Versioning console to do this. To summarize:

1. From your Provisioning Service management console right-click one of your vDisks in Standard Image Mode and select 'Versions'.
2. In the 'Versions' menu select 'New'.

3. You will see a new version being created with access set to 'Maintenance'.

4. Next you go to the Master Target device, which is used for updating vDisks and change its 'Type' to 'Maintenance'.

5. Assign the vDisk you want to update to the Master Target device.

6. Power on the Master Target device and select the proper vDisk from the boot menu.

7. Login to the Master Target device and make your changes / updates.

8. Run any disk sealing tasks and power off the Master Target device.

9. Again, from your Provisioning Service management console right-click the vDisk in standard image mode and select 'Versions'.

10. Highlight the vDisk you have just updated and promote it to test first (this step is optional, you can also promote it to production right away).

    a. Here you either select 'Immediate' or 'Scheduled'. With 'Immediate' the Target devices will need to be rebooted first before they will be able to use the new updated vDisk. With 'Scheduled' they will need to be rebooted after the scheduled time and/or date.

11. Think about replicating your vDisk files to your other PVS servers. This is something that PVS can help you with as well; it has a built-in mechanism for this.

12. Select one of your Target devices and configure it to boot from the 'Test' vDisk.

13. When testing is done and successful, promote the vDisk to production as per the steps mentioned above.

14. After multiple updates have taken place, also meaning that multiple vDisks / differencing disks have been created it is time to merge.
15. As before, from the PVS management console go into 'Versions' and this time select 'Merge'.
    a. From the 'Merge' menu you have the option to either choose 'Merged Updates', which will merge multiple differencing disks into a new file linked to the original base file, or 'Merge Base'. The latter will merge the original file and all of the differencing disk files into a single new file without any linked files attached.
    b. Also, you need to select if you are merging it into: Maintenance, Test or Production.
16. Again, think about replicating everything to your other PVS servers.
17. If the merged vDisk is still in maintenance or test, promote it to production.
18. Once you are done you can manually delete the older versions. However, do note that once they are deleted you will not be able to revert back to one of these versions, which is also possible using PVS Versioning.

It is not uncommon to see some of the more 'old school' system administrators using the manual (copying and editing multiple vDisks) approach. Also, in larger enviroenments a hybrid deployment is often used as well. Here you would use versioning for your test and development environments and for production you would apply the manual (full vDisk copy) approach, something I would recommend doing as well. In both cases it is important to first get yourself formiliarized with the process and steps involved, one at the time.

> **FMA fact:** Be aware that while promoting the version, PVS will actually open up the vDisk and write to it. This it can lead to inconsistencies if you are storing vDisks locally and replication can be complicated.

Write cache

When working with 'normal' PCs, or server systems for that matter, we normally don't think about this too much, but when a machine boots and also after it has entered its steady state, it will need to write certain information to base Operating System.

The same applies to applications and other software being used. If the earlier mentioned vDisk is in read-only mode, where will it store those writes? For this they created something that is referred to as the target device's write cache. As with MCS, where all the writes to the base OS are stored on a differencing disk, all writes to a read-only vDisk will be stored in its accompanying write cache.

Each target device will have its own write cache and, depending on the OS used and the type of deployment (RDSH or VDI), its size will vary. What is also worth noting is that when a Standard Image mode machine gets rebooted, its write cache is cleared; it will start out fresh again. Logically this does not apply to machines in Private Image mode where all changes made during the session will be persistent.

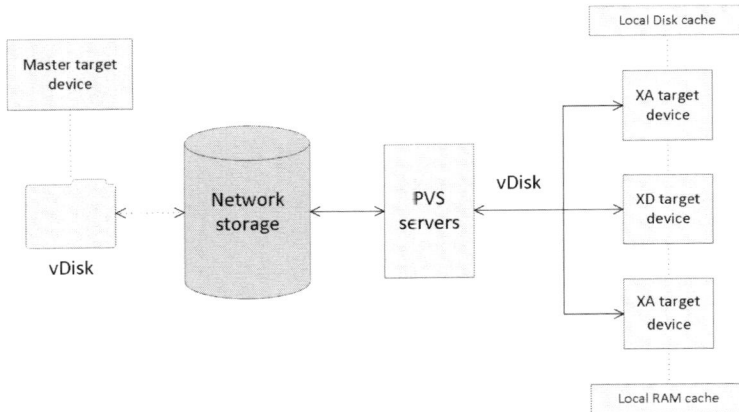

Figure 26: Provisioning Services architecture

Adding write cache to a target device can be done in multiple ways and during the last couple of years Citrix has made some impressive improvement in this area. The following section is meant to provide you with an overview on the various write cache options available.

Cache on device hard drive

The write cache file is stored on the local hard drive of the target device itself; this can be a virtual or physical machine and thus a virtual or physical hard drive as well. No additional software is needed to enable this feature; it is configurable from the PVS management console. As mentioned, the write cache file is only temporary, as it gets refreshed when the machine reboots unless it is set to Private Image Mode. A common and recommended approach when cache in RAM is not possible.

Cache on device hard drive persisted

Here we are basically talking about the same set-up as cache on device hard drive, but this time no changes will be lost when the machine reboots. Note that a different bootstrap file (will be discussed shortly) will be needed for this method. If you want use PVS for persistent desktops, I would recommend to also have a look at the 'Personal vDisks' section over at page 241.

Cache on a server

The write cache file can also be placed on the provisioning server itself, meaning that all writes will be handled by the PVS server. This can increase the overall disk IO and network bandwidth needed, something to consider. It also means that all writes will need to traverse the network back to the PVS server as opposed to writing them on the local hard drive of the target device itself. Personally I wouldn't recommend this setup.

Cache on server persistent

If a vDisk is set to cache on server persistent, each target device that accesses the vDisk automatically has a device-specific, writable disk file created. All changes will be persistent, so after a reboot no changes will be lost. You can also assign a target device to multiple vDisks. To be honest, persistent desktops based on PVS, or MCS (PvD) for that matter isn't a common approach. While personal vDisk might be optional, I would recommend using full VMs instead.

Cache in device RAM

Writes will be temporarily stored in the RAM of the target device. As you can probably imagine, this is by far the fastest method out there today. Besides cache in device RAM with overflow on HDD, this is the preferred way to implement PVS write cache.

Cache in device RAM with overflow on HDD

As soon as the target device runs out of free memory space to store any writes the system will switch to the local hard drive (cache on device hard drive). This method uses the VHDX

232

differencing format. When enough RAM is available, the target device will write to RAM first. When RAM is full, the least recently used blocks of data will be written to the local disk to accommodate newer data on RAM. The amount of RAM specified is the non-paged kernel memory that the target device will consume. The more RAM you assign, the more writes can be stored in RAM and, as a result, the better the overall user experience will be. This has been a very popular approach throughout the past year or so. The more RAM you have available for caching purposes, the better of you will be.

The boot mechanism

When a target device starts it needs to somehow be able to find and contact a provisioning server to eventually stream down the appropriate vDisk. This information is stored in a so-called Bootstrap file named ARDBP32.BIN.

It contains everything the target device needs to know to contact a PVS server so that the streaming process can be initialised. For one, it will contain information about the login servers (with a maximum of four IP addresses), which will be used by the target device to logon to PVS. However, that doesn't mean that one of these (potentially) four servers will also be used for streaming purposes. That is decided in the next phase where the login server will notify the target device about actual streaming server. You will find all the steps involved a few paragraphs down.

The Bootstrap file is delivered through a TFTP server, this also (partly) applies to the alternative BDM (Boot Device Manager) approach, which will be discussed in more detail as we progress. There are some distinct differences between the two.

TFTP

When using TFTP the target device needs to know how and where it can find the TFTP server to download the Bootstrap file before being able to contact a PVS server. Secondly, since this is a critical step you want to make sure that the TFTP server isn't a single point of failure, meaning that you would like to implement some form of high availability. Throughout the next section I'll list some of the options you have in achieving this (delivering the Bootstrap and HA).

FMA fact: Provisioning Services has its own built-in TFTP server. However, you are free to use whatever you prefer.

One of the most popular approaches in delivering the TFTP server address to your target devices is through DHCP, but there are other options as well:

- You can use DHCP option 66 to enter the TFTP's server address. However, note that you will only be able to fill in one server address: no HA here.
- You can use DHCP option 66 combined with DNS round robin. Here you put in a hostname that has multiple A (host) records (PVS servers) in DNS, which will then be rotated in a round robin fashion. Has its flaws (not all PXE clients are able to handle multiple host entries for example) but works.
- Using PXE (broadcast) services. PVS also offers the ability to configure a PXE service when initially configuring Provisioning Services. When a target device boots it will send out a broadcast message to find a suitable PXE server. This way, if one of the two PVS

servers (also hosting the PXE services) is down, the other one will respond and deliver the Bootstrap file. Instant HA without needing to touch DHCP: a very popular approach. Again, note that there are various PXE clients out there and that they do not all offer the exact same functionalities.

- And finally the Citrix NetScaler. Using the NetScaler you have multiple options in making your TFTP server highly available.

BDM

There are actually two different methods to make use of the Boot Device Manager. Let's start with Provisioning Services. PVS offers a quick wizard, which will generate a relatively small .ISO file (around 300KB). Next you configure your target devices to boot from this .ISO file, using their CDROM/DVD players, for example, by specifying its (shared) network location.

This method uses a two-stage boot process where the PVS location will be hardcoded into the bootstrap generated by the BDM. The rest of the information (like the PVS device drivers) is downloaded from the PVS server using a proprietary download protocol based on TFTP (UDP, port Nr. 6969). Here, TFTP will still be used. This works with virtual as well as physical machines.

As of XenDesktop version 7.0, when using the XenDesktop setup wizard we can create and assign a small BDM hard disk partition, which will be attached to the virtual machine as a separate virtual disk. Using this method the above-mentioned two-stage approach is no longer needed because the partition already contains all the PVS drivers.

This way all the information needed, as discussed previously, will be directly available without the need for PXE, TFTP and/or DHCP. Advised for virtual machines only.

> **FMA Fact**: As an added advantage, using the BDM method will also decrease boot times by around 5 to 10 seconds since we don't have to wait for PXE and TFTP.

PVS logon and boot steps summarized

When we sum up the whole process from start to finish it comes down to this:

- First the target devices boots and acquires an IP address.
- The target device first identifies a TFTP server.
- Next the Bootstrap file will be downloaded and the target device will boot from it.
- The target device will contact and log onto one of the PVS servers.
- The logon server will notify the target device about the streaming server.
- Target device starts streaming the vDisk from the PVS server.

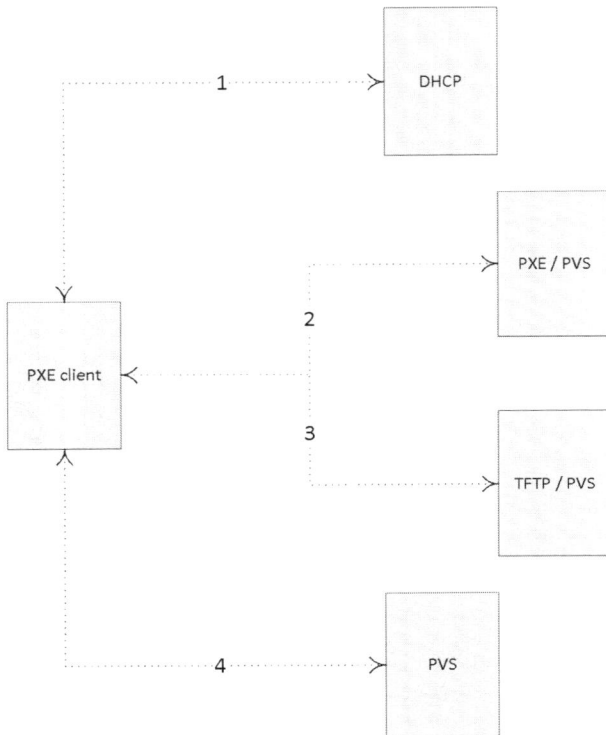

Figure 27: PVS logon and boot process

High Availability

When dealing with highly available PVS environments, there are multiple components to consider. First of all, PVS needs an SQL database, which somehow will need to be made highly available, secondly, you will at least install and configure two PVS servers and configure / enable HA within the PVS software itself, which is done from the management console, and last but not least, the storage where your vDisks reside also needs to be shared, or made highly available. And of course when making use of TFTP for Bootstrap delivery, that will need to be made HA as well, as we have seen in the previous section.

As a side note, Multiple PVS servers can also be used for load-balancing purposes with regard to the streaming traffic they handle – active / active.

> **FMA fact**: When vDisks are stored locally on the Provisioning Servers, you will need to implement some sort of replication mechanism so that all PVS servers will be able to offer the exact same vDisks. This can also be done manually from the PVS management console. Recommended automation methods include both DFS-R and Robocopy.

When it comes to the SQL database you have multiple options:

- PVS offers a built-in offline database support mechanism. It uses a snapshot of the database when the database becomes unavailable. Note that this feature is disabled by default.
- Database mirroring, SQL Clustering and SQL AlwaysOn are all valid options as well.

To conclude, here is a shortlist of components to consider when implementing HA for PVS:

- The Provisioning Services SQL database.
- Your physical or virtual Provisioning Servers.
- Storage used to store your vDisk files, PVS servers and/or target devices.
- The TFTP servers for Bootstrap delivery.

Provisioning wizards

Once you have set up your base Provisioning Services infrastructure, your Master Target Device, or multiple, and configured a vDisk, the time has finally come to (auto-) provision multiple virtual target devices using the streamed VM set-up wizard or the XenDesktop set-up wizard. Ultimately, the devices, which end up using one or multiple of your vDisks, are referred to as device collections: also see the next section for more information with regard to some of the basic terminology used with Provisioning Services. Of course PVS can be used with physical machines just as easily; the way this is set up is just slightly different.

The streamed VM set-up wizard

This wizard is accessed directly from the PVS management console. With the streamed wizard we can create multiple virtual machines, or target devices, to where the vDisks will be steamed (a preconfigured template VM will be needed for this): it will create the target device objects within the appropriate device collection (a collection needs to present) and finally it will assign a vDisk in Standard Image Mode to the virtual machines. It goes without saying that the vDisk will have to be made beforehand as well.

> **FMA fact**: The streamed wizard supports the following Hypervisors: XenServer, Hyper-V through SCVMM and ESX through vCenter.

During the wizard session you will be able to select the Hypervisor to connect to the VM template on which the newly provisioned VMs will be based, the device collection to where the VMs will be added during creation, choose the number of

VMs to create, the number of CPUs and the amount of memory each VM will be assigned, and finally you have the option to let the system create new or add-in existing Active Directory computer accounts.

Make sure to read through all of the prerequisites before you start using the wizard. I would suggest the Citrix E-docs website as a good starting point.

The XenDesktop set-up wizard

To be able to use the XenDesktop wizard you need to make sure that your Delivery Controllers and Provisioning Servers are both on the same version. The XenDesktop set-up wizard, just as with the streamed VM set-up wizard, creates VMs on a XenDesktop hosted Hypervisor (Host Connection) making use of a preconfigured template VM machine.

It will also create target devices within a new or existing device collection, which will take on the name of the corresponding XenDesktop Catalog. It will assign a Standard Image vDisk to the VMs within the device collection, and at the same time it will add all virtual desktops to the XenDesktop Machine Catalog within Studio. Once you have gone through all the steps in the wizard, this in a nutshell is what happens next:

- First, if needed, it will create a new XenDesktop Machine Catalog.
- Create VMs on a host's Hypervisor using the preconfigured machine template.
- Create BDM partitions, if specified.
- If using a Streamed with personal vDisk Catalog, create a personal vDisk, and then attach the personal vDisk to the VM. This will be discussed in the next session;

personal vDisks are somewhat special.

- Create a write cache disk of the specified size (make sure to check out all prerequisites and write cache considerations beforehand).
- Create Provisioning Services target devices, and then assign the selected vDisk to those devices.
- Add the target devices to the selected Provisioning Services Collection.
- Add the VMs to the XenDesktop Catalog.
- Boot each VM to format the newly created write cache disk.

Personal vDisks

While using Provisioning Services (or Machine Creation Services) to configure persistent desktops, either through persistent write cache or by attaching a Personal vDisk, isn't a very popular approach within larger enterprises, there are tons of smaller companies who are interested in this type of setup. If you talk to Citrix, they would normally advise you to use PvDs for no more then a 100 to max 125 machines, primarily to prevent things from getting too complicated. If more are needed, fully cloned VMs are preferably used instead. Also, on my website I get a lot of questions around PvDs and related technology. That's why I decided to include the subject in here as well.

A Personal vDisk, or PvD in short, offers a way for users to store their changes when working on a virtual, pooled static machine (the PvD is assigned or attached to a virtual machine and then the user is assigned a virtual machine on first use). When PVS is used, streaming is only possible to virtual

machines; streaming to physical is not supported. PvD
technology can be used with PVS as well as MCS.

> **FMA fact**: Personal vDisks can only be assigned to an
> desktop Operating System; server OSs are not supported
> at this time.

An overview

With Personal vDisks we still use one base (master) image just
like before but we now get an extra Personal vDisk attached to
our VM on which all our 'personal' changes, will be stored.
These will include all file level and registry changes including but
not limited to: installed or streamed applications provisioned by
SCCM, App-V (think cache) or XenApp but also things like:
desktop wallpapers, Start menu settings, favourites etc. It
basically stores all changes made under C:\Users as far as the
user profile is concerned and everything else when it comes to
applications that get installed / updated.

Split in two

The PvD VHDs, by default, are split in two when it comes to
storage allocation for personal (profile-related) changes and
application installs and/or updates. If your PvD is 10 GB in size
it will allocate 5 GB for profile / personal storage and the other
5 GB for application installs / updates etc. This can be changed
(Registry setting) into 70 / 30, 90 / 10, or 99 / 1 even; give this
some thought and adjust accordingly. When used in
combination with user profile management and/or folder
redirection, there's not that much left and it would be a waste of
space.

When an administrator needs or wants to edit the underlying base (master) image: no problem! He or she simply updates or installs an application, service pack, security update or whatever needs fixing and the Personal vDisk will take it from there. The user will see all the changes he or she made (stored on the PvD) in conjunction with the base (master) image even if it's being updated live, although the administrator must still roll out these changes to the end-users from Studio like before, so the VM will still need a reboot. It allows all of the user changes to persist over the base image changes.

The Personal vDisk communicates with the XenDesktop Personal vDisk agent, which is installed on the base (master) image during (Catalog) creation. This agent tracks what's installed and available on the base (master) image versus what's installed and changed on the Personal vDisk and will blend these two together once the base (master) image has been updated and rolled out, or applied, to the end-user. This way we get the persistence of dedicated desktops together with the management advantages of pooled desktops.

Some characteristics

If a conflict exists, for example, when a user installs the same application on his PvD as the Administrator does on the base (master) image, then the system will make a note of this and remove the software installed by the user, keeping the PvD as small in size as possible. Note that this is a default setting and is customisable the way you see fit. PvDs can be resized afterwards. Their default size and location are selected during the Catalog creation wizard (selecting MCS as the provisioning mechanism) from XenDesktop Studio or the PVS set-up wizard when PVS is applied.

They end up smaller in size than the 'normal' provisioned differencing disks created with dedicated desktops.

Thin provisioning is supported, so PvDs can be attached to any storage target as defined within your Hypervisor: this means that PvDs can be on different (storage) locations than your actual VMs, enabling you to spread out the IOPS load.

A PvD can be used as a simple profile management solution for small-sized environments, although Citrix recommends using a separate profile management solution alongside. It's compatible with almost all profile management solutions out there.

PvDs allow for easier management but with the flexibility of dedicated desktops. They are 100% persistent with pooled VDI storage and management. As mentioned earlier, PvDs are compatible with most PC life cycle management systems like SCCM, and application virtualisation solutions like Citrix XenApp. And just so you know, PvDs are also available in VDI-in-a-Box, which is still supported by Citrix.

Basic Provisioning Services terminology

Below I will go over some of the terminology that goes with configuring, managing and maintaining Citrix Provisioning Services, some of which you have already come across during the previous sections.

- Farm: This represents the top level of a PVS infrastructure. All sites within a Farm share that farms Microsoft SQL database. A Farm also includes a Citrix License Server, local or network shared storage, and collections of target devices.

- Site: A Site represents a logical grouping of all Provisioning Servers, Device Collections, target devices and storage.
- Stores: This is where you physically store your vDisk files. This can be on either local storage, on the PVS server (s) itself or shared storage in the form of a SAN. When a vDisk is created from the PVS management console you will need to assign it to a store.
- Device Collections: They enable you to manage a large number of devices as a logical group. They simplify administration since administrative tasks can be executed at Device Collection level instead of on a per device basis. A Collection can also represent a physical location or a specific subnet range.
- Target Devices: All devices, both virtual as well as physical, that get a vDisk streamed over the network. The device used to create and maintain the actual vDisk is referred to as a Master Target Device.

Key takeaways

- Provisioning Services streams a base image over the network down to either virtual or physical machines.
- It works for both desktop as well as server Operating Systems.
- A device using a vDisk is also referred to as a Target Device.
- The machine used to create and maintain the vDisk is referred to as the Master Target Device.
- Target Devices are managed using Device Collections.
- Dozens, hundreds or thousands of Target Devices can share a single vDisk.
- The life cycle of a vDisk consists of creation, deployment, maintenance and finally retirement. For this we can leverage the built-in PVS Versioning mechanism.
- Give your write cache sizing and location some consideration: you will be glad that you did.
- Although PVS vDisks can also be streamed in Private Mode, where any changes made to the vDisk will be saved, this isn't a very popular approach.
- Provisioning Services can seem complicated and challenging at first. Take your time and take it step by step, you will be fine. There are many excellent resources out there to help you on your way.
- Make sure to make your PVS infrastructure highly available.
- While PvDs have their use, apply them wisely: it's not for everyone. And while this may be somewhat off topic, in many cases where VDI is being considered, RDSH might make more sense.

- Make sure to check out CTX117372 for some best practices around PVS networking.
- While in the past it was always considered a best practice to use physical machines for your Provisioning Servers, today virtual machines are almost always recommend by Citrix. This has a lot to do with the enhancements around standard networking.
- The same applies to isolating your PVS traffic, again mainly due to the advancements that have been made on the networking and virtualisation side of things during the last couple of years. Keep it simple. One of the main reasons why isolation might still make sense is because of security considerations.
- CTX131611 lists a bunch of Known Hardware Related Provisioning Services Issues.
- Check out CTX124185 for best practices around antivirus on PVS vDisks.

Machine Creation Services

Machine Creation Services is simple to operate: it is integrated right into XenDesktop and you don't have to build and maintain a separate infrastructure like with PVS. Also, while MCS was originally developed and meant for the provisioning of VDI-based VMs, as of XenDesktop 7 it now also supports the provisioning of server Operating Systems. Never mind if it's on-premises or in the cloud, since MCS can do both.

FMA fact: While I use the term 'provisioning' do not confuse the provisioning of machines with MCS with that of PVS (see previous chapter). In general, provisioning means providing or making something available. A term widley used in a variety of concepts within IT.

Breakdown

Next to Provisioning Services, MCS is the second option that we have regarding (automated) desktop image delivery and single image management within XenDesktop. MCS is designed in such a way that it will communicate directly with the Hypervisors Application Program Interface, or API to take care of things like VM creation, the starting and stopping of VMs (power management), delete VMs and so on.

It supports Microsoft's Hyper-V using SCVMM, VMware's vSphere through vCenter and Citrix's XenServer by directly communicating with the Pool master and/or XenCenter.

As with PVS, it all starts with a master VM, template machine, golden image or whatever you would like to call it. A master VM is nothing more than a virtual machine with everything installed; applications, antivirus, patches etc. and configured exactly the way you want to present it to your users.

This will also include the amount of compute (vCPU, Memory, Disk space etc.) assigned to the VM. Next, when you create a new Machine Catalog from Studio (based on MCS technology) you will be asked to select this master VM, which will then serve as the base image from where all other VMs will be (automatically) provisioned.

During these steps you will also have the option to change some of the earlier made configuration choices with regard to the amount of compute assigned to VM (a more detailed overview regarding the steps involved can be found on page 251). MCS is based on Differencing Disk technology, which is similar to that of Linked Clones, used by VMware for example. Using MCS we can provision three different types of desktops (Catalog), see the table on the next page for an overview.

Table 11: MCS desktop types

Desktop type	Desrciption
Pooled-Random	A Desktop will be assigned randomly when a user logs on. When they logoff the desktop will become free for use and any changes made will be lost completely
Pooled-Static	A desktop will be permanently assigned to a user at logon. It will stay with the user even after logoff. Any changes made will be discarded during reboot / logoff
Dedicated	A desktop will be permanently assigned to a user at logon. It will stay with the user even after logoff. Any changes made will be saved to the VM no matter how many times it gets rebooted / refreshed

When provisioning new machines using the Machine Catalog wizard from Studio, from a technical point of view it will work like this: MCS will first take a snapshot of your master VM (template machine) or you can take one manually, which has the added advantage that you can name it yourself. Next, this snapshot is consolidated (merged) and a temporary virtual machine will be created.

This virtual machine will then boot so that certain tasks can be taken care of (DHCP, KMS etc...) before it will be copied over to all datastores known as part of your VM deployment. All

VMs created as part of the provisioning process will consist of a Differencing Disk and an Identity Disk: both will be attached to the VM (how this is handled technically slightly differs per Hypervisor). The Differencing Disk is meant to store all changes made to the VM (it functions as a write cache) while the Identify Disk is meant to give the VM its own identity used within Active Directory. During this phase MCS will also take care of machine account creation in Active Directory. And finally the actual VMs, based on the information provided during the wizard will be created / provisioned on your underlying Host Connection.

1. Create / configure master VM:
   a. Install Operating System.
   b. Install VM tools.
   c. Join Domain.
   d. Install VDA.
   e. Install applications.
   f. Anti virus scan.
   g. Other...
2. Create Machine Catalog in Studio:
   a. Select Operating System type (server, desktop, remote PC).
   b. Select machine management (PVS, MCS, other service or technology.
   c. Desktop experience (random or static assigned desktops).
   d. Select master VM.
   e. VM config (compute: vCPU, RAM, Disk space), # of machines.
   f. AD location for machine accounts plus the account-naming scheme.
   g. Summary, hit finish.

3. Automated (or manual) snapshot creation.
4. Temporary VM is created. This will boot so that certain tasks like DHCP, KMS etc. can be taken care of first.
5. Full copy of snapshot.
6. Snapshot is copied to accompanying data stores.
7. AD identities are generated.
8. Desktops are added to Active Directory.
9. VMs are provisioned and disks get attached.
10. Depending on the amount of machines and the type of storage platform used this can take up to serveral hours. Done!

Why this matters

Each time you create a new master VM, or update an existing one, for that matter, this process repeats itself, meaning that if you have multiple master VMs, let's say two for VDI (Windows 7 and 8) and two for RDSH (Windows Server 2008 R2 and 2012 R2), the system will create a snapshot of every master VM, four in this example, which will then need to be copied over to all of the datastores as part of your VDI / RDSH deployment.

As mentioned, when updating an existing master image, the same process is repeated. The system will basically treat the updated master VM as a new master VM and, as such, a snapshot will again be created and copied over to the accompanying datastores accordingly. For obvious reasons, a few questions go with this.

- How many master virtual machines will you be managing – meaning the different types of virtual machines, Windows 7, 8 and so on?
- How many datastores will you be using?

- How many times, per week, month, year will your master VM(s) need to be updated? However, this will always be a hard question to answer.
- Does your storage platform support thin provisioning? If not, then every provisioned VM will be as big as the master VM it is based on.

By answering these types of questions you will have at least an indication of the amount of storage needed and the administrative overhead that comes with maintaining your virtual infrastructure based on MCS.

Host Connection

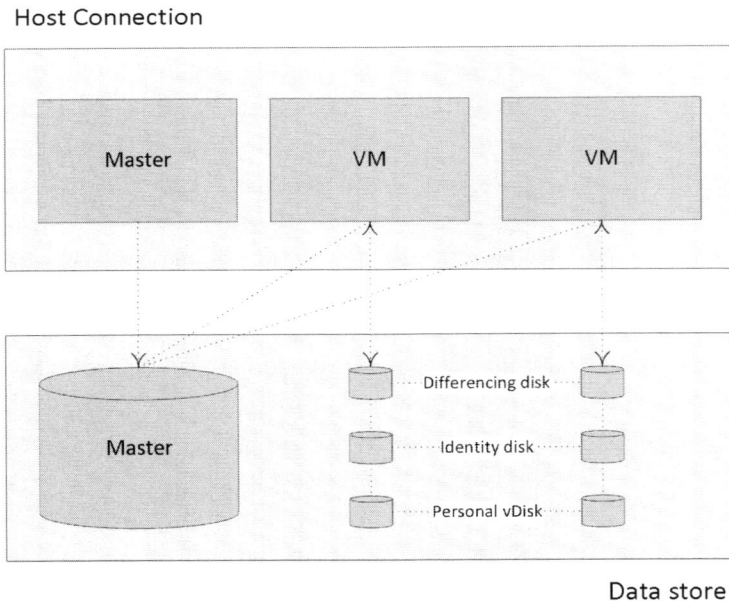

Data store

Figure 28: MCS Differencing Disks

Your workloads

As we all know, virtualising 100% of your application workload is not going to happen anytime soon. And even when a large part is virtualised, using App-V, for example, applications might be pre-cached, meaning you will still need to (potentially) 'break open' the base image they reside on if the application itself needs to be updated, patched etc. in some way. Of course the same applies when applications and/or plug-ins are installed in the base image.

Now imagine managing 4 (or more) different base images (master VMs), all with a relatively intensive maintenance cycle perhaps caused by a bunch of 'home-made' applications that need to be updated on a weekly basis.

Every week these images, or master VMs, need to be updated at least once, meaning a new snapshot per master image that will need to be copied down to all the participating datastores for each image type, taking up CPU resources, causing a peak in IO and network resource usage. This alone can be a time-consuming process depending on the number and size of your images and the number of datastores involved.

FMA fact: Today technologies like application layering and containerisation can help us overcome most of these application-related issues; however, the general adoption of these kinds of technologies and products will still take some time.

254

Rollbacks

Rollbacks are treated the same way (there is a rollback option available in Studio specific to MCS) in that they are seen as yet another image that is different from the one your VMs currently rely on. This means that the whole process as described previously will repeat itself.

Some more considerations

When a master VM / image is updated. copied over to all datastores etc. and assigned to the appropriate VMs, these VMs will first need to be rebooted to be able to make use of the new or updated master VM. While this may sound as a relatively simple process there are some things you need to take into consideration.

- When rebooting a couple of hundred virtual machines (or more) this can have a potential negative impact on your underlying storage platform. Also referred to as a boot storm. This is not something you want to risk during work hours.

- Some companies have very strict policies when it comes to idle and disconnect sessions. There might still be some user sessions in a disconnect state at the time you want to reboot certain VMs, but when the company policy states that users may not be logged off (forced) unless they do so themselves or automatically when the configured disconnect policy kicks in, you will have to reschedule or reconsider your planned approach. Not that uncommon, trust me.

- All this might also interfere with other processes that might be active during the night.

- And while not on topic, all this applies to Provisioning Services as well.

Storage implications

I already mentioned a couple of things to consider with regard to your underlying storage platform when using MCS, but I am pretty sure I can come up with few more, so let's have another look.

- MCS is, or at least can be, storage-intensive with regard to the (read) IOPS needed. On average it will need around 1.6 times more IOPS when compared to PVS: again, mainly read traffic from the master VM as mentioned earlier. However... and this is often where the confusion starts, the 1.6 number is based on the overall average, meaning that it also takes into account boot and logon storms (that's also why they are mainly read IOPS). If we primarily focus on the so-called steady state IOPS, then it's closer to 1.2: a big difference, right?

- While the above shouldn't be too big an issue with all modern storage technologies available today, it's still something you need to consider.

- The ability to cache reads is a very welcome storage feature! Don't be surprised if you end up hitting a read cache ratio of 75% of higher, boosting overall performance.

- Consider having a look at IntelliCache, a technology built into XenServer, when deploying non-persistent VMs on NFS-based storage.

- Clustered Shared Volumes Cache (Hyper-V) is also (very) helpful. In fact, it would probably outperform Provisioning Services all together, with the exception of cache in RAM that is.

- When looking up IOPS recommendations based on Citrix best practices, be aware that these are (almost) exclusively based on steady state operations.

- A medium workload (based on the medium login VSI workload) running on a Windows 7 or 8 virtual machine (provisioned with MCS) will need around 12 IOPS during its steady state with a read/write ratio of 20:80. During boot, these numbers will be the other way around: 80:20.

- Running the same workload on a Server 2012 R2 virtual machine will lead to 9 IOPS during its steady state with a read/write ratio of 20:80. Note that this is on a per user basis. And again, during boot this will probably be closer to 80:20 read/write.

- Collect as many (IOPS / workload-specific) data as possible and consult with one or multiple storage administrators. See what they think.

- Remember that there is more to IOPS than just the read/write ratios. Also consider the different types of IOPS like random and sequential, the configured storage block sizes used, and the actual throughput available.

- Often multiple datastores are created to spread the overall IOPS load on the underlying storage platform. Think this through. Remember that each time a new master VM is created or one is updated, it will need to be copied over to all datastores as part of your VM deployment.

- Load testing can provide us with some useful and helpful numbers with regard to performance and scale. However, don't lose track of any potential resource-intensive applications that might not be included during some of the standard baseline tests. You don't want to run into any surprises when going live, do you? Include them.

- Whenever possible, try to scale for peaks, meaning boot, logon and logoff storms.

- If needed, schedule and pre-boot multiple VDI VMs, as well as any virtual XenApp servers, before the majority of your users start their day.

- Try to avoid overcommitting your host's compute resources as much as possible. And while overcommitting your physical CPUs / cores is fine, never overcommit memory: there is no need.

- Failing over VMs while using MCS isn't a problem, but if you would like to move the accompanying virtual machine disks / files as well, using Storage vMotion, Live Storage Migration and/or Storage XenMotion, you are out of luck. This is not supported.

- The renaming of network connections and Data Stores is also not possible.

- There is a strong dependency between the VM and the Disk ID / datastore it resides on (information stored in the Central Site database): once broken or interrupted, your VM will not be able to boot properly.

- Consider implementing storage technologies and hyper-converged solutions like Nutanix, Atlantis, VSAN, VPLEX (there are plenty more out there), enabling you to move around your MCS-based VMs, including their disks, either automated or manually, while maintaining the VM Disk ID dependency using and combining features like Shadow Clones, Data Locality, Data synchronisations and so on. SDS is key.

- The ability to thin provisioning the earlier discussed

differencing disks would be preferred. This will initially save you a lot of disk space, and if your environment isn't that big (< 1000), re-provisioning your VMs once or twice a month might be optional as well. You might be able to get up to a few hundred machines per hour. This is something that your storage platform will need to support.

- The same applies to compression and de-duplication.
- I/O offload for writes and a caching mechanism of some sort for reads will greatly enhance the overall user experience.
- Monitor the growth of your differencing disks and size your storage platform accordingly. Do not forget to include the duplicate images of your master VM copied over to each datastore when it comes to free GBs needed. When using Hyper-V a differencing disk cannot be marked as exposable. As a result, when the VM is rebooted, the disk will be detached, a new disk will be attached and the old one will be deleted.
- Also, when an image is updated, at least temporarily, there will be two full images / master VMs residing in each datastore: do not forget to include these into your GB calculations as well.
- As soon as all VMs within the datastore are using the new or updated image, the 'old' one will be deleted automatically. By default, this will happen after a time period of six hours, but this is configurable through PowerShell.
- Think about a reboot schedule for your XenApp servers. Each reboot will 'refresh' the differencing disk, making them start from zero. Reboot your VDI VMs on a daily basis or make them automatically reboot once a user

logs off.

- Consider your underlying and supported Hypervisor when using MCS. You can use NFS for XenServer and ESXi or Clustered Shared Volumes for Hyper-V. However, at this time no thin provisioning on XenServer with block-based storage. Do note that some interesting new developments surrounding block-based storage in the latest XenServer Tech Preview, a.k.a. Dundee are on their way.

- MCS combined with Hyper-V local storage is also optional. Simply configure a cluster without shared storage. A copy of your master image will be placed on one of your local drives, C:\, D:\ etc.

- Citrix used to recommend using NFS exclusively to go with MCS, but that was more geared towards the inability of XenServer to thin provision disks based on block-based storage than anything else. While NFS will be more straightforward to configure and maintain, block-based storage with MCS is also supported and used in many production environments as well.

Updating

When you update the master VM/image of a persistent virtual machine, or multiple, only newly provisioned persistent VMs will be able to use the updated master image. All of the existing persistent virtual machines will continue to rely on the 'old' master VM. When dealing with non-persistent VMs this works different. Once the new or updated image is assigned and the VMs reboot, the old image will be discarded (and eventually deleted once it is no longer in use) and the new one will be used from then on.

Key takeaways

- MCS is considered to be easy. It is managed and configured directly from Studio and you do not need any additional infrastructural components as you do with PVS.
- MCS is based on differencing disks technology.
- Your base or golden image will be copied over to all datastores, which are part of the virtual machine deployment. Take this into account when thinking about your storage needs.
- When application virtualisation is not an option, often forcing you to install applications into your base image, think about using application layering as an alternative.
- When using MCS, rollbacks are created the same way as a new or updated base image: they will again need to be copied over to all datastores involved. Note that in some cases the previous image might still be in use by some machines. If so, than no full copy will be needed.
- Give your Idle and Disconnect session policies some thought. This will make it easier to reboot your machines during night-time, depending on company policy, of course.
- Go over the earlier mentioned list of storage implications a couple of times: there is a lot to consider.

FMA Core services deep dive & the ICA / HDX protocol

The FMA core services

The FlexCast Management Architecture is the true foundation of Citrix's applications and desktop (virtualisation) platforms and probably will be for many years to come. It has always been the next generation architecture for VDI, at least from Citrix's point of view, and it has evolved over the years to now also include and support XenApp / RDSH workloads: in fact we are up to version 7.8 of XenDesktop and XenApp already. It is robust, scalable and flexible at the same time and of course it (almost) goes without saying that its main goal is to securely manage and deliver or broker applications and desktops to our users all over the world from every device thinkable.

The FMA takes care of itself. Think about this. Most people have no idea how many services and components are involved when installing and configuring XenDesktop for example, and still they are capable of running huge environments without to much trouble. Often consisting of thousands of desktops and users.

The FlexCast Management Architecture is built up around eleven core services. The FMA, like other platforms and technologies, is constantly being improved and enhanced and as such is undergoing constant change. As a result, if we look back over the past five to six years or so we can see that the FMA evolved from six services back in 2010 up to eleven services today, an impressive ride to say the least. However, the problem that we often see with rapid evolving platforms, is that over time as features and functionalities are being added they become much harder to manage and maintain.

That is why the FMA has been designed using a set of clearly defined standards where new functionality can be introduced by adding new services, or build on top of existing ones if needed.

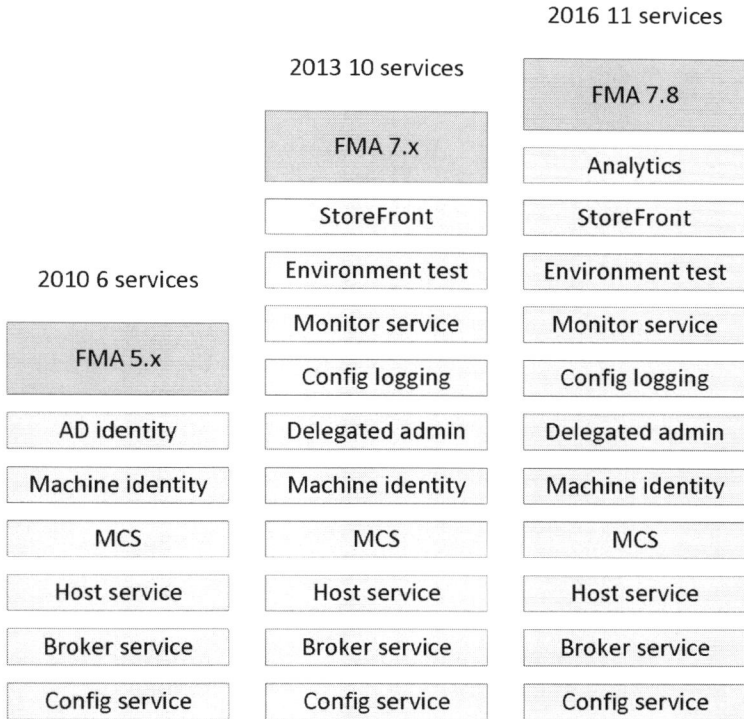

	2010 6 services	2013 10 services	2016 11 services
			FMA 7.8
		FMA 7.x	Analytics
		StoreFront	StoreFront
		Environment test	Environment test
		Monitor service	Monitor service
	FMA 5.x	Config logging	Config logging
	AD identity	Delegated admin	Delegated admin
	Machine identity	Machine identity	Machine identity
	MCS	MCS	MCS
	Host service	Host service	Host service
	Broker service	Broker service	Broker service
	Config service	Config service	Config service

Figure 29: FMA services evolution

The Delivery Controller is often referred to as the heart of the FMA: this is mainly because the mentioned services, all eleven of them, live or reside on your Delivery Controllers, making it an extremely important component. Next to these eleven services, which we will have a closer look at in just a minute, both VDAs (desktop and server) also host several services, which communicate with your Delivery Controllers as well.

These will be discussed in more detail as we progress throughout this chapter.

Internal communication

Although FMA services run completely isolated from eachother, internal communications between the different services takes place using WCF (Windows Communication Foundation) end points (also referred to as service interfaces) over port 80 (default). Here I would like to note that port 80 can be changed into any port number you might prefer and that encryption is supported as well.

The endpoint address is represented by the EndpointAddress class, which contains a Uniform Resource Identifier (URI) that represents the address of the service, an Identity, which represents the security identity of the service, and a collection of optional Headers.

Each service has the ability to interact with all other services in order to carry out important tasks and actions throughout the FMA. As a best practice you will deploy two or more Delivery Controllers, avoiding a single point of failure and providing scalability where and when needed.

As we will shortly see, there are four services that have a special place within the FMA and take on a more prominent role than the others (a.k.a. core services). These are the Broker, Configuration, Delegated Administration and the Configuration Logging service.

FMA fact: While all services closely interact with and depend on each other, at the same time they are also completely separated from each other. Each service is configured to communicate to the Central Site database using its own individual DB connection string. If one service fails, unless they depend directly on each other, it will not affect any or most of the other services.

One of the biggest differences between the IMA and FMA is that with the FMA the Delivery Controller is only responsible for managing and brokering connections to managed as well as unmanaged VDAs installed on your server and desktop machines. It doesn't host any sessions of its own.

Also, all the ICA / HDX bits, bytes and related services (actually controlling the HDX functionality throughout a session) reside on the VDA itself, again relieving the Delivery Controller from any additional tasks. As a result of this approach, it is also easier to maintain the code and different operating systems can be deployed within the same site.

FMA fact: Keep in mind that if you change something for one specific service, like the DB connection string for example, you will have to do this for all of the other FMA services as well.

The FMA's eleven

Let's go over each and every service one at the time. Where applicable I'll elaborate a bit more on the inner workings, any special considerations and/or relations to other services like the XML / STA service.

FMA fact: All FMA services run under the NT AUTHORITY\Network service account. Also, when authenticating to the Central Site database (this is where the Configuration Service plays an important role as well) all services use the local computer account of the machine that they are currently running on.

On the next page you will find an overview of all eleven main FMA services, as they reside on your Delivery Controllers.

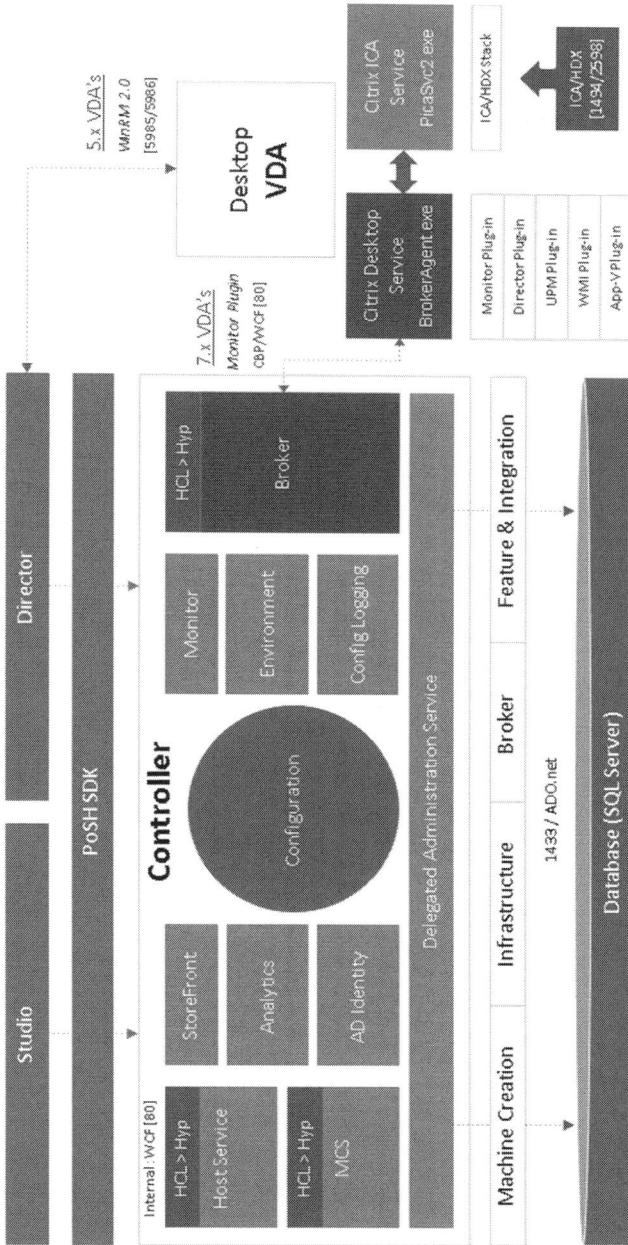

Figure 30: FMA main services overview

1. Broker service

The broker (XML) service (a.k.a. the Desktop service) is probably the best-known one. From a Delivery Controller point of view, it brokers new and manages existing sessions, handles resource enumeration, the creation and verification of STA tickets and user validation, disconnected sessions, and so on and so forth. From a VDA point of view it takes care of all communication to and from the Delivery Controller. It does this by communicating with the VDA Citrix Desktop Service, a.k.a. BrokerAgent.exe, which is part of the desktop as well as server VDA.

Note that the STA (service) is also part of the Broker service, and has been as of Presentation Server 4.0. Before that it was written as an ISAPI extension for Microsoft Internet Information Services, or IIS. As of XenDesktop 4.x the XML service (ctxxmlss.exe) has been rewritten in .NET and became part of the Broker service as well. So the Broker service is actually built up of three separate services, all handling different tasks: it brokers connections, it enumerates resources, and it acts as the Secure Ticket Authority, generating and validating STA tickets; however, this only applies to user connections made externally through a NetScaler.

Main responsibilities

As mentioned, the broker service has some huge responsibilities within the FMA. As such, my FMA partner in crime, Mister Mick Glover a.k.a. XDtipster on Twitter, often refers to the broker service being the workhorse of the FMA. Besides some of the tasks already highlighted, one of its most important tasks is the actual registration of all VDAs, including ongoing management from a Delivery Controller perspective. To give you a complete overview of the main tasks and responsibilities of the broker service, have a look below.

- As already mentioned, VDA registration, resource allocation, connection brokering, licensing enforcement.
- During the initial user logon process it will validate the end-user's identity, based on credentials received through StoreFront.
- It is involved in HDX policy management.
- It manages the overall power state of desktops and server machines when run virtually, starting and stopping VMs based on usage and on administrator configuration, including idle pool management.
- It temporarily stores user credentials to allow users to be logged into virtual desktops without having to re-enter credentials (single sign-on).
- It keeps track of virtual desktop state, based on information received from virtual desktops. As such, it will take appropriate action when needed.
- It will participate in the initial load-balancing process, deciding which desktop or server to connect to. This information will eventually end up in an ICA launch file.
- Administrators will use the broker service, although they may not actually know it to log off sessions, define Machine Catalogs and publish virtual desktops based on computer identity.
- It exposes Hypervisor state and alert information.
- It will also handle all power management features, including but not limited to: power policy rules, reboot schedules and cycles, pool/buffer size management, and remote PC wake on LAN.

The broker service Site services

The Broker service is somewhat special in that it also houses multiple Site services, let me explain. Site services provide Site-wide maintenance and housekeeping functionalities within and a XenDesktop Site. They take care of things like managing connections to your Host Connections, cheking up on session idle times, managing reboot schedules, cache maintenance (refresh) and more.

Before I go any further you need to krow that there are eighteen Site services in total, with eac1 having its own responsibility, or multiple in some cases. They are part the Broker service. More specifically, each individual Site service will only run on one of your Delivery Controllers (within a Broker service), creating a distributed model. As soon as a Delivery Controller misses a heartbeat with the Central Site database, all Site services running on that particular Delivery Controller will be transferred to one of the other active and still considered healthy Delivery Controllers. Again, they will be moved from one Broker service to another. A heartbeat message is exchanged between the Delivery Controller and the database every 20 seconds with a default timeout of 40 seconds.

FMA fact: While it is considered a best practice to keep all Delivery Controllers equally configured, Site services are the exception to the rule, so to speak.

At runtime, when a Delivery Controller becomes active the Site services will automatically be divided between all active Delivery Controllers within your Site. Do note that although you as an Administrator have the ability to assigr certain Site services to a particular Delivery Controller if you want or need to – this is not a recommended or supported approach. The election mechanism is controlled by the contents of the Central Site database, the FMA will take care of this for you. Remember?

The eighteen Site services are:

1. ControllerReaper.
2. ControllerNameCacheRefresh.
3. Licensing.
4. BrokerReaper.
5. RegistrationHardening.
6. WorkerNameCacheRefresh.
7. AccountNameCacheRefresh.
8. PowerPolicy.
9. GroupUsage.
10. AddressNameResolver.
11. RebootScheduleManager.
12. RebootCycleManager.
13. ScopeNamesRefresh.
14. FeatureChecks.
15. RemotePC.
16. IdleSessionManager.
17. LeaseReaper.
18. Hypervisor connection.

Broker Service   Broker Service

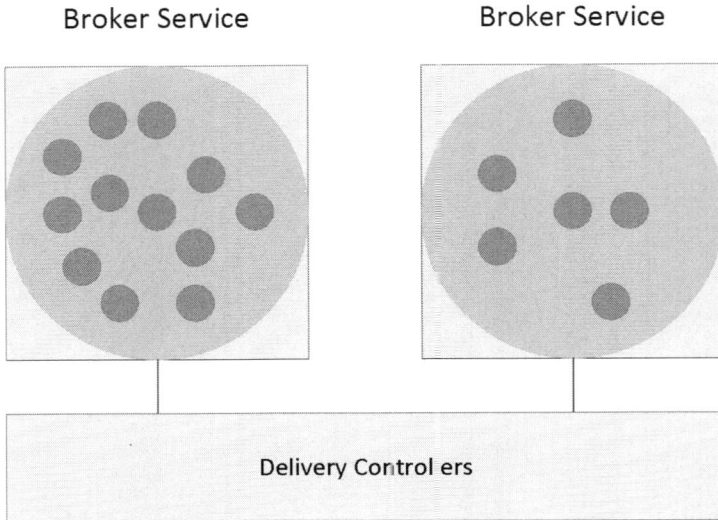

Delivery Controllers

Figure 31: Broker service - Site services

Hypervisor Connection Site service

This one is different from the other Site services. The Hypervisor Connection Site service is the only service which can exist on multiple Delivery Controllers within the same Site and can be controlled, or configured using the PowerShell SDK. As the name implies it manages your Host Connection configured through Studio. It allows you to configure which Delivery Controller manages and takes ownership of a specific Host Connection, or multiple when desired

Multiple controllers can host and manage multiple Host Connections, either assigned by you (through the Hypervisor Connection Site service) or they can be automatically load balanced over your Delivery Controllers, which will happen by default, again, the FMA is that smart. Technically you could also assign all of your Host Connections to be managed and owned by a single Delivery Controller, which might be better equipped for the task at hand, compute and resource-wise. However, you might want to check with Citrix if this is a supported setup.

2. Configuration service

All FMA services need to register with the configuration service on start-up so that it knows they are all good to go. This is one of the main reasons why the Configuration service has such a prominent role: it handles all inter-service communication within the FMA. Again, I would like to quote Mr Glover on this one: the configuration service is the glue holding the FMA together.

Located at the centre of the FlexCast Management Architecture, it holds and manages a list of all FMA services, allowing them to advertise their WCF addresses, or end points (service interfaces), including the functionality that they provide. Only after a service successfully registers with the configuration service, when adding more Controllers after a reboot or during Site creation, for example, will it become active and able to communicate with other FMA services.

Once all services have successfully registered themselves, the configuration service will share a listing of all active and registered services as being active Site members, including their main responsibilities, or capabilities and service (communication) interfaces.

As soon as an individual FMA service needs to communicate with one of the other FMA services it will first (need to) contact the Configuration service to get a copy of the services listing mentioned earlier.

After an FMA service successfully queries the Configuration service and the listing has been received, this information will be cached for five minutes. This is mainly to ensure that the system isn't being overwhelmed with service listing requests, preventing the Configuration Service from becoming a potential bottleneck. At this point the requesting service knows where to find the other services, what they are capable of and how to communicate with them.

As a side note, the Machine Creation Service and the Machine Identity Service both communicate through the Host service to find out about the configuration and connections of the underlying Host Connection, or Hypervisor, if any, including the storage and network configurations needed for virtual machine provisioning. This information will be cached for one minute as opposed to the five minutes mentioned earlier.

FMA fact: Each FMA service can query the configuration service to look up other services using the listing mentioned earlier. In short, service registration and communication are both reliant on the configuration service. It will also store configuration metadata for all services, relieving Active Directory.

Permissions

The Configuration service directory stores the Active Directory machine account identifier (SID) for each service that has succesfully registered with it. At the same time, this infromation will also be stored in the Central Site database where it will be accessible to all Delivery Controllers including the services that they host. Only when the machine SID of the accompanying

FMA service is listed, and known by the Configuration service will communication between FMA services be possible.

When a service with an unregistered machine account contacts the Configuration service for the services listing it will receive an access denied. The only exception to this is the 'Network service' account: it is always allowed. Viewing and validation the successful registration of FMA services can be done through the PowerShell SDK. Use the following syntax:

Get-ConfigRegisteredServiceInstance -InterfaceType sdk | select serviceaccount, interfacetype, servicetype | format-table

FMA fact: If you would like to refresh the cache of one of the FMA services (remember the five minutes), all you have to do is restart the accompanying Windows Service. The cache (services listing) is retreived during service startup.

3. Configuration Logging service

Monitors and logs all configuration changes made within a XenDesktop Site, including all Administrator activity. Depending on its configuration, no Site changes are possible when its database is unreachable, making it one of the four core services as mentioned earlier. The data itself can be stored within the central site database or a separate database can be created, which would be the recommended approach. As of XenDesktop version 7.7 a separate location / database can be selected during the initial installation configuration process.

4. Delegated Administration service

While at first sight it may not seem this way, the Delegated
Administration Service is also considered to be one of the
FMA's more critical services. All other FMA services will need
to communicate with the Delegated Administration service in
order to validate if they have all the proper permissions and/or
rights needed to make the necessary changes to the Central Site
database. Next to this, it manages the configuration and
administration of all delegated administrative permissions. As a
result, if this service becomes unresponsive or unavailable site-
wide configuration changes will not be possible.

5. AD Identity service

Handles all Active Directory computer accounts related to
XenApp / XenDesktop virtual and physical machines.

6. Machine Creation services

Handles the creation of new virtual machines. When this service
is unavailable no additional virtual machines can be created, at
least not using MCS. Also note that MCS is only capable of
creating virtual machines, not physical. If you want to be able to
create physical machines you will need to use Provisioning
Services.

FMA fact: If you do not configure a Host Connection
within Studio, when creating a new Device Catalog, the
option to use MCS as a provisioning mechanism will not
be available (greyed out).

See the 'Machine Creation Services' chapter for a more detailed
description of how MCS works and what to think about when
implementing.

7. Host service

Manages all connections between the physical hosts, the Delivery Controllers, and the underlying Hypervisor. This can be either vSphere, XenServer or Hyper-V. This is where your virtual server and/or desktop VMs live. Physical machines are still optional as well, but again you'll use PVS instead of MCS. As we have seen earlier, the Host service is also responsible for discovering and managing the connections and configurations of the Hypervisor, network and storage that are required, and used by the machine provisioning operations.

7.1 Hypervisor Communications Library

The HCL is used by a number of FMA services, the Broker, Host and MCS to be a bit more precise to provide an abstract Application Programming Interface, or API for interacting with the underlying Hypervisor, or multiple. This will ensure a consistent and consequent representation of the configured Hypervisor (Host Connection) including network and storage resources. While multiple Hypervisors are supported this also adds to the complexity of the code, this is where the HCL comes in, it fucntions as an abstraction layer. As a result, when a new version of a hypervisor is released, Citrix can quickly add support without the need to replace the code in multiple places.

8. Environment Test service

Takes care of all Site-wide tests, initiated from Studio. You can runs tests on your Delivery Groups, Machine Catalogs or even on your entire Site configuration, and more.

9. Monitor service

Monitors the overall FMA architecture and produces alerts and warnings when it finds something potentially wrong. These will pop up in Studio or Director. Note, however, that, although these alerts will tell us that something is potentially wrong, they won't tell us what is wrong or where to look for answers. Therefore, FMA services are best checked using PowerShell code typed in directly from a PowerShell Command Prompt.

For example, try using the Get-BrokerServiceStatus and/or Get-ConfigServiceStatus cmdlets to view the status of the Broker and Configuration service. There is a 'Get-' command for each FMA service.

10. StoreFront service

This takes care of your StoreFront deployment, which can be added as well as managed directly from Studio. Note that your StoreFront can and probably will appear twice within Studio. Once under the console root as an integral part of Studio, which is needed to be able to configure the Citrix Receiver on your published hosted shared desktops directly from a Delivery Group. And a second time (as a separate node) enabling you to manage your StoreFront deployment as if you were using the separate, MMC based StoreFront management console.

11. Analytics service

The analytics service does as the name implies: it collects analytical data. It is leveraged by the Citrix Customer Experience Improvement Program (CEIP), which can be enabled voluntarily and will be disabled by default, as well as the Citrix Call Home functionality. All data will be shared anonymously, encrypted and, as always, will be used for the greater good.

Studio and Director

The FMA services can be easily configured and monitored using PowerShell. The same holds true for both Director and Studio as they also rely heavily on the PowerShell SDK for both managing and monitoring all that is going on within your Site. The FMA is powered by PowerShell. If you have a look at the Director main dashboard you will see that some of the more important FMA services are being monitored. This is also PowerShell doing its magic in the background. In fact, every button you click within Studio and/or Director is a pre-configured PowerShell scripts being executed in the background (while Citrix Studio is written in C# it also leverages PowerShell). Here I would also like to quote Mr. Martin Zugec, FMA architect over at Citrix:

In the past, we were struggling to automate something that was available only from the GUI – the GUI provided you with more functionality than the CLI. In FMA, it's opposite. You have more functionality available from the CLI than you have from GUI. The purpose of Citrix Studio is to make the most common tasks easily accessible, while the SDK allows you to do a lot more.

The Desktop VDA

As mentioned in the 'The Virtual Delivery Agent' chapter, the VDA is a relatively small piece of software that gets installed on all virtual and physical machines running a Windows server and/or desktop operating system within a XenDesktop Site (note that there is also a Linux based VDA). It serves multiple purposes, as we will find out shortly, but only after a VDA is able to successfully register itself with one of your Delivery Controllers.

VDA registration

As soon as a Virtual Delivery Agent starts up, meaning the desktop or server Operating System boots, it will try and register

itself with one of the Delivery Controllers known within the
Site. For this to happen there needs to be a mechanism in place
that tells the VDAs which Delivery Controllers are part of the
same Site and how they can contact or reach them. For this,
Citrix introduced the 'auto-update' feature, which will be
enabled by default. It will keep all VDAs updated when Delivery
Controllers are added or removed (go offline) from the Site.
Each VDA maintains a persistent storage location to store this
information. Also see the section named 'Desktop VDA ICA
stack services' over at page 286 for some more detailed
information regarding the VDA registration process.

When the auto-update feature is disabled, or does not supply the
correct information, the VDA will check the following locations
(in this order):

- Through configured policies.
- The ListOfDDCs Registry Key.
- OU-based discovery (legacy).
- The Personality.ini file created by MCS.

If a VDA is unable to register itself with a Delivery Controller
or communication between the VDA and the Delivery
Controller fails for any reason, you will not be able to connect
to it.

Here I would also like to note that VDA registration is the Nr.
one issue reported over at Citrix support, and as such deserves
some extra attention. Make sure to also have a look at the
'Troubleshooting the FMA' chapter for some more details
around the potential troubleshooting steps involved when
dealing with VDA registration issues.

This is also where the Citrix Desktop service, as part of installed VDA plays an important role. The Desktop service communicates directly with the Broker service over at the Delivery Controller and takes care of the initial VDA registration process through the Connection Brokering Protocol (CBP). The CBP is a collection of WCF (Windows Communication Foundation) end points defined to exchange information and handle the registration process.

FMA fact: Restarting the Citrix Desktop service on the VDA triggers the registration process and can be used to force re-registration when needed.

Launching a VDI desktop

Let's have a closer look and see what happens when a VDI-based virtual machine is launched from a trusted, internal network. The XML service will again play an important role throughout the whole process.

- Let's assume that the VM is pre-subscribed and already present on the user's (StoreFront) home screen. Here it does not matter how we are connected: using a locally installed Receiver or using the Receiver for Web sites.
- After the user clicks the desktop icon the StoreFront server will contact the Broker (XML/STA) service to check if any registered VDAs are available. It (the Broker service) does this by communicating with underlying Hypervisor platform through the Host service on the Delivery Controller.
- If needed it will first start / boot a VM. It's not uncommon to pre-boot a few VMs, since, as you can probably imagine, this will positively influence the

overall user experience. Understanding the usage
patterns of your users allows you to boot enough
machines before they're needed.

- In between the VDA will register itself with the Delivery
  Controller handling the initial request. It will do so by
  leveraging the Connection Brokering Protocol (CBP)
  and communicating with the Broker service over at the
  Delivery Controller, as highlighted earlier.

- Next the Delivery Controller, or Broker (XML/STA)
  service, will contact one of the VDAs and send a
  StartListening request. By default, the VDA isn't
  listening for any new connections on port 494 or 2595
  until it gets notified that a user wants to connect.

- As soon as the VDA is listening, the Broker
  (XML/STA) service will send this information back to
  the StoreFront server in the form of an XML file.

- Based on this information, the StoreFront server will
  then generate a launch.ica file (it uses the default.ica file
  as a template) containing the IP address of the VDA and
  a whole bunch of other connection properties that are or
  might be needed. This is sent down to the user.

- The locally installed Receiver (or HTML5-based
  Receiver) will read and autolaunch the launch.ica file,
  initiating a direct connection from the user's end point
  to the VDA.

- The installed VDA will verify its license file with the
  Delivery Controller.

- The Delivery Controller checks with the Citrix License
  Server to verify that the end-user has a valid ticket. A big
  change when compared to the IMA where every Session
  Host would communicate with the license server.

- At this time any applicable session policies will be passed on to the VDA and the session is launched.

What happens inside the VDA

Let's take it one step further and see what happens inside the VDA during launch time. The process below assumes that Session Reliability is enabled and that a desktop OS VDA gets launched as we've seen in the previous section. Remember that as of XenDesktop 7 there is also a server OS-based VDA, which we will have a closer look at in the next section.

- The CGP service will receive the connection and sends this information on to the tcpip.sys, which will forward it to the ICA stack.
- The ICA stack will notify the ICA Service a.k.a. the PortICA service (picaSvc) that a connection has been made after which the picaSvc will accept the connection.
- Then the ICA Service will lock the workstation because the user needs to be authenticated to ensure that the user is allowed access to that particular machine.
- As soon as the user logs onto the workstation, the PortICA service will communicate with the display manager to change the display mode to remote ICA, this request will be forwarded to the ThinWire driver.
- In the meantime, the PortICA service will hand over the 'pre-logon' ticket data, which it received from the ICA stack, up to the Desktop service and from there back to the Delivery Controller in exchange for 'real' credentials.
- The Desktop service receives the user's credentials, which are sent back to the PortICA service.
- The PortICA service contacts the authentication service to log on the user.

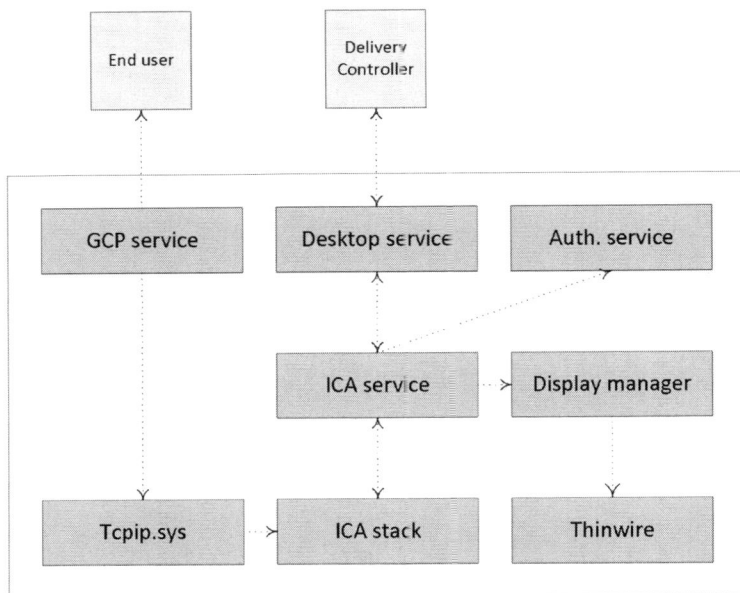

Figure 32: VDA: what happens during launch

Desktop VDA ICA stack services

If we have a closer at the Desktop VDA (check the main overview image) we can see that it consists of multiple FMA core services and plug-ins. The two main services are the Citrix Desktop Services a.k.a. BrokerAgent.exe and the Citrix ICA Service a.k.a. PicaSvc2.exe; together they control all HDX functionality for the duration of the session.

The Citrix Desktop service

The Citrix Desktop service communicates directly with the Broker service over at the Delivery Controller and, as highlighted earlier, takes care of the initial VDA registration process through the Connection Brokering Protocol (CBP), which is a collection of WCF (Windows Communication Foundation) end points defined to exchange information and handle the registration process. Once the VDA has been registered successfully the Citrix Desktop service will continue to communicate regularly with the Broker service on the Delivery Controller, also including a number of different feature plug-ins.

The Citrix ICA service

The Citrix ICA service implements the actual ICA protocol bits and bytes within the VDA, or the biggest part of it anyway. It will receive instructions through the Citrix Desktop service protocol coming from the Broker service over at the Delivery Controller. As soon as it is notified of a new connection request, and after AD authentication has taken place, and ticketing, licensing and HDX policy information has been successfully exchanged, the ICA stack will start listening for incoming connections allowing the launch request to complete.

Both Director and Studio also communicate with the underlying FMA services through WCF over port 80. Here it is also worth noting that when working with older VDAs (5.x and below) these will require WinRM listening to be enabled on port 5985 or 5986 to be able to communicate with Director and Studio. With 7.x VDAs this information is provided by the monitor plugin through the CBP protocol highlighted earlier.

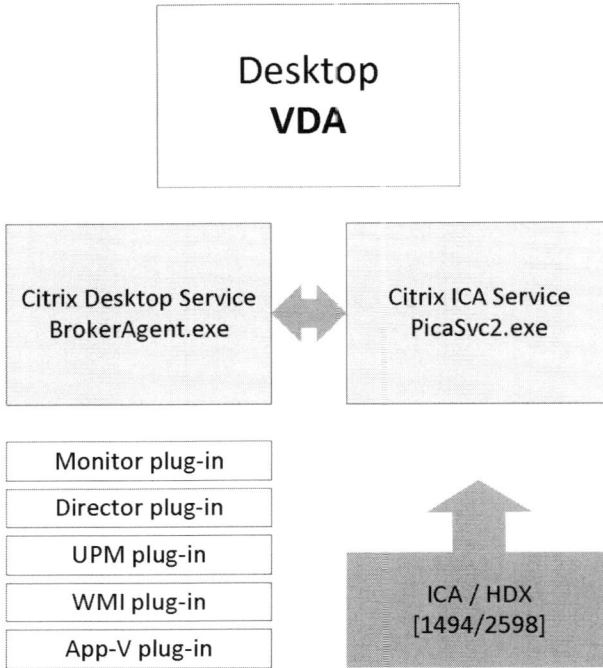

Figure 33: Desktop VDA services

The Server VDA

Although the new FMA-based Server VDA has been built from the ground up it still has a lot of similarities when compared to the 'old' ICA protocol stack deployed with XenApp 6.5 and earlier versions. However, unlike XenApp, the VDA (Virtual Delivery Agent) directly communicates with the Delivery Controller: it does this through the Broker Agent, basically the same way as we are used to with the Desktop VDA (PortICA) as previously discussed.

FMA fact: As opposed to the Desktop VDA, which has been around for a couple of years now, there is no PortICA service within a Server VDA, it simply does not exist.

Head to head

One of the biggest differences between the Server and the Desktop VDA is its ability to accept and manage multiple user sessions at once, hence the RDSH (XenApp) model, whereas the Desktop VDA, also referred to as PortICA, can only handle one ICA session at a time.

Both Server and Desktop VDAs communicate directly and exclusively with the Delivery Controller, and as such they do not need access to the Central Site (SQL) Database or license server.

Also, the underlying OS of an RDSH / XenApp server does not have to be the same as that of the Delivery Controller. And of course we can use multiple Operating Systems throughout our Site if needed or desired. As mentioned, for server machines Citrix now includes a multi-user ICA stack, which extends the Windows Remote Desktop Services with the HDX protocol.

This is the same ICA protocol stack developed for Citrix XenApp 6.5, just with a different management interface to make it compatible with XenDesktop 7.x controllers. Have a look at the table on the next page for some of the biggest differences between the two agents.

Table 12: Server VDA vs. desktop VDA

Server VDA	Desktop VDA
Build from ground up	Existing / updated
Multiple sessions/users	One user per session
Desktops and application.	Desktops and applications
CTX Stack Control service / ICA stack	PicaSvc2.exe a.k.a. PortICA
Desktop service a.k.a. BrokerAgent.exe	Desktop service a.k.a. BrokerAgent.exe
Server OS only	Desktop OS only
Non-brokered RDP and ICA connections allowed	Non-brokered RDP connections are allowed; non-brokered ICA connections are not allowed, except in HA mode
Server OS can be hosted using a server VDI configuration / set-up (niche)	

What happens during installation

During Server VDA installation one of the things it will do is register the Broker Agent Service (used for direct communication with the Delivery Controller), which is similar to the Desktop VDA process. Next it will install the multi-user ICA stack, as it does with earlier XenApp versions, which will then become part of Termsrv, creating the ICA stack listener waiting for new ICA connections.

The ICA stack itself has changed very little with the introduction of the FMA: one of its biggest changes is to be found in its communication interface, which is now better known as the earlier mentioned Broker Agent.

Last but not least, it will install and configure the Citrix Stack Control Service: this is its display name within the Windows services overview. As you will see in the graphical overview on the next page, the abovementioned Citrix Stack Control Service, a.k.a. SCService64, will act as an interface between the Broker Agent (a.k.a. BrokerAgent.exe and part of the new FMA) and the ICA stack running in Termsrv, mapping a direct COM interface between the two.

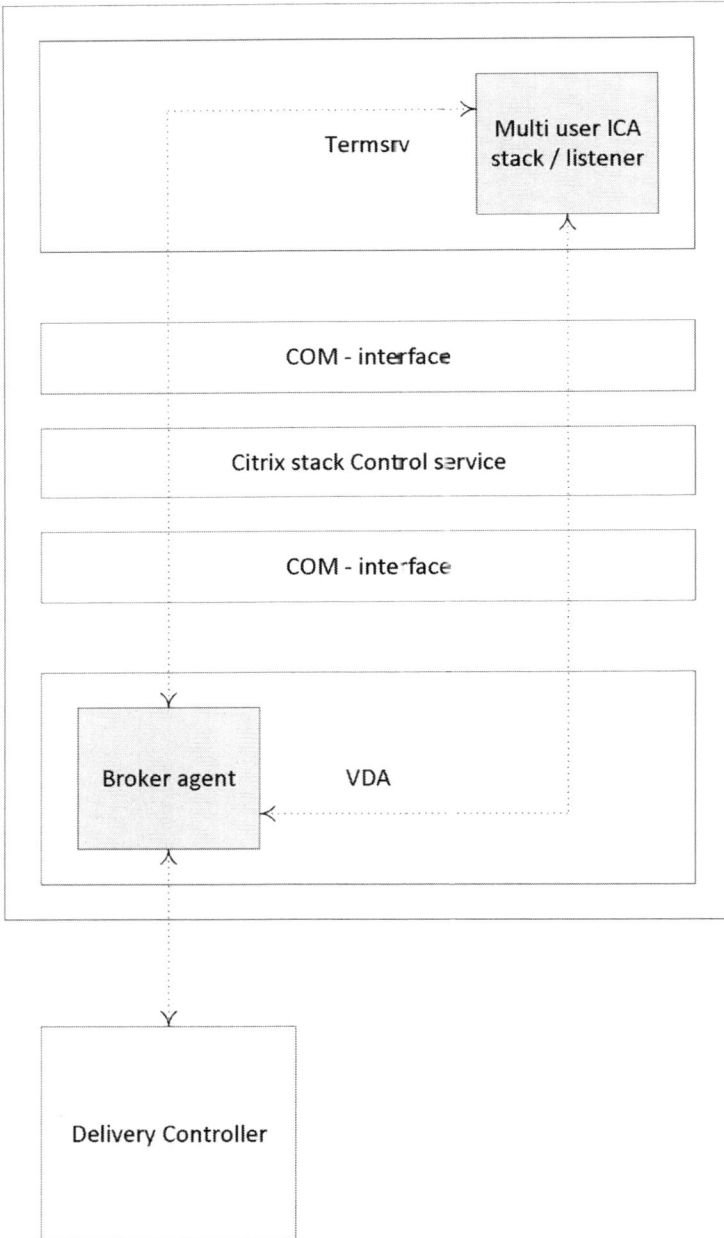

Figure 34: Server VDA internals

So to a certain extent you could say that the SCService64.exe takes on a few of the responsibilities similar to those of the PortICA service in a Desktop VDA. Obviously this is new behaviour and was first introduced with XenDesktop 7 (FMA 2.0). The same can be said for the PortICAsvc.exe as part of XenDesktop 5.x: as of XenDesktop 7 it has been slightly altered and renamed as picaSvc2.exe.

FMA fact: Each Terminal Server protocol (like Citrix's ICA) will have a protocol stack instance loaded (a listener stack awaiting a connection request). When installed, the Server VDA basically extends Microsoft's RDS protocol with the ICA/HDX feature set / protocol.

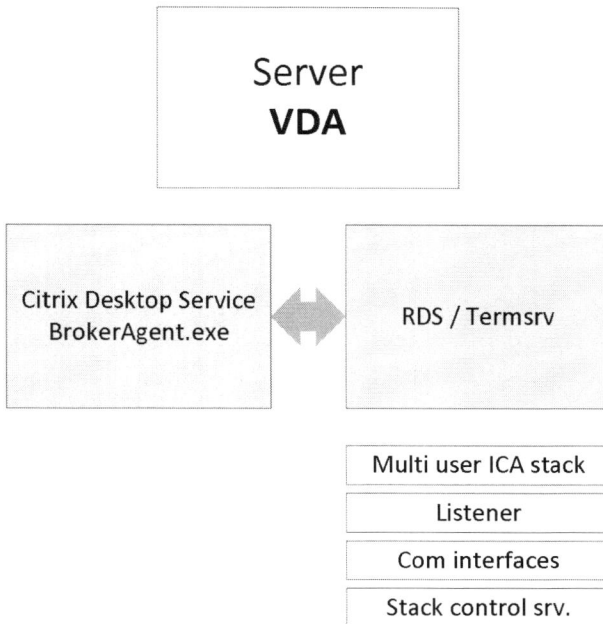

Figure 35: Server VDA services

Making the FMA services highly available

As we've established earlier, a XenDesktop Site consists of eleven main services and each individual service, also referred to as a service instance, will run on every active Delivery Controller within your Site.

As a way to make these FMA services highly available, each service will need to register itself with a so-called peer service group, which contains all registered service instances of the same type. For example, if you have four Delivery Controllers you will also have four Broker services, of which only one will be active at a time.

All four Broker services will register themselves with the above mentioned service group (the Broker service, service group), and they will do so at startup. After registration is succesfull this information is written to, and storred in the Central Site Database so that all active Delivery Controllers including their services will have access to this information whenever needed. This way, if the active Broker service fails for some reason, one of the other Broker services can and will take over. This basically means that there will be a service group for every main FMA service, all eleven of them, the same principle applies.

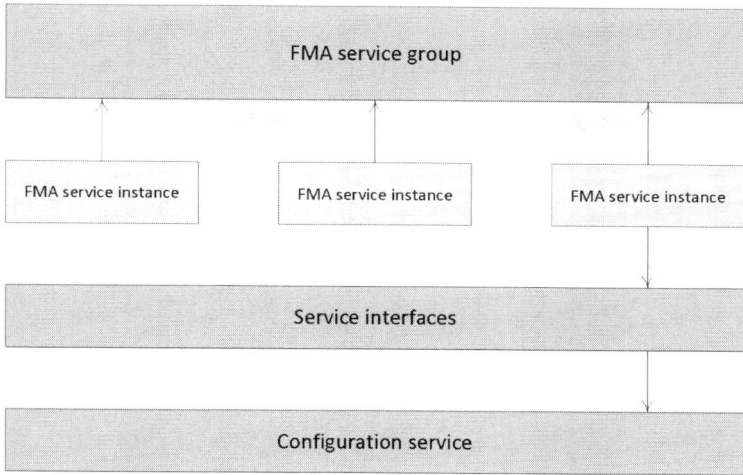

Figure 36: FMA service group

FMA fact: Each service group has a unique identifier, which can be queried using the PowerShell SDK if and when needed.

Conclusion

As you can see there is a lot going on under the covers when it comes to the FlexCast Management Architecture and its services. Hopefully this chapter has answered some of the questions that you might have. For this chapter a special thank-you goes out to my FMA partner in crime, Mick Glover, and Martin Zugec as they were able to answer just about every question I had.

Key takeaways

- FMA stands for FlexCast Management Architecture and, as of XenDesktop version 7, includes a Desktop as well as a Server VDA.
- It is the next generation architecture for XenDesktop and XenApp VDI and/or RDSH-based deployments.
- Over the years it has evolved from six up to eleven main services in total.
- Internal communication takes place over port 80 using Windows Communication Foundation end points.
- Each service runs complete separated from the other services, as a result each service also has its own separate database connection string: if one service fails it will not directly affect any of the other services.
- There is a distinct difference in architecture when compared to the IMA. All of the HDX / ICA bits and bytes are installed as part of the VDA on the Session Host and VDI based VMs while the Delivery Controllers primarily concerns itself with brokering, maintaining and optimizing existing sessions.
- All services run under the NT AUTHORITY \ Network account and use the local computer account for database authentication purposes. One of the benefits this brings is that password are automatically changed every 30 days. This is a big deal, as service accounts are usually very dangerous.
- The Broker service includes the XML as well as the STA service.
- There are 18 active (sub) site services in total, all running within the Broker services, taking care of various Site housekeeping tasks.

- There needs to be a way that VDAs can track and contact the various Delivery Controllers within a Site to be able to register themselves. Citrix uses the auto-update feature for this.

- As we have seen, the PortICA, or picaSvc2.exe, service is an important one during the VDA launch and user login process.

- The PortICA a.k.a. PicaSvc2.exe and the Citrix Desktop Service a.k.a. BrokerAgent.exe services are the two main FMA services within the Desktop VDA.

- The Connection Brokering Protocol (CPB) plays an important role in the VDA registration process. It is basically a collection of WCF end points.

- The Server VDA does not have the PortICA service; however, it does have a Broker service.

- It basically uses the same ICA stack as with XenApp 6.5, but with a different management interface to make it compatible with the 7.x Delivery Controllers.

- Service groups make FMA services highly available.

The ICA / HDX protocol

Citrix is an American software company founded back in 1989 by Edward Lacobucci, a former IBM developer. Citrix's first office was located in Richardson, Texas, and would later that year be relocated to Coral Springs, Florida, housing 18 FTE already. While they actually started out as Citrus Systems, shortly after an existing company claimed the trademark rights to that name they changed it to Citrix, as we know it still. In its early days the company primarily focused on developing remote access products for Microsoft Windows Operating systems, OS/2 at the time. As a result, and after two years of development, Citrix released their first product, named Citrix Multiuser, which was actually an extension to the OS/2 platform. This is where the ICA protocol, or the Independent Computing Architecture was born.

> **FMA fact**: The ICA protocol originated with Citrix Multiuser, around 1990 / 1991, meaning that the ICA protocol is actually over 25 years of age already.

They acquired / licensed the OS/2 source code from Microsoft (and basically became BFFs from then on) and built the ICA protocol from the ground up, the main ingredient for Citrix Multiuser version 1.0 at that time. The software allowed multiple users to work from separate computers remotely accessing software from a server: sounds familiar, right? Today they provide server, application and desktop virtualisation, networking, Software as a Service (SaaS), and cloud computing technologies. It has been quite a journey.

The agreement

Around the same time that Citrix released their Multiuser product, Microsoft announced to move away from the OS/2 platform over to Windows. This basically left Multiuser version 1.0 useless unless some significant changes were to be made to its base code, making it compatible with both Windows and DOS. While Citrix was on the verge of closing, multiple investors (including Microsoft) kept them on track, leading up to their second big release, Citrix Multiuser version 2.0, also referred to as Multi-Win back in 1992: fully compatible with Microsoft DOS and it allowed up to 5 users simultaneously.

In the meantime they signed a license agreement with Microsoft (which has been renewed multiple times) allowing them to use the Microsoft NT (3.5) source code for building an even more robust remote access protocol, improving the ICA, which by then was already patented by Citrix. Citrix basically modified Windows NT, turning it into a multi-user platform. And while there were some struggles between the two, since Microsoft basically funded Citrix to develop the ICA protocol and now they wanted their piece of the pie, eventually they became friends again and Microsoft 'licensed' Citrix's ICA protocol for use with Windows NT 4.0, 5.0 and onwards. However, at this time Microsoft was still empty-handed from a remoting protocol point of view.

With this renewed agreement, for which they paid good money, by the way, Microsoft regained the opportunity to make use of Citrix's ICA technology and to come up with a potentially competing protocol themselves; this is where the RDP protocol found its origin, based and built on the technology and ideas of Citrix.

Anyway, shortly after that, in 1993, they launched a new product named WinView, which was able to run both DOS and Windows applications and the company grew to over 65 employees in total during 1994. In the meantime they also launched their first Citrix-authorised re-seller programme, signed up Tech Data as their first official national distributor and achieved a net revenue of 10 mMillion $, impressive to say the least.

This all led up to the 1995 launch of Citrix WinFrame, a true multi-user Operating System based on Microsoft's NT technology: at that time it allowed up to 15 users simultaneously, and I guess the rest is history.

In 1997 they opened a new headquarters in Fort Lauderdale, Florida, and after serving as the Vice-President of Marketing, Mark Templeton became the new Citrix CEO, a role which he had up until 2015, and with great success, I might add. Many love Mark; unfortunately I never had the pleasure to meet him personally. When Citrix celebrated their 20th anniversary they put together a PDF document highlighting all of their milestones during those 20 years. You will find it here:

https://www.citrix.com/content/dam/citrix/en_us/documents/go/citrix_timeline.pdf

The Independent Computing Architecture

Now that you know some of its history, let's have a closer look at some of its subcomponents, how they all fit together and what happens on the inside. Let me start with a short statement on what the ICA protocol actually does from a (very) high-level perspective.

In its most simple form, the ICA protocol transports keystrokes, mouse clicks and screen updates (using standard protocols like TCP/IP, IPX, NetBEUI, SPX) from the server to the client in a highly controlled and secure manner.

It is optimised for Wide Area Networks with high latency and offers various levels of Quality of Service. These types of protocols, since there are more besides ICA, are often referred to as remoting protocols.

FMA fact: By default, the ICA protocol uses TCP port 1494. If Session Reliability is enabled a.k.a. the Common Gateway Protocol, or CGP then ICA traffic will be encapsulated through TCP port 2598. Note that any network traces that you might run will also show 2598 instead of 1494.

When Citrix released WinFrame back in 1995 it also introduced ICA version 3.0, which included ThinWire 1.0. Back then, ICA functionality was still limited to ThinWire (screen updates), printing, client drive mapping and audio. Before that there was the ICA version 1.0 in 1992 and the ICA version 2.0, which was also released in 1992 as part of the Citrix Multiuser launch discussed earlier.

Virtual Channels

I already touched on the ICA protocol and its 32 virtual channels in the chapter 'The Citrix Receiver' as part of the nine main FMA components. This is where the client-server set-up highlighted earlier becomes even more apparent. Let's do a quick résumé since the virtual channels are an essential part of the ICA protocol stack.

A big part of the communication between the client and server takes place over and through what Citrix refers to as virtual channels. This is where most ICA / HDX features live. Each virtual channel consists of a client-side virtual driver (Receiver) that communicates with a server-side application (the VDA). I say 'most', because Receiver also offers and supports a whole bunch of additional features and functionalities that do not involve or need a virtual channel.

Virtual channels (there can be 32 channels in total) are mainly used for some of the bigger well-known features where a bigger than average and direct communication path between the client and server is needed, like client drive mapping, smart cards, clipboard, printing, audio, video and so on.

FMA fact: As a (security) best practice Citrix recommends disabling any virtual channels that are not in use.

And of course from time to time, new virtual channels are released with new versions of XenDesktop and Receiver to provide additional functionality. Take Framehawk and ThinWire Plus, for example. Those were released as part of Feature Pack 2 and 3, respectively, for XenDesktop 7.6, including a new Receiver on the client side. Each virtual channel represents a specific feature or functionality on its own.

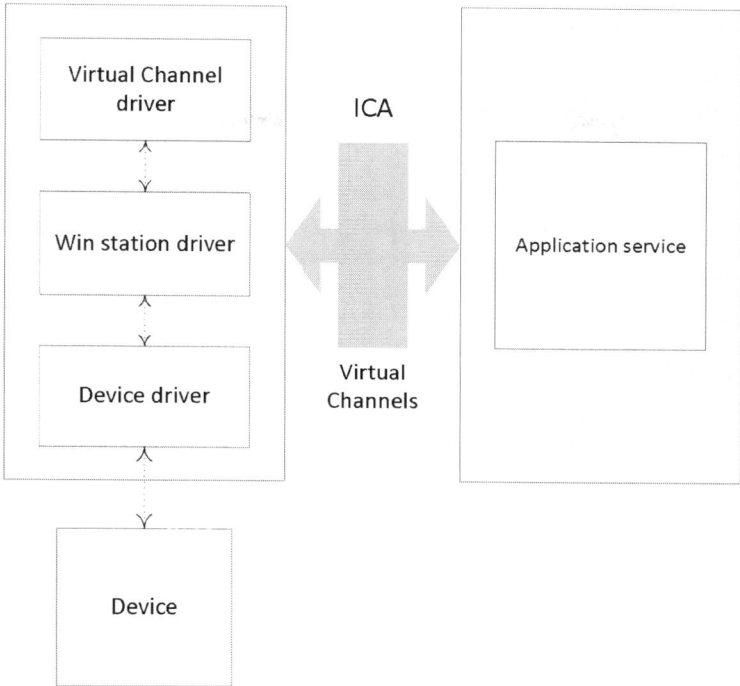

Figure 37: Virtual Channels - Client / Server overview

What happens in a nutshell

- When a new session is established, at client load time, first the client (Receiver) connects to the XenDesktop / XenApp Server (VDA).

- The client passes information about the virtual channels it supports to the server. This is where the version of the Receiver combined with VDA installed matters.

- The server-side application starts, obtains a handle to the virtual channel, and optionally queries the client for any additional information about the channel.

- As soon as additional data has been sent and received, the server virtual channel application is completed and it closes the virtual channel to free up any resources that may have been allocated.

The above is also referred to as the client server handshake.

The earlier mentioned client-side virtual drivers can be found in the following Registry Key:

HKEY_LOCAL_MACHINE\SOFTWARE\Citrix\ICA Client\Engine\Configuration\Advanced\Modules\ICA 3.0

If you would like to disable certain client functionality, you can do so by editing the Registry Key mentioned above. Simply remove the functionality you would like to disable, like clipboard (clipboard mapping) or ClientDrive (client drive mapping).

FMA fact: As mentioned, there are 32 virtual channels in total; however, Citrix reserves 17 of those. Third-party companies and customers who want to design and implement their own virtual channels are free to use the other ones. These are also referred to as dynamic virtual channels or DVCs.

Most features and functionalities configured at server level (mainly through policies) will need to be supported at the client side as well; there is a strong dependency between the two (think about the ICA handshake mentioned earlier).

Creating your own

Although XenDesktop / XenApp products ship with various virtual channels included, supported by both the VDA and Receiver, they are also designed to allow customers and third-party vendors to create their own virtual channels by using one of the provided SDKs, or Software Development Kits. When you want or need to create a virtual channel of your own you basically have two choices. One: you can use the Virtual Channel SDK; or two: you can use the ICA Client Object (ICO) SDK. Citrix offers several resources for you to leverage when it comes to creating your own VC. Here is a shot excerpt from the Virtual Channel SDK page:

> The Citrix Virtual Channel Software Development Kit (VCSDK) allows software engineers to write both host-side applications and receiver-side drivers to support additional virtual channels using the Citrix ICA protocol. The host-side virtual channel applications run on XenApp or XenDesktop, and the client-side portion of the virtual channel runs on the local device where Citrix Receiver resides. This SDK provides support for writing new virtual channels for the Citrix Receiver.

Citrix offers the following online resources:

- The Citrix Virtual Channel Software Development Kit (login with My Citrix needed).
- CTX113279 – How to Allow Custom Virtual Channels Created with ICO in Version 10.0 of the CTX Windows Client. Although somewhat outdated, it does provide some offer some interesting additional information.

- Client Object API Specification Programmer's Guide.
- The Citrix Developer Network. Home of all technical resources and discussions involving the use of Citrix SDKs.

Life is all about priorities

As we have seen, the ICA protocol consists of various virtual channels each offering its own functionality. By default, each of these virtual channels is given a priority, ranging from 0 to 3: the lower the number, the higher the priority.

For example, printing has a default priority of 3, which means that it has the lowest priority and will therefore be allowed less bandwidth then virtual channels with a higher priority (lower number) like Audio and ThinWire (Windows screen updates).

While it is possible to manually change these priorities, it isn't that common to do so. You need to be aware that when giving a higher priority, and thus more bandwidth to one virtual channel it also means that you are taking away potential bandwidth from another virtual channel. However, in the rare occasion when you may want to assign a higher priority to one of the virtual channels, this is how it is done. In Registry locate the key:

HKLM\System\CurrentControlSet\Control\Terminal Server\Wds\icawd\Priority.

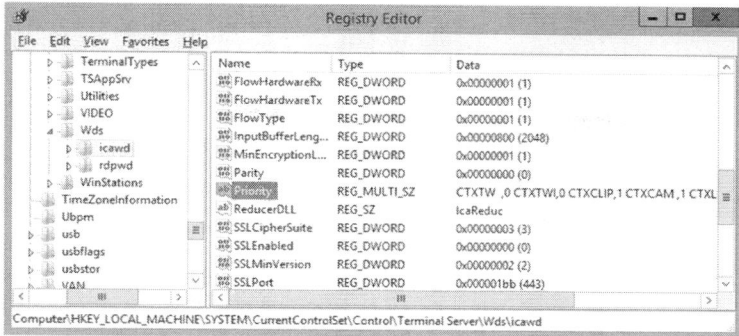

Figure 38: Virtual Channels (priority) Registry Key

There you will find various abbreviations like: CTXCAM, CTXTWI, CTXFLASH and so on, accompanied by a number ranging from 0 to 3 (their current priorities). These two combined represent a single virtual channel.

By simply changing the number, you will change the priority of the associated virtual channel. These priorities, 0 to 3, are also commonly referred to as priority groups. And remember, always be careful when editing the Registry, make sure to back up the key, or keys beforehand.

FMA fact: Other ways to accelerate ICA traffic would include Citrix policies, which can then be applied either per user or per server, or to the whole Site. Implementing a physical accelerator like the Citrix CloudBridge, formerly known as Branch Repeater, is always optional as well.

Multi-Stream ICA

While this (see previous section) does offer us some level of control with regard to ICA traffic acceleration, it is still fairly limited. By implementing, or activating a feature named Multi-Stream, or Multi-Port ICA we can configure true Quality of Service (QoS) on all or parts of the ICA / HDX traffic sent throughout our network. Note that I am referring to network-based QoS, which is different from prioritising a single virtual channel. Here we would like to be able to accelerate ICA traffic on an network (TCP/IP port) level rather than from within the ICA protocol itself. Without Multi-Stream ICA we can only accelerate ICA traffic as a whole on TCP/IP port 1494 or 2598 (Session Reliability) as discussed previously.

With Multi-Stream ICA enabled we can assign separate TCP/IP ports to each of the earlier mentioned priority groups a.k.a. streams within Multi-Stream ICA. This means that we can configure and assign a TCP/IP port for all priority 0 virtual channels, and another separate TCP/IP port for all priority 1 virtual channels, and so on. Meaning that there can be four Multi-Stream ports in total.

Each virtual channel will by default already have a priority assigned to it, as we've seen, ranging from 0 to 3, which correlates to very high (real-time activities, such as webcam content), high (interactive elements, such as screen, keyboard, and mouse), medium (for bulk processes, such as client drive mapping) and low (background activities, such as printing). This is true for single-stream ICA traffic (without Multi-Stream ICA enabled and configured) as well as Multi-Stream ICA traffic (with Multi-Stream ICA enabled and configured). However, as highlighted earlier, these priorities can be manually changed if and when needed.

The accompanying Multi-Stream ICA Registry Key, when enabled, can be found at:

HKLM\SYSTEM\CurrentControlSet\Control\Terminal Server\Wds\icawd\MultiStreamIca

It will consist of two subkeys: Stream and VirtualChannels.

Within the Stream Registry Key we can manually configure the various stream priorities and assign them to be either primary or secondary. Or we can use the default configuration instead. The format used is *Stream#, Stream type*. For example: 0,S will mean; all virtual channels with the priority 0 will be secondary, and 1,P means that all virtual channels with a priority of 1 will be primary and so on. Note that there can be only one primary stream, the rest will be secondary. The default configuration is: 0,S;1,P;2,S;3,S.

Within the VirtualChannel Registry Key we can manually configure the virtual channel stream pairs (binding a VC to a stream), which basically means that we assign a priority to a virtual channel, just like before. Or we can leave the default configuration in place. The format used is: *VirtualChannelName, Stream#*. CTXCAM,1 means that the virtual channel CTXCAM has been assigned to the stream 1. As a result, it will be part of the stream pair 1,P, as highlighted earlier. The default configuration is: CTXCAM,0; CTXTW,1; CTXTWI,1; CTXLIC,1; CTXVFM,1; CTXPN,1; CTXSBR,1; CTXSCRD,1; CTXCTL,1; CTXEUEM,1; CTXMM,2; CTXFLSH,2; CTXGUSB,2; CTXCLIP,2; CTXCDM,2; CTXCCM,3; CTXCM,3; CTXLPT1,3; CTXLPT2,3; CTXCOM1,3; CTXCOM2,3; CTXCPM,3; OEMOEM,3; OEMOEM,2.

Multi stream ICA

| Priority group 0 / P |
| Priority group 1 / S |
| Receiver | VDA |
| Priority group 2 / S |
| Priority group 3 / S |

QoS

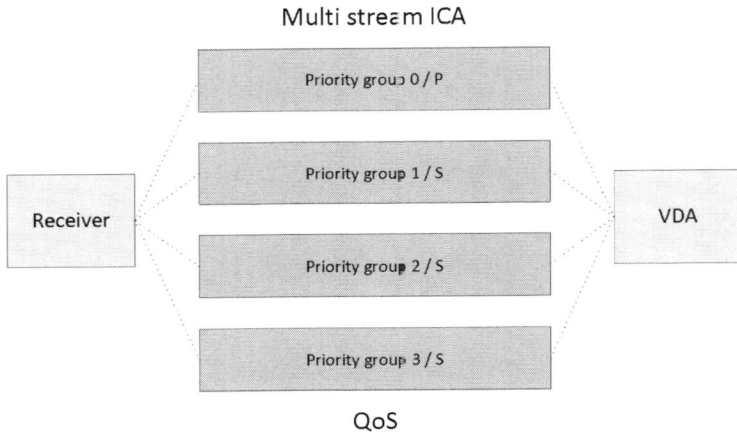

Figure 39: Multi-Stream ICA

FMA fact: When not using a CloudBridge appliance, formerly known as Branch Repeater, Session Reliability must be enabled for Multi-Stream ICA to function.

Once you have set up and configured the stream priorities and pairs you will have to configure a so-called multi-port Citrix policy where you configure separate TCP/IP ports to the primary (one) and secondary (three) streams as explained in the previous section.

Once that is out of the way you can actually go on and configure and apply QoS policies at network level on a per TCP/IP port level. This way you can apply QoS on grouped ICA virtual channels instead of a single or a couple of virtual channels within the ICA protocol.

Session Reliability

I already mentioned this feature once or twice throughout this chapter; here I will address it in a bit more detail. When Session Reliability is enabled, the ICA Client tunnels its ICA traffic inside the Common Gateway Protocol (CGP) and sends the traffic to port 2598 instead 1494. The XTE service acts as a relay; removing the Common Gateway Protocol layer and then forwarding traffic to the ICA listener on port 1494 internally as shown below:

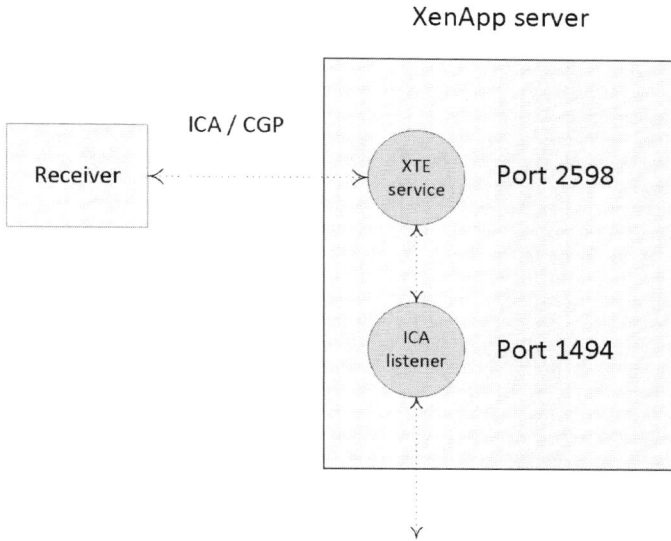

Figure 40: Session Reliability

Internally, all ICA traffic coming from the XenApp server destined for the end-user's client device will be sent through or via the XTE service as well; it basically works the same way, only vice versa. Session Reliability has the ability to buffer ICA traffic when the CGP connection between the client and the XTE service is somehow broken; it will then temporarily store all ICA data until the connection is restored. During that time, as long as the XTE service is buffering the ICA data, the user session will not go into a disconnected state; instead the session will remain active on the server.

From a client perspective, the session seems frozen while the client is attempting to reconnect with the XTE service over the Common Gateway Protocol. Once the session is restored, all buffered ICA data will be flushed and sent over to the client device and the session will continue as usual.

Configuration specifics

By default, Session Reliability (SR) is configured via policy and set to 180 seconds, or three minutes before the user session will be dropped and put into a disconnected state. However, this time-frame can be changed when needed. The default port used by SR is TCP/IP port Nr 2598 but can also be changed when desired.

> **FMA fact**: When Session Reliability is enabled users will be automatically reconnected as soon as the network connection is reinstated, and they will do so without needing to reauthenticate. Configuring the 'Auto client reconnect authentication' policy to prompt users to reauthenticate can change this behaviour.

Auto client reconnect is a feature used to detect unintended disconnected ICA sessions and will reconnect the user session automatically. As mentioned, users then do or do not have to reauthenticate, depending on how you configure the accompanying policy. If both Session Reliability and Auto client reconnect are used they will work in sequence, meaning that first the Session Reliability policy will be applied, and as soon as the user session disconnects because the configured SR time-frame has elapsed, the Auto client reconnect policy will kick in. As an alternative to Session Reliability you can also configure ICA Keep-Alive. This feature prevents a session from going into a disconnected state when a session seems broken. If configured, it will send a constant stream of ICA packages every few seconds (configurable) to detect if the user session is active. Only after the session has been marked as inactive will the session be put in a disconnected state. However, in practice Session Reliability is almost always preferred over ICA Keep-Alive.

Citrix HDX

I just wanted to briefly touch on HDX (High Definition Experience) since it is more than 'just' the ICA protocol and it is often misunderstood. In fact, HDX technologies are built on top of the ICA protocol: and they are not meant as a replacement at all. HDX technologies extend the ICA protocol. According to Citrix: HDX technologies offer a set of capabilities that deliver a 'high-definition' experience to users of centralised applications and desktops, on any device and over any network. It does this by trying to optimise the user experience, decrease the overall bandwidth consumption, and increase the user density per server. The HDX portfolio offers several innovative and industry-first technologies further enhancing and extending ICA, still the Nr. 1 remoting protocol in the industry today. A couple of examples of HDX technologies are: Flash and Windows media redirection, 4K monitor support, HDX 3D Pro GPU acceleration and sharing support (separate VDA), acceleration of printing and scanning, optimisation of USB traffic and more.

FMA fact: Remember, Citrix HDX isn't a replacement for the ICA protocol. HDX technologies are meant as an extension and as such operate on top of the ICA protocol.

There are two HDX-related technologies, which I would like to highlight in particular: these are ThinWire compatibility mode and Framehawk.

ThinWire compatibility mode

Although this may sound like something completely new, ThinWire on its own has been part of the ICA protocol almost from the beginning: it was part of the WinFrame release back in 1995, or ICA 3.0 as mentioned earlier in this chapter. Then again, the technology introduced with ThinWire compatibility mode is indeed (very) new, innovative even. ThinWire compatibility mode, which has had various names along the way, like project snowball, enhanced ThinWire, ThinWire Plus, and so on, was released as part of Feature Pack 3 for XenDesktop / XenApp version 7.6. It delivers a great user experience while keeping the CPU and bandwidth footprint as small as possible. In fact with the release of version 7.8 of XenDesktop / XenApp it has again been improved with enhanced lossless visual quality, sharpening fuzzy images at a faster rate when compared to version 7.7.

ThinWire compatibility mode is actually a fallback mode for the current 'video codec for compression' which is used by default. It uses H.264 compression and delivers a high-quality and superior graphics and video experience for most users by default. The accompanying policies (based on templates) are configured out of the box and aim to deliver the best user experience possible. However, there is a trade-off to all this. This method consumes a lot more resources to encode and decode, which requires a relatively high-power processor on the client side and impacts user density on the server side.

If the default method fails to kick in, because the user's end point device doesn't have enough compute / CPU power on-board, for example, or an older unsupported version of Citrix Receiver, then the ThinWire compatibility mode will be leveraged automatically, hence the fall-back mentioned earlier. And since it uses a combination of low-cost algorithms, which are compatible with almost every Operating System out there, it can be used in almost all circumstances. As highlighted, it also offers a very effective, and above all efficient CPU and bandwidth footprint. So even when the default mode does work you might want to consider switching to compatibility mode anyway, enhancing user density, saving on valuable resources and network bandwidth in general.

FMA fact: Make sure you check out the HDX policy templates in Studio. There are 6 in total.

Framehawk

Framehawk was first introduced with Feature Pack 2 for XenDesktop / XenApp version 7.6 combined with a new Receiver, version 4.3. And while it has been around a bit longer than ThinWire compatibility mode, it is still considered fairly new and is constantly being improved. Framehawk is mainly aimed at mobile workers who depend on Wi-Fi / 4G networks where things like packet loss and high latency are usually a problem. Framehawk can fix this for you. I have read about latency's reaching up to 500 ms and situations where 35% of packet loss was no exception and Framehawk still delivered a more than acceptable user experience. That is pretty impressive.

FMA fact: If you go to YouTube and search for Citrix Framehawk you will find multiple comparison clips of Framehawk vs. other technologies. Guess who comes out on top?

On average Framehawk does tend to consume a lot more bandwidth and CPU resources when compared to ThinWire compatibility mode. However, with the latest 7.8 releases Framehawk has again been improved significantly with reductions in memory footprint of 40% and up to 20% in CPU efficiency.

They also gained up to 50% in bandwidth efficiency when scrolling via touch input, once again improving the overall user experience. Framehawk is now also compatible with the latest, or near latest, release of NetScaler Gateway (including the Unified Gateway as of release 11.0-F) and the Citrix Receiver for Windows and iOS. Just be aware that there will still be a difference between the two, and it will all depend on the use case at hand.

Key takeaways

- Edward Lacobucci founded Citrix in 1989.
- Initially they started developing a multi-user platform for Microsoft's OS/2.
- Citrix actually started out as Citrus.
- They licensed the OS/2 source code from Microsoft and started developing Multiuser, which would later become their first major release.
- ICA was introduced when Citrix Multiuser was launched, which was around 1990 / 1991.
- Shortly after Citrix launched Multiuser, Microsoft announced that they would drop OS/2 and move to Windows.
- With some help of other companies, Microsoft included, Citrix managed to stay in business.
- In the meantime Citrix patented ICA and they started working on a new and improved version of ICA.
- Eventually a new agreement was signed giving Microsoft access to the ICA source code. This is how the Microsoft RDP protocol came to exist.
- ICA supports most, if not all, standard protocols today.
- It uses TCI/IP port 1494 by default, and is tunnelled through port Nr. 2598 when Session Reliability is enabled.
- The ICA protocol consists of 32 virtual channels in total, 17 of which are reserved by Citrix.
- The client capabilities are negotiated at session launch time, also referred to as the handshake.
- Virtual channels consist of, and communicate through, virtual drivers at the client side and server-side applications on the server side.

- Customers and other third parties have the ability to develop their own virtual channels.
- Each virtual channel has a default priority assigned to it, ranging from 0 to 3, with 0 being the highest, or most important. A higher priority means more bandwidth.
- By editing the registry you can manually change priorities. Be careful with this, giving more priority to one VC means you also take away priority (bandwidth) somewhere else.
- Multi-Stream ICA works by assigning separate TCP/IP ports to groups of priorities, or streams, establishing true QoS.
- Session Reliability ensures that the user session is not disconnected and that the user's session freezes, while in the background the ICA traffic is buffered.
- All buffered ICA traffic will be flushed out to the user's device once the user session reconnects.
- Session Reliability can leverage the Auto client reconnect feature to enforce users to reauthenticate when a session is reconnected.
- HDX is an extension to the ICA protocol and is in no way intended to replace ICA. It works on top of the ICA protocol.
- The Citrix ThinWire technology had multiple names: it is known as ThinWire Plus, ThinWire Advanced, Legacy ThinWire and ThinWire compatibility mode. They all have one thing in common: ThinWire is all about compressing data and enhancing the overall user experience.
- ThinWire has a small CPU and memory footprint and doesn't need much bandwidth.

- Framehawk is all about packet loss and high latency connections, delivering a more than acceptable user experience under challenging circumstances.
- In general, Framehawk needs more CPU and bandwidth than ThinWire, although this has been greatly enhanced with the latest 7.8 release.

Application delivery

As we have already seen in Studio, we have a couple of options
when it comes to delivering applications to our users. Here it is
important to note that I'm not talking about the ability to
publish an application; no, I am focusing on the mechanism
used to deliver the application after it has been published to a
user's desktop. As a side note, I will leave out any potential
EUC solutions that might be used to manage the end-user
environment, including the ability to assign installed /
virtualised applications to your users. This chapter is meant to
give you an idea of some of the options you have and to provide
you with an overview of the technology and components
involved.

We basically have three 'main' flavours to choose from (I know
there are more):

- We can leverage locally installed applications. Here I am
  referring to applications installed as part of the base
  image (MCS and/or PVS are both optional) of our
  RDSH and/or VDI deployment (s). Locally installed
  applications can then be published out to our users.
  Once launched, these applications will be started from
  the base image using local compute resources.
- We can apply 'true' application virtualisation using
  Microsoft App-V, for example. There are multiple
  software virtualisation products out there, like ThinApp,
  but App-V is favourite by most and above all supported
  and advised by Citrix as well. In fact, if we look forward
  to XenDesktop 7.8 they have made some really nice
  enhancements to Studio and the FMA with regard to
  App-V integration.

- Citrix AppDisks is Citrix's application-layering technology, which was introduced with XenDesktop / XenApp 7.8 and will be available with all XenDesktop and/or XenApp editions. Of course other application-layering vendors are optional as well, there are multiple. Since application layering is still a relatively new and unknown concept to most, I will elaborate a bit more on this as we progress.

FMA fact: Note how I say 'true' application virtualisation. This is because solutions like XenApp are also often referred to as application virtualisation solutions, so it is really a matter of perspective.

Locally installed applications

I assume we all know what I mean by this. When we prepare our master image used to provision our RDSH and/or VDI workloads, we manually install certain applications, plug-ins and add-ins etc. And while I say 'master image', this can just as easily be a single virtual or physical machine with a VDA installed, from where our applications would then be published and launched.

Microsoft App-V

Let's first start with a quick summary of what is involved when we are talking about XenDesktop and/or XenApp combined with Microsoft App-V application virtualisation. App-V consists of the following components:

- Management server – Provides a centralised console to manage App-V the infrastructure and deliver virtual applications to both the App-V Desktop Client as well as a Remote Desktop Services Client. The App-V management server authenticates, requests, and provides the security, metering, monitoring, and data gathering required by the administrator. The server uses Active Directory and supporting tools to manage users and applications.

- Publishing server – Provides App-V clients with applications for specific users, and hosts the virtual application package for streaming. It fetches the packages from the management server.

- Client – Retrieves virtual applications, publishes the applications to the client, and automatically sets up and manages virtual environments at runtime on Windows devices. The App-V client is installed on the VDA and stores user-specific virtual application settings, such as registry and file changes in each user's profile.

- And let's not forget about licensing. When using Citrix XenApp, Microsoft RDS CALs will be needed. As an added bonus, App-V will be covered as part of your RDS licenses as well (note that this does not apply to VDI based environments). This changed when Microsoft switched from Terminal Service (TS) to Remote Desktop Services. With TS CALs App-V still needed to be licensed separately.

By manually adding the Microsoft App-V Management and Publishing servers into Citrix Studio we can publish virtualised App-V applications right onto our users' desktops. These applications will then be 'streamed' over the network using your App-V set-up of choice. Applications can be pre-cached or prepublished and the use of a so-called shared content store is also optional, allowing us to stream directly from a central shared content source without having to stream the App-V package to the local platform.

FMA fact: Published App-V applications can be configured to be launched from the Start menu, through Citrix Receiver, using the locally installed (image) App-V client or from the StoreFront web interface.

Alternatively the Citrix Connector for System Center Configuration Manager is also optional. It is compatible with XenDesktop / XenApp 7.1, 7.5 and 7.5 and just recently Citrix announced support for both versions 7.7 and 7.8 as well.

The Connector is integrated with the Configuration Manager console to provide a single place where each user's access to applications can be defined and managed. To be a bit more precise, it can be used to:

- Synchronise XenDesktop Catalog and Delivery structures within Configuration Manager
- Deploy software to all types of XenApp and XenDesktop Catalogs
- Leverage MSI and App-V applications already defined in Configuration Manager
- Report application deployment success and failure
- Publish applications to StoreFront and Receiver directly from the Configuration Manager console
- Deploy HDX-delivered applications to PCs already managed by Configuration Manager.

App-V in XenDesktop 7.8

As of XenDesktop version 7.8 you can use Citrix Studio to manage the distribution of App-V applications to VDI based virtual desktops or XenApp servers without the requirement of a separate App-V server and database infrastructure, greatly simplifying administrative processes and eliminating additional infrastructure costs, a big step forward. When manually adding in App-V packages directly from Studio, all you have to do is fill in the accompanying UNC path and you are good to go, again, no further infrastructural App-V components needed. Ctxappvlauncher.exe will take care of everything.

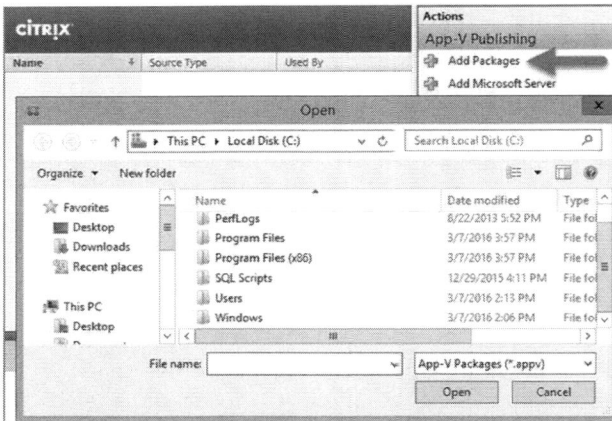

Figure 41: Adding App-V packages from Studio

Citrix AppDisks

Throughout the next section I would like to talk about what application layering actually is and also highlight some of the issues we often run into when using the more traditional approach when it comes to delivering applications to our users.

Let me first quote Citrix on their AppDisks technology:

> AppDisks is a technology that enables administrators
> to package and manage their apps independently of
> their golden images. This in turn reduces the number
> of golden images required. With AppDisks, instead of
> installing the application into the golden image, the
> application is installed (or more specifically the data is
> redirected) into a virtual disk – a VHD or VMDK
> depending on your Hypervisor. And once this
> AppDisk is created, it can be assigned across multiple
> golden images. Yes, that means across Windows
> versions. So long as the application can handle the
> respective Windows versions, then so will AppDisk.

Of course this is spot on, but, as I mentioned earlier, AppDisks
is one of multiple solutions or products that can produce these
layers for you. The next few sections will apply to almost every
application-layering product out there, with a few exceptions of
course.

FMA fact: AppDisks will be available with all
XenDesktop / XenDesktop editions, Advanced,
Enterprise and Platinum. Note that AppDNA will be for
Platinum-licensed customers only.

Application layering in more detail

Application virtualisation (mostly App-V and ThinApp) has
been around for some time now; application layering, however,
as mentioned, is still relatively new. Although assumed by some
and theoretically possible in some cases, application layering is
not meant as a replacement for application virtualisation.

In fact, you could say that they go hand-in-hand. Today there are multiple layering solutions available, and while they all take a slightly different approach, the concept is the same, in most cases anyway.

One of the biggest issues when it comes to application virtualisation is that simply not all applications can be virtualised. The more applications a customer has the harder this will be, which makes sense. Note that I'm primarily focusing on RDSH / VDI deployments. Research has shown that being able to virtualise around 50-60% of all applications on average is hard enough, let alone even higher.

From what I have seen personally at various customer sites it's not uncommon for a mid-sized to larger company to have (at least) a few hundred different applications. And if 'only' 60% of those applications can be virtualised (again, on average) you are left with dozens, potentially hundreds even, of applications that you will have to 'present' to your users in some other way. And while cloud-based applications (SaaS) are becoming more and more popular, they won't fit all use cases and primarily apply to new(er) applications in general. Many older, legacy (Windows) applications simply can't be replaced that easily, meaning you will still need to come up with a way to 'present' those apps to your users. This is where application layering can help.

The big, bad image

So what happens with applications that cannot be virtualised or replaced in another way? Right, they end up in your 'base' image. Not something to get very excited about. Let's have a brief look at some of the cons associated with this approach:

- It will make your applications harder to maintain and manage. When an application needs to be updated / patched you will always have to make those changes on your 'production' image. This could also be true for some of your virtualised applications, which might be pre-cached, for example, but at least you have a choice.

- Although, based on permissions, your users will only be able to see and start what they are allowed to (at least that's what they think): there will (potentially) be a whole bunch of applications on the base image that need to be shielded and/or hidden so users will be unable to locate and start them. Not to mention that, although they are not used by everyone, all applications will still need to be patched and updated.

- The same applies to adding new and removing old applications: it's not dynamic at all.

- You will have a hard time installing and maintaining multiple versions or editions of the same software.

- Your image might potentially grow up to hundreds of GBs. This doesn't have to be an issue per se, but it sure can be.

- I have come across (multiple) applications that needed to be updated on a weekly basis, or twice per week even. Queuing the updates and applying them once every two weeks or perhaps only once a month is far from acceptable in most cases. Can you imagine the horror?

- It's not that hard to see how all this will negatively impact production and not to mention your users. Think about it, when updating and thus changing a production image, with most companies it will need to be retested and 'accepted' each time before taken back into production as part of their standard 'change' protocol.

This will take one or two days at a minimum, and that's fast: trust me!

- This could easily force you to create multiple images / silos, based on departments, for example, while it should be 'less is more'.
- Another consideration might be the use of fat clients (niche software) or another form of persistent desktops, which you might not want to do, preferably.
- So-called 'Reverse-Seamless' technology could also be used. Here an application will be installed on the end point device and made available as part of the virtual sessions. Again, not ideal but worth considering. Application life cycle management becomes much harder.

Bring on the layers

Although this section isn't meant to give you a detailed technical explanation on how layering works, and this will also differ per product (vendor), here's a simplistic explanation on what it is about... First an application gets installed / captured on a VHD or VMDK file (virtual hard disk). This virtual disk will then be mounted onto a virtual machine (assigned to a user or machine; this also differs per layering solution). In some cases an in-guest mount is also optional, making layers available to physical machines as well.

Almost without exception, all application layer vendors make use of (mini-) filter drivers a.k.a. write filters residing in the base Operating System to 'manage' the file system containing C:\ etc. These 'filters' will also make sure that all application layers mounted to a machine will be seamlessly merged into the file system, making them appear as if they were installed locally, including any .ini, .dll, registry entries and other files that may come with it. From there on, any 'calls' made to the file system, when launching an application, will be 'filtered' and directed to the appropriate application layer, or VHD / VMDK file.

How they help

Some might argue that using an application-layering solution adds yet another product to the stack: it's another 'technology' and potential interface that admins need to get familiar with. It will also come at a certain cost with regard to purchasing the product, licenses and so on. Applications will not be isolated like with app virtualisation. However, these cons, if you can call them that, are soon forgotten when you have a look at some of the pros that come with application layering. To name a few...

- As for the 'another product to the stack' argument, yes that's true, but if you forget what is going on under the hood technology-wise, which is easily done, then learning how to deal with layers (creating, assigning and updating them) will probably only take you a couple of hours max.

- Another GUI? Perhaps. But if you are a VMware or Citrix shop, for example, then go with App Volumes or AppDisks (which will be integrated into Studio). The impact on your existing product stack will be minimal. And who cares about 'another' GUI if it helps you solve some major issues.

- About the costs. I don't have any list prices to share, (AppDisks will be included for free as part of all editions) but just think about what you would have to do, and how much time and effort it will take managing all your applications, or environments that you might be managing as a consultant, when taking the 'traditional' route.

- No isolation. Yes. But if applications can't be virtualised there's usually a reason for this. I mean, being able to interact with the underlying OS and any applications or other resources that might reside on there can be an advantage just as easily.

What about some of the (other) pros…?

- No more applications in your base image, with a few exceptions free for you to choose.
- You might end up with just one 'golden' image, maybe two.
- Applications can be managed completely independently from each other, on a per layer basis if you will, even on different time schedules or 'on the fly' if needed, without impacting your production environment.
- It also works for drivers, add-ons, plug-ins and so on.
- Depending on the technology used, applications can be added and removed dynamically: the user does not have to log out, reboot etc. When a layer has been added the application icon will appear almost instantly on the user's desktop, same with removing layers.
- They all work on top of your existing infrastructure, leveraging Active Directory for layering assignment to users, groups of users, machines and so forth.
- Non-persistent desktops are now more 'achievable' then ever.
- Support for all Hypervisors (does depend on solution chosen) and works for all major RDSH and VDI platforms out there.
- When combined with a personal data / AppDisk

(optional in most cases), you can achieve persistent desktops but still maintain all the advantages of non-persistent.

- Most application-layering products have built-in application life cycle management capabilities.
- Reduces storage, compute and network costs, and not to mention the time it takes to rapidly 'package' and provision applications to users, including overall management.
- Layering and application virtualisation go hand-in-hand. Application Layering is easy; you don't need to have any specific knowledge (or a lot less anyway), as apposed to App-V packaging, which can be an art on its own. As an added advantage the application layering packaging process can easily be delegated to other teams when needed.

Layering questions to ask

Although the primary focus is on AppDisks, when thinking about implementing an application-layering solution in general there will always be a few (basic) questions you have to ask yourself (or out loud) with regard to the platform you are supporting or going to support.

- To start, is it Citrix XenApp / XenDesktop, VMware Horizon / View or maybe 'plain' Microsoft RDSH that you want to support?
- The same goes for supported Hypervisors. Depending on what you are using, your options might be limited to a few vendors.
- Is there a steep learning curve?
- Does it need to work for persistent as well as non-

persistent?

- Do we need to be able to assign layers to users, machines or both?
- Does it support both VHD and VMDKs?
- Can we assign layers to virtual as well as physical machines?
- How about the rest of the vendor product portfolio: do they offer anything else that might benefit us combined with application layering?
- Do they offer a (persistent) personal data / app disk solution? Would I like to use it?
- A user profile solution (based on layering as well) perhaps?

FMA fact: Citrix AppDisks is available as of XenDesktop / XenApp version 7.8

Key takeaways

- Although I narrowed it down to three ways of application delivery, there are of course a lot more flavours to choose from, especially when talking virtualisation, layering and containerisation. Search for the Application Virtualization Smackdown whitepaper, or visit rorymon.com. You will be amazed by the options you have.

- AppDisks is Citrix's approach to application layering.

- AppDisks will be available for all licenses. AppDNA integration with AppDisks will be for Platinum customers only. AppDNA will automatically check your AppDisks for any potential compatibility issues with the underlying Operating System and/or any other software, including applications, security updates and patches etc. already installed and running. When applicable it will tell you what is wrong and how to correct it.

- Application layering is not meant as a direct replacement for application virtualisation: they go hand-in-hand. In practice you will probably use all three, base image-installed applications, virtualised and layered apps.

- Application layering does not isolate applications like App-V does, for example.

- Think of it as just another tool in the toolbox to make life a little easier.

- Remember that, although a single master image is great to have, it is also a utopia in most cases. Just don't go nuts: keep the number of images to manage to a minimum. Less is more.

Login, resource enumeration and Citrix printing demystified

The user login process

When troubleshooting a XenDesktop environment/architecture it's important to know which components and services are involved, how they interact and what is supposed to happen during normal operations. In fact, I guess it's safe to state that that goes for all problems in life: if you don't know or understand the basics of what you are dealing with, then you're bound to get lost, fast.

Throughout the next few sections I will zoom in on the user login and resource enumeration process as well as the steps needed to actually launch a desktop and/or application and talk about what happens during some of the most common day-to-day operations and processes, so common that in most cases we don't even think about what's going on under the hood until… it stops working!

I have already discussed the user authentication process from a StoreFront and Web Interface perspective, but just to be sure we are all on the same page I'll highlight them here as well.

User authentication

With StoreFront, users are authenticated by the authentication service, which is an integral part of StoreFront. Users can authenticate to StoreFront using different methods: usernames and passwords, domain pass-through, NetScaler pass-through, using smart cards or by enabling unauthenticated user access. As soon as a user logs in by filling in his or her username and password (on the StoreFront web page using the so-called Receiver for website configuration, or using a locally installed Citrix Receiver), the StoreFront authentication service will pick up the user credentials and authenticate them with a domain controller.

Once authenticated, StoreFront will forward the user credentials, as part of an XML query, to one of the configured Delivery Controllers, assuming you configured at least two, of course. In between, StoreFront will check its local datastore for any existing user subscriptions and store them in memory. Next, the Delivery Controller receiving the credentials will again contact a domain controller, this time to validate the user's credentials before responding to the StoreFront server.

If we look at Web Interface, user authentication works a bit different, since it has no internal authentication service. When a user logs in by filling in his or her username and password, Web Interface will immediately forward these credentials, as part of a XML query, to a Delivery Controller where a domain controller will be contacted to authenticate the user before responding to the Web Interface server.

As before, Web Interface can also authenticate users to, and enumerate and aggregate resources from, multiple XenApp Farms and XenDesktop Sites; no App Controller, though.

FMA fact: Knowing the architecture, the components, the way traffic flows throughout and expected behaviour is the only way to successfully troubleshoot your FMA-based infrastructure.

StoreFront 3.x

As of StoreFront 3.0 Citrix reintroduced XML-based authentication. By simply running a few PowerShell scripts, user authentication falls back to the XenDesktop / XenApp XML service, as with Web Interface, useful when StoreFront is not in the same Domain as XenDesktop / XenApp or when it is not possible to set up an Active Directory trust, for example. Again, this method will be disabled by default, at least now you have options.

External user authentication through NetScaler

Let's take it step by step and see what happens when someone logs in externally. I'll assume that your NetScaler Gateway is set up and configured to integrate your StoreFront server(s), you have Receiver installed, SSL certificates are present, and that an STA / XML / Broker service address (Delivery Controller) and a domain controller for authentication purposes are also configured.

Perhaps you want to load balance your StoreFront and/or Delivery Controllers by creating and configuring virtual load balance servers on the NetScaler, adjust the theme of the NetScaler's Web Interface and, last but not least, you'll probably have to configure your StoreFront deployment to accept pass-through authentication from NetScaler. Where port Nr. 443 (SSL) is used, you can also use port 80, although 443 is recommended.

1. *A user opens up a web browser and connects to the external URL of the NetScaler Gateway (using SSL over port Nr. 443) where he or she fills in his or her username and password. A locally installed Citrix Receiver can also be used to establish a direct connection to the NetScaler Gateway. Citrix Receiver uses Beacons to determine if a connection is internal or external and handles it accordingly.
2. The NetScaler will take the user credentials and authenticate them (session ticket) against Active Directory over TCP port Nr. 389. The NetScaler has its

own authentication service just like StoreFront mentioned earlier. LDAPS or LDAP TLS are also both optional, or preferred even (port Nr. 636). This will also enable password changes from your NetScaler.

3. Once authenticated, the user session gets redirected to StoreFront where it will first perform a callback to the NetScaler that handled authentication to validate the user. The authentication details will then be sent over to the StoreFront server.

4. From here the user credentials will be forwarded, as part of the earlier mentioned XML query, to the configured Broker (XML) service on one of the Delivery Controllers. Both these transactions will use either port Nr. 443 / SSL or 80 / HTTP.

5. In between, StoreFront will check its local datastore for any existing resource subscriptions and stores these in memory.

6. The Broker (XML) service will again contact a domain controller (port Nr. 389 / 636) to validate the user credentials: note that this is different to the user authentication process, as we've established earlier. During this process it will find out to which security groups the user belongs.

7. With this information the Delivery Controller or Broker (XML) service will contact the Central Site database to find out which resources have been assigned to the user. It does this over port Nr. 1433 / 1434.

8. The Broker (XML) service will return an XML file to the StoreFront server including all assigned resources.

9. StoreFront will generate a web page containing all the assigned resources, which will be routed through the NetScaler Gateway and presented to the user. The user's home screen will be populated with any pre-subscribed

resources (Keywords). Depending on how you are connected, your resources will be displayed either directly using a Receiver for Web sites, or you'll find them within the locally installed Citrix Receiver instead. The user will be able to browse his or her own personal app store for any assigned resources to which he or she can subscribe and then launch.

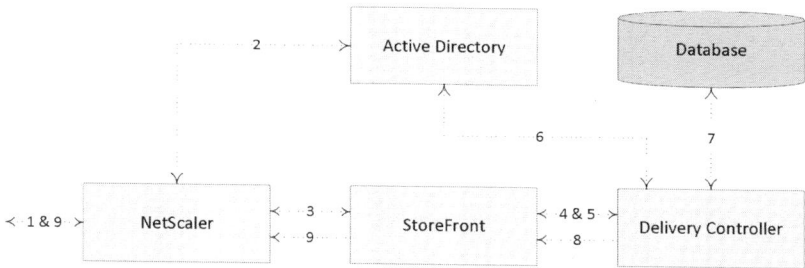

Figure 42: External user authentication

FMA fact: *If you don't enable authentication on the NetScaler's login page the NetScaler will contact StoreFront and the user will be presented (through the NetScaler) with the StoreFront login page (Receiver for Web sites). The user fills in his or her credentials and authentication will be handled by StoreFront.

Internal user authentication through StoreFront

Now that you have an idea of what happens when a user logs in externally by contacting a Citrix NetScaler, let's have another (detailed) look at what happens when a user does the same but this time internally by contacting the StoreFront server directly.

1. A user opens up a web browser and connects to the internal StoreFront URL where he or she fills in his or

her username and password. This method is also referred to as Receiver for Web sites, as mentioned above (don't confuse this with the HTML5-based Receiver for web;: they're not the same). A locally installed Citrix Receiver can also be used to establish a direct connection to StoreFront, which is probably the preferred method whenever possible. The earlier mentioned (NetScaler) Beacon functionality applies here as well.

2. Next the StoreFront authentication service will pick up the user credentials and contact a domain controller to authenticate the user in Active Directory over TCP port Nr. 389. Here I'd like to note that if domain pass-through authentication is enabled on the StoreFront server, this step would automatically be skipped. LDAPS or LDAP TLS are also both optional, or preferred even (port Nr. 636).

3. Once authenticated, the user credentials, as part of the XML query, will be sent to a Delivery Controller.

4. In between, StoreFront will check its local datastore for any existing resource subscriptions and store these in memory.

5. During the next phase the Broker (XML) service will again contact a domain controller (port Nr. 389 or 636) to validate the user credentials; this is different to the user authentication process, as we've established earlier. During this process it will find out to which security groups the user belongs.

6. With this information the Delivery Controller, or Broker (XML) service, will contact the Central Site Database to find out which resources have been assigned to the user. It does this over port Nr. 1433 / 1434.

7. The Broker (XML) service will return an XML file to the

StoreFront server over port Nr. 443 / SSL using
HTTPS, or port Nr. 80 when using 'plain' HTTP.
8. StoreFront will generate a web page containing all the
assigned resources, which will be presented to the user.
The user's home screen will be populated with any pre-
subscribed resources (Keywords). Depending on how
you are connected, your resources will be displayed
either directly using a Receiver for Web sites, or you'll
find them within the locally installed Citrix Receiver
instead. The user will be able to browse his or her own
personal app store for any assigned resources to which
he or she can subscribe and then launch.

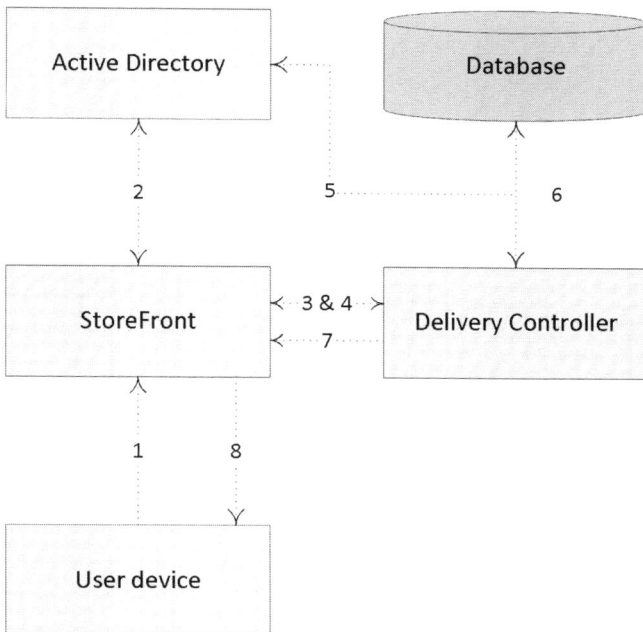

Figure 43: Internal user authentication

The actual resource launch process

Here we basically pick up where we left off at the end of the resource enumeration process as highlighted earlier. Just as with the authentication process, there are some differences between the internal and external resource launch process. Also, when launching a hosted shared desktop or a published application there is an additional load balance step involved. Let's start with an external hosted shared desktop session launch through NetScaler.

The Secure Ticket Authority

Before we continue… You might have heard about something called the STA, or the Secure Ticket Authority in full. It was first introduced with one of the earlier Secure Gateway editions over ten years ago. It (the STA) runs as a service and is part of the Broker service on the Delivery Controller just like the XML service. During the resource launch sequence the StoreFront server as well as the NetScaler will both need to be able to communicate with the STA. As such, you will need to configure the NetScaler as well as the StoreFront server(s) or Web Interface server(s) to point to the same XML/STA service(s)/Delivery Controller(s).

Once a user launches a resource, externally through NetScaler Gateway, at one point a secure ticket will be requested. As we will see shortly, the STA ticket will eventually end up in the launch.ica file generated by StoreFront and/or Web Interface. Once generated, the Delivery Controller hosting the STA service will hold the STA ticket information in memory for a configurable amount of time. As soon as a secure session is established the NetScaler Gateway responsible for handling the session only has to check the STA ticket (as part of the .ica launch file) with the STA service that originally generated the ticket. It (the STA service) does this from memory where the ticket was stored after it was created and sent back to the StoreFront server as part of the XML file mentioned earlier, more (detail) on this in the overview below.

FMA fact: The STA is only used when traffic traverses a NetScaler, so you don't have to worry about the STA service and its tickets when authentication takes place internally.

Launching a resource externally

1. Assuming that the login and enumeration process finished without any issues the user is free to subscribe to and launch any applications and/or desktops that have been assigned to him or her. As an example, let's say that the user tries to launch a (XenApp) hosted shared desktop session.

2. After the user clicks the icon the launch request is sent to the NetScaler Gateway from where it will be forwarded to the StoreFront server.

3. The StoreFront server will contact the Broker (XML/STA) service, or Delivery Controller, to find out if and where the resource is available and where it can be best started. This is where the well-known XenApp load-balancing mechanism comes into play. Which as of the FMA needs to be configured through policies.

4. During this time the StoreFront server will also request an STA ticket from the Broker (XML/STA) service. It will include the user, domain and resource name it wants to start. It will also request a 'least loaded' server as part of the load-balancing process.

5. The Broker (XML/STA) service will query the Central Site database (ports Nr. 1433 and 1434) to find out which server is able to offer the requested resource. The Delivery Controller will use this information, together with its load balance algorithm to decide which server to connect to.

6. At this time the Broker (XML/STA) service will create the STA ticket mentioned earlier. This will include information on the server and resource to connect to, as discovered in the previous steps mentioned.

7. Next the Broker (XML/STA) service will send this information back to the StoreFront server in the form of an XML file.

8. Based on this information, the StoreFront server will then generate a launch.ica file (uses the default.ica file as a template) containing the STA ticket and a whole bunch of other connection properties that are, or might, be needed. This will also include the FQDN/DNS name of the NetScaler Gateway itself.

9. StoreFront passes on this information down through the NetScaler Gateway onto the locally installed Receiver, which initiated the connection to begin with.

10. *The locally installed Receiver will read and autolaunch the launch.ica file to set up a connection to the NetScaler Gateway (443 / SSL).

11. From here the NetScaler Gateway will first contact the Broker (XML/STA) service (this address is configured on the NetScaler as well) to verify if the earlier generated STA ticket, as part of the launch.ica file, is still valid.

12. The Broker (STA) service will validate the STA ticket from memory. Once verified, it will send back the IP address, port Nr. Resource name etc. of the machine and the resource it needs to connect to. Once done the

STA ticket will be deleted.

13. The NetScaler Gateway will set up a new ICA connection using port 1494 (ICA) or 2598 (CGP) Common Gateway Protocol) depending on configuration.

14. The installed VDA will verify its license file with the Delivery Controller.

15. The Delivery Controller checks with the Citrix License Server to verify that the end-user has a valid ticket. This will also be done for any Microsoft (CAL) licenses, with regard to HSD and published applications that might be involved.

16. At this time any applicable session policies will be passed onto the VDA applying them to the session.

17. Finally the HSD is launched and the NetScaler Gateway acts as a proxy between the user and the XenDesktop resource in the data centre.

18. Somewhere in between the session/connection, information will be passed on and registered in the Central Site Database where it will be used for future load balance purposes.

FMA fact: The STA ticket gets generated and sent back after a user launches an application/desktop, and not during the resource enumeration process. It also includes information on the resource to be launched, including the server to launch the application on (load balance).

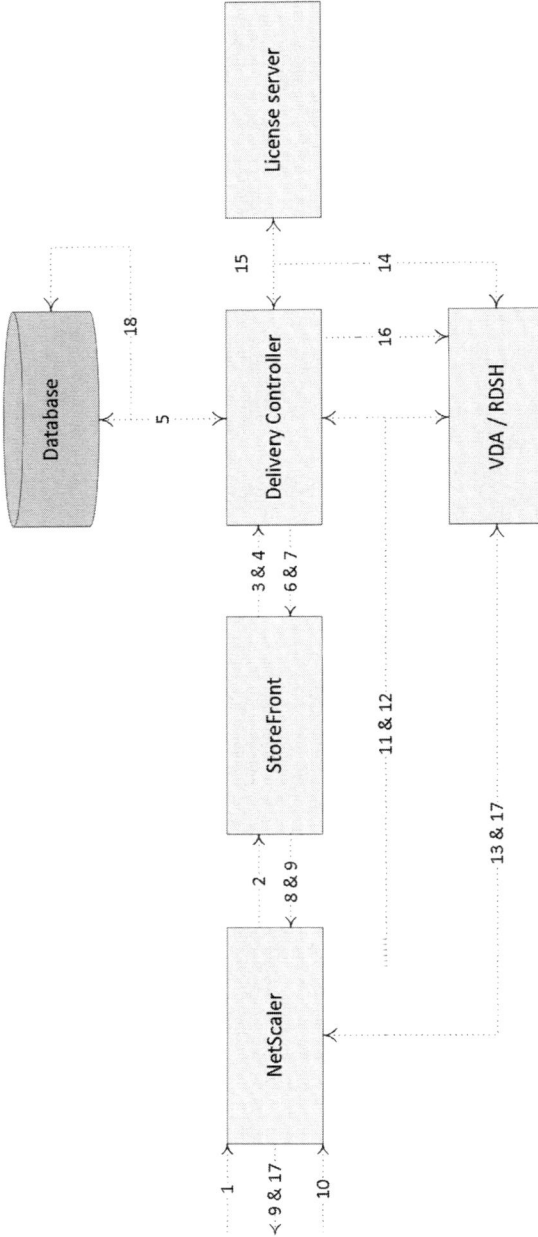

Figure 44: Launching a resource externally

The Windows authentication process

As I am primarily focusing on the Citrix side of things here I
deliberately left out the Windows / Domain Authentication
process. However, you do need to be aware that every time you
initiate a fresh Citrix session, by launching a hosted shared
desktop session, for example, or by starting published
applications, a few things happen in the background from a
Windows perspective as well. When you launch a resource you
are basically logging in on the server machine where that specific
application or desktop is being published. As a result, you will
be logged on as a normal Windows / domain user before your
resource will actually start. The steps involved in the
background do not differ when compared to logging into a
'normal' Windows server or desktop machine. These steps
include:

- User logon and authentication
- Profile load
- GPO processing
- Startup scripts
- Drive mapping
- Printer mappings

Receiver and HTML5

From my previous examples I assume that you already have the
Citrix Receiver installed locally, which is a pretty common
scenario. But if you don't, you have a few options. First (we
already covered some if this earlier) when you connect to
StoreFront, either directly or through the NetScaler Gateway as
we've talked about, it automatically checks if there is a Receiver
installed locally and which Operating System you are running. If

not, it will guide you to a download section or page (usually Citrix's) where you will be able to download the Citrix Receiver. There are a few ways administrators can implement this.

HTML5 to the rescue

If, for whatever reason, you are unable or not allowed to install a Citrix Receiver locally, Citrix offers the Receiver for HTML5. You will still be able to connect to StoreFront / NetScaler and launch your resources without any loss of functionality. Although not enabled by default, StoreFront has a built-in HTML5-based Receiver, which will kick in at launch time.

It does this by fetching the HTML5 engine from the StoreFront and making it part of the local browser. Note that you must use an HTML5-supported browser for this to work. So basically your browser becomes your Receiver handling the launch.ica file. When you close the browser, you close the session. Even when your users will have Receiver installed you can enable it anyway, as it will function as a fallback mechanism.

Do note that when enabling the HTML5-based Receiver some additional configuration steps will be needed.

As highlighted earlier: you will have to enable and configure ICA WebSockets through Citrix policies using Studio for example. The same applies to your external users connecting through a NetScaler, a separate HTTP Profile with WebSockets enabled (disabled by default) will need to be created. When using Provisioning Services these policies will need to be applied at vDisk level.

The Broker, XML and STA

Be aware that the STA (service) is also part of the Broker service, and has been as of Presentation Server 4.0. Before that it was written as an ISAPI extension for Microsoft Internet Information Services, or IIS. I also highlighted the XML service multiple times.

I put the XML and STA services between brackets because as of XenDesktop 4.x the XML service (ctxxmlss.exe) has been rewritten in .NET and became part of the Broker service as well. So the Broker service is actually built up of three separate services, all handling different tasks: it brokers connections, it enumerates resources, and it acts as the Secure Ticket Authority, generating and validating STA tickets.

FMA fact: Make sure that the Broker (XML/STA) service on the NetScaler and the StoreFront server is configured identically. The same applies to the load balance/fail over order in which you configure them.

Launching a resource internally

Now that we've seen which steps are involved when launching a resource externally, a hosted shared desktop in this case, let's have a look and see what happens when we launch a pooled VDI-based virtual machine internally.

After this we will have looked at an external and internal resource launch, an HSD, which is comparable to a published application, and a VDI virtual machine. Again, user authentication and resource enumeration have successfully completed, here we go (again).

1. As mentioned, we will launch a pooled VDI virtual machine this time. Let's assume that the VM is pre-subscribed and already present on the user's home screen, never mind how we connected: locally installed Receiver or using the Receiver for Web sites.

2. After the user clicks the icon, the StoreFront server will contact the Broker (XML/STA) service, or Delivery Controller, to check if any registered VDAs are available. It does this by communicating with the underlying Hypervisor platform through the Host service on the Delivery Controller.

3. If needed, it will first start / boot a VM. It's not uncommon to pre-boot a few VMs, since, as you can probably imagine, this will positively influence the overall user experience.

4. Next the Delivery Controller, or Broker (XML/STA) service, will contact one of the VDAs and send a StartListening request. By default, the VDA isn't listening for any new connections on port Nr. 1494 or 2598 until it gets notified that a user wants to connect.

5. During this phase the VDA will also try and register with the Delivery Controller.

6. As soon as the VDA is listening, the Broker (XML/STA) service will send this information back to the StoreFront server in the form of an XML file.

7. Based on this information, the StoreFront server will then generate a launch.ica file (it uses the default.ica file as a template) containing the IP address of the VDA and a whole bunch of other connection properties that are, or might, be needed. This is sent down to the user.

8. The locally installed Receiver (or HTML5-based Receiver) will read and autolaunch the launch.ica, file initiating a direct connection from the user's end point

to the VDA.

9. The installed VDA will verify its license file with the Delivery Controller.

10. The Delivery Controller checks with the Citrix License Server to verify that the end-user has a valid ticket.

11. At this time any applicable session policies will be passed on to the VDA and the session is launched.

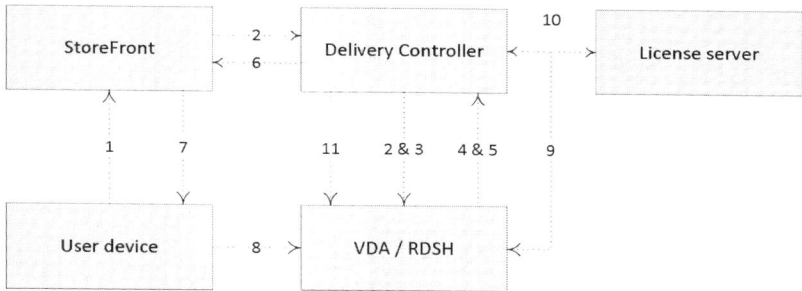

Figure 45: Launcing a resource internally

Site policies

When we publish resources, either hosted shared desktops, VDI-based virtual machines or published applications, we normally would use a combination of Catalogs and Delivery Groups to grant or allow access to these resources. Although this works fine in most cases, using PowerShell we can get a bit more granular.

Entitlement policies – These apply to pooled and shared desktops. With entitlement policies you can explicitly deny a certain user from a group of users' access to a pooled and/or shared desktop. Let's say you have a group of 50 users and you want to exclude five users, using these policy rules you won't have to create a separate group of users to exclude, you can just exclude those five users without affecting any of the other users.

There are two types of Entitlement policies:

1. BrokerEntitlementPolicyRule: this one is issued for access to desktops.
2. BrokerAppEntitlementPolicyRule: this one is used to control access to applications.

Assignment policies – These basically do the same thing as the Entitlement policies described above, only they apply to dedicated private desktops. Again, there are two policies:

1. BrokerAssignmentPolicyRule: this one is issued for access to desktops.
2. BrokerAppAssignmentPolicyRule: this one is used to control access to applications.

Before we move on to the Site Access policy I'd like to point out another Entitlement policy gotcha: Once we've configured a Delivery group with the Desktops and Applications delivery type we can use PowerShell to limit access to the HSD. Let me explain what I mean here.

By default, when you create a delivery group with the delivery type set to Desktops and Applications, Studio creates one Desktop Entitlement Policy Rule and one App Entitlement Policy Rule for the group, meaning that each user is entitled to one desktop session and one app session. Studio doesn't expose the user filter on these objects, so both are available to all users of the delivery group.

Using the PowerShell command: Set-BrokerEntitlementPolicyRule we can change this behaviour. It can set the IncludeUserFilterEnabled parameter to True instead of False, enabling the user filter, and it also lets you add an AD security group, this way limiting access to just that group and that group alone, as opposed to all users who are members of the Delivery group.

Site Access policies

Site Access policies – This isn't directly about the users connecting, it is more about connections in general and the conditions that need to be met once a connection gets established: things like client IP addresses, the protocol used, Smart Access filters, hostnames etc. Based on this information, connections can be excluded or denied access as well.

FMA fact: When a Delivery Group gets created, two access rules are created and added by default, one for direct connections and one for connections through NetScaler. Using PowerShell we can look at and change these access rules, as we see fit.

To see what your Site Access policies currently look like, open PowerShell and type:

Get-BrokerAccessPolicyRule followed by the - DesktopGroupName command, so that you won't get overloaded with all Access policies currently enabled. To edit these policies you will use the Set- BrokerAccessPolicyRule command.

Key takeaways

- There are two main authentication points within a Flex Management-based Architecture: NetScaler (optional) and StoreFront.

- Knowing the difference between the IMA and the FMA, how traffic flows throughout each component, and the way they are supposed to interact is or can be vital to successfully troubleshooting the FMA.

- As of version 3.0, StoreFront can also use the XML service for authenticating users.

- Note that there is a distinct difference between authentication and verification. Authentication is to make sure that somebody is who he or she claims to be. Verification is done to find out which resources are assigned (permissions) to the user, which will then be displayed in the user's store, ready for subscription.

- User authentication and resource enumeration basically go hand-in-hand.

- The STA only applies when connections are coming in externally through NetScaler.

- The STA service is part of the Broker server, and so is the perhaps better-known XML service.

- The HTML5-based Citrix Receiver, as part of your Internet browser, can offer the exact same functionality and features as a natively installed Receiver.

- The Windows authentication process is also involved when launching a Citrix published resource.

- Site policies allow us to exclude certain users or to apply certain policies when specific conditions are met. PowerShell can be used to manage and configure Site policies.

A deeper look into Citrix printing

A user clicks 'print', what happens next? When Citrix is thrown in the mix, things work a bit differently. Although the Microsoft print basics still apply, and I'll discuss them shortly, the way that print traffic will or can be routed throughout your environment depends on, one: the physical set-up of your machines; and two: the Citrix (print) policies configured. Note that I will only focus on native Citrix printing, and won't go over any of the third-party solutions out there.

Microsoft print file formats

First things first, Microsoft supports two so-called print file formats, EMF and XPS. EMF stands for Enhanced MetaFile and XPS stand for XML Paper Specification. A print file format basically refers to the type of print output an application produces and how it will be handled (routed and rendered) afterwards by the print subsystem. Although considered legacy, EMF is still widely used today, perhaps the most, even.

This is mainly because up until Windows XP and Server 2003 this is all we had, so you can probably imagine the number of applications that depend on EMF. XPS was introduced later with Vista and Server 2008.

The way an application is written, coded or compiled etc. will determine which print file format will be used. Win32 (Windows API) applications, meaning that they are based on a C-based framework for creating applications, depend on and leverage the EMF print file format. WPF (Windows Presentation Foundation), representing a graphical subsystem for rendering user interfaces in Windows-based applications, uses the XPS print file format. As you would expect, both behave somewhat different.

Some more differences between the two

XPS applies compression by zipping the print data into a .zip file. EMF does not apply compression at all. Also, EMF needs to separately draw each image it encounters, even if the image is used multiple times within the same document. XPS, however, can reference a single image multiple times. For XPS to be used, assuming your application supports it, both the print driver as well as the physical print device itself need to support XPS, otherwise it will be converted back to EMF.

After a user clicks 'print'

Again, this is still from a Microsoft printing perspective. Once a user clicks 'print' the application will produce some form of print output, a.k.a. print data. This data will contain all characters, fonts, colour schemes, images and so on, which will then need to be 'translated' into something that the physical print device can understand and handle. As explained earlier, depending on how the application is written / coded, this data will either be EMF- or XPS-based.

With EMF the print output will either be processed by the GDI (Graphics Device Interface), turning it into a metafile (XML-based) or it will, together with a locally installed print driver, render the data into a printable format before handing it over to the (local or remote) print spooler service However, with EMF the mentioned GDI intervention is most common.

FMA fact: With XPS, the earlier mentioned print output is already in an XML format and will be sent over to the print spooler service right away. See image on the next page for an overview.

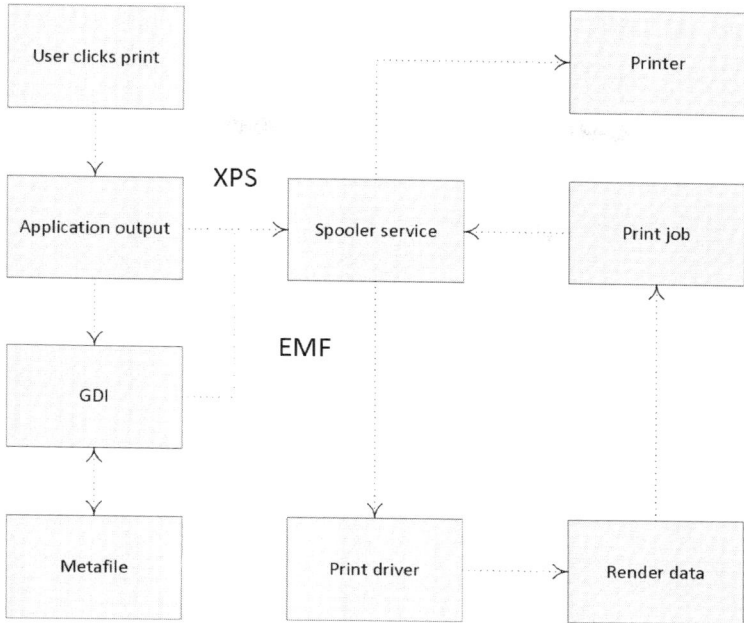

Figure 46: What happens after a user clicks print

From there the print data will (again) be handed over to a locally installed print driver, further rendering the data (if needed), which will turn it into an actual print job before sending it back to the print spooler service. During this phase it will also determine if the target printer is locally attached or remote through a print server before sending it over to the actual physical print device.

Print Spooling

The process where the application print output is received by the spooler service, which hands it over to a print driver, rendering it into a print job, and sends it back to the spooler service and then over to the physical print device, is what we actually refer to as print spooling. Of course this is still somewhat high-level, but it does give you a good indication of what is taking place under the hood.

Local and remote print spooling

When, from a client perspective, print spooling takes place locally it will also consume local compute resources. On a PC with a locally attached printer, spooling will be local to the client. When that same PC uses a network-provisioned printer connected through a print server, spooling will take place remotely on the print server, also meaning it will consume remote resources on the print server.

Another example would be when we have a session on a XenApp server. Here we could also have a network-provisioned printer, meaning that from a client perspective spooling will take place remotely on a print server.

When spooling takes place remotely, not only will remote compute resources of the print server be used, it will also generate a certain amount of network traffic between the client (which can be a XenApp server) and the print server with every individual print job. You need to take both into account when sizing your print architecture set-up.

Some history

If we look back a couple of years, and perhaps even today, then most print issues were related to badly written print drivers. They were not optimised for multi-user environments; not tested or signed; services would hang (spooler and Citrix Print Manager); blue screens would pop up; the auto-creating of printers would fail; we would experience high CPU loads; and so on.

Back in the Windows NT days all we had were version 2 kernel-mode drivers, which of course ran in kernel mode. It isn't that hard to imagine what happened if one of those drivers went bad.

You would simply lose the whole system and everything on it. Luckily with Windows 2000 came version 3 user mode drivers, which are still widely used today. Version three print drivers run in user mode, so if something were to go wrong with one of these drivers it would not affect the system kernel. Although this could still leave the server useless, the impact is less than with kernel-mode drivers.

With Windows Server 2008 R2 Microsoft introduced a mechanism, which automatically blocks the installation of version 2 kernel-mode drivers: a good thing. They also introduced a feature named Print Driver Isolation, and it can do exactly as the name implies: isolate your print drivers. When using Print Driver Isolation you have three separate modes to configure and apply, None, Shared and Isolated.

Print Driver Isolation

With the None mode (which will be applied by default) nothing changes, all drivers will still be able to interact, and if one goes bad it can still potentially bring down the whole machine, or the biggest part of it anyway.

With Shared mode, however, we have the ability to group a certain number of print drivers and let them run in a process completely separated from all other print drivers including the Print Spooler and CTX Print Management Service.

These print drivers will run isolated in a process named
'PrintIsolationHost'. This also means that if something were to
go wrong, only the drivers within that _solated process would be
potentially affected. And since it also runs separately from the
Spooler and CTX Print Management Service, it won't affect any
of the other users on the same system. The same rules apply to
the Isolated mode, only here the isolation part will get applied
on a per print driver basis. For each print driver a separate
'PrintIsolationHost' process will be created and will run
completely separate from all other drivers and services as
mentioned above.

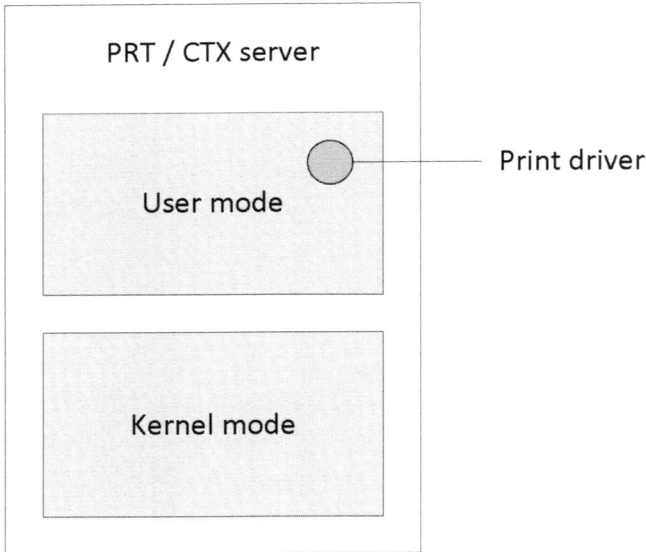

Figure 47: Print driver runs isolated in user mode

When isolating multiple print drivers on a one to one basis, meaning a separate 'PrintIsolationHost' process per print driver, more local resources will be consumed and thus needed, something to be aware of before implementing. Also, and this is not just me talking, you might want to think about why a specific print driver might need to be isolated from all others in the first place, and if it's worth implementing such a driver onto your production environment at all.

> **FMA fact**: Perhaps you are better off using None and Shared mode in production and use Isolated for troubleshooting purposes only, which of course could apply to production as well, only temporarily.

Version 4

As off Windows Server 2012 we also have version 4 mode drivers, which are still user-based print drivers and can also be isolated. So basically all of the above applies here as well. They are designed to handle the more modern Metro-style applications and are based on the XPS print file format exclusively. They are supposed to support a larger number of different printer types; they are more stable, or so I have been told, support enhanced printer sharing, and should be a lot easier to install and maintain.

Citrix Print Management Service

It was first introduced in 2005, which was around the same time as the EMF-based universal print driver. It has multiple responsibilities, capabilities and handles a few different tasks with regard to the CTX print process. For one it directly communicates with the Print Spooler service, see image on the next page.

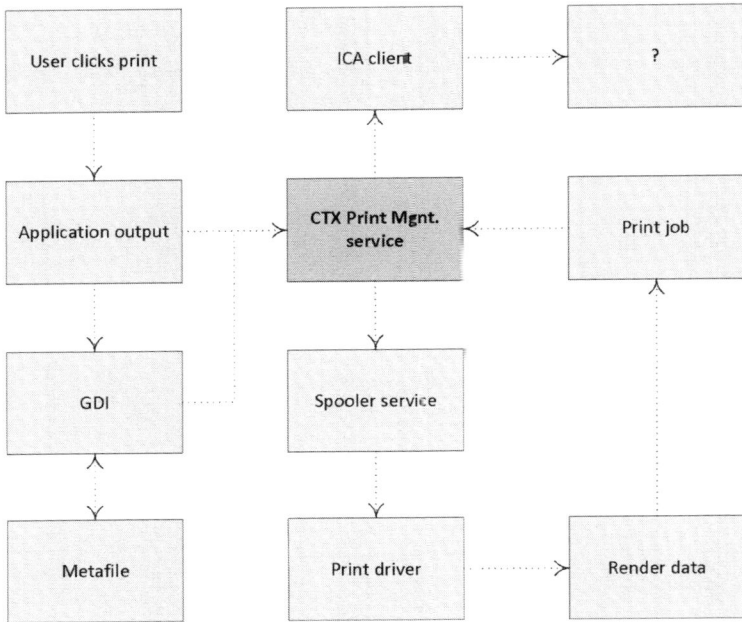

Figure 48: Citrix Print Management service

It can communicate with the locally installed ICA Client when needed (when the client printing pathway is used) and also compresses data before it is sent over the ICA channel. It is in charge of the ICA virtual channel for client printer mapping / creation within your CTX session. Which is good to know when troubleshooting auto-create printer failures.

What's wrong today?

Now that we've talked about some of the (Microsoft) print specifics that come into play when dealing with printing in a Citrix-orientated environment, what is wrong today when dealing with Citrix printing? Well, to be honest, not that much has changed. We still have to deal with delayed logons and printing, services that crash, blue screens, CPU spikes, auto-creation failures, and more. And if we can related these types of issues back to Citrix printing (since there can be dozens of reasons why all this may happen) then in most cases it is still because of faulty print drivers and badly designed print architecture set-ups.

The Citrix Printing Pathways

A printing pathway basically defines how print traffic can or will be routed throughout our environment. It also tells us where a job gets processed, spooled and so on.

Depending on the types of end points we use, the way we provision printers, including the physical set-up of our XenApp and/or print servers and physical print devices, we can partly influence how print traffic will be routed, and use it to our advantage. Before we have a look at both pathways, client and network, I'd like to start with a set-up referred to as server local printers: see below.

Server local printers

A server local printers configuration is nothing more than attaching a physical printer directly to a XenApp server. Probably a set-up you won't come across that often, but potentially useful nonetheless. From a client perspective, when a document is printed, spooling will take place locally on the XenApp server, leveraging local resources, before sending the output to the actual physical print device.

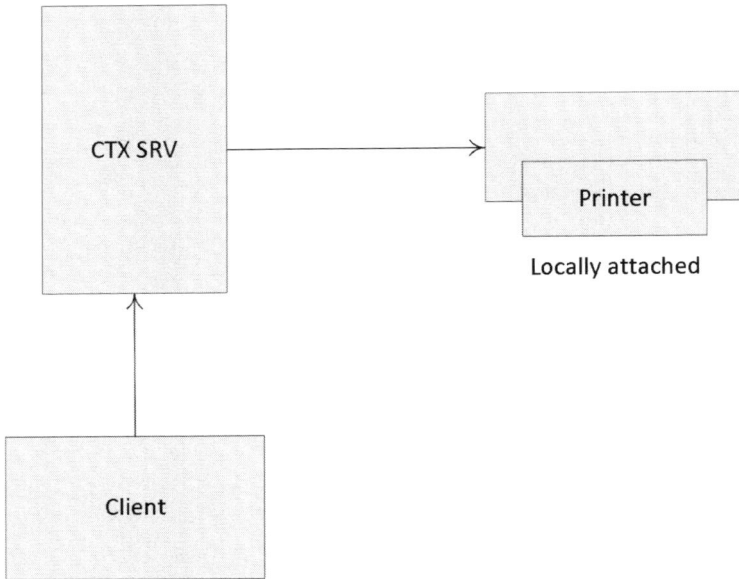

Figure 49: Server local printers setup

The client printing pathway

Although you have a few options with regard to configuring the client printing pathway (we'll get to those in a minute), the best way to explain and illustrate how it works is by assuming that, on the users client device a locally attached printer has been configured. By default, there is no print server involved. The client part refers to print traffic generated on the Citrix (XenApp) server being redirected back to the client device from where it will be forwarded to the actual physical printer.

This is what happens... A user will have a session on the Citrix (XenApp) server. As soon as he or she clicks 'print', the application print output will be spooled / rendered on the Citrix server (turning it into an actual print job) before sending it back (over ICA) to the client device. From a client / user perspective this means that spooling takes place locally, again leveraging local resources on the XenApp server.

Here it is important to note that both the client device as well as the Citrix (XenApp) server will have the Citrix Receiver / ICA protocol installed. When the spooled print job is sent back from the Citrix (XenApp) server to the client device this is done using, or over, the ICA protocol / virtual channels, and thus the data sent can be controlled, meaning compressed, limited etc. This is very useful, especially when the client device and the XenApp server are physically separated from each other. See image below.

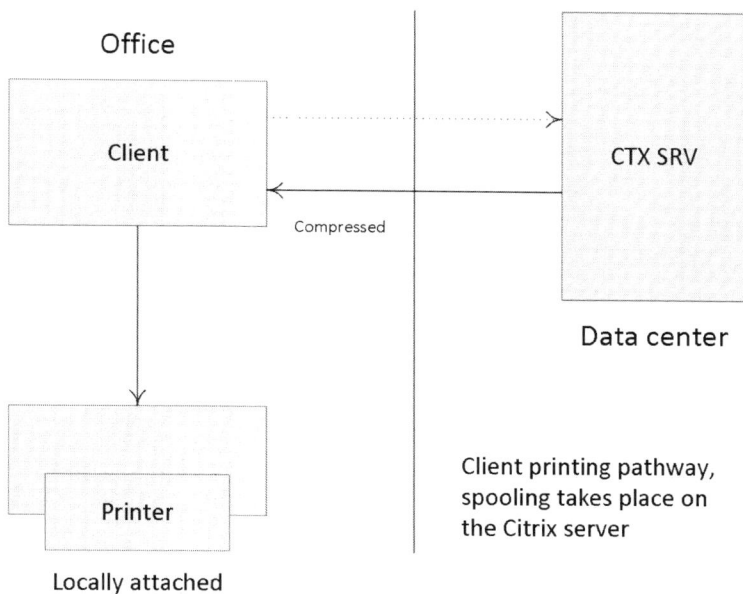

Figure 50: The client printing pathway

> **FMA fact**: As a side note, most thin client devices are
> based on Linux, as a result they will not be able to locally
> handle and process the earlier mentioned print jobs. As a
> result of this, the client printing pathway will only work
> with Windows-based (fat) client devices.

Also note that when a locally attached printer is configured, and
again this will only work on a Windows (fat) client device – the
client printing pathway – will be enforced, meaning that the
application print output / the print job will always be sent back
to the client device.

Stay tuned because we have a few more 'use cases' to discuss
when it comes to the client printing pathway.

The network printing pathway

When using network-provisioned print devices (print server) by
default, Citrix will try and use the network printing pathway
whenever possible. The process... Again as a user you will have
an active session on one of the Citrix (XenApp) servers. This
time, after you hit print, the print output will be sent over to the
print server (spooler service) where it will get spooled /
rendered into a print job before being sent over to physical print
device.

From a client perspective, spooling will take place remotely,
leveraging remote resources. As opposed to the client printing
pathway, here only the Citrix (XenApp) server will have the
Receiver / ICA protocol installed: the print server does not
know how, and is unable to communicate using the ICA
protocol / virtual channels. As a result, all traffic sent between
the XenApp server and the print server will be unmanageable
and thus uncompressed.

When the XenApp server and the print server are situated close together this won't be too big an issue.

But when the XenApp server is located in the data centre and the print server is near the users, in one of the branch offices, for example this might cause a potential problem, as we will see in another example coming up.

Another thing that needs to be taken into account is that the print job sent from the print server to the physical print device will also be sent in an uncompressed state. So again, when the print server is located near the users, in the branch office as mentioned above, this won't be an issue. But if the print server is located back in the datacentre, near the XenApp server, this is something to keep an eye on as well.

Office

Client ....> CTX SRV

Network printing pathway,
spooling takes place on the
print server.

Uncompressed

Printer

PRT SRV

Network provisioned

Data center

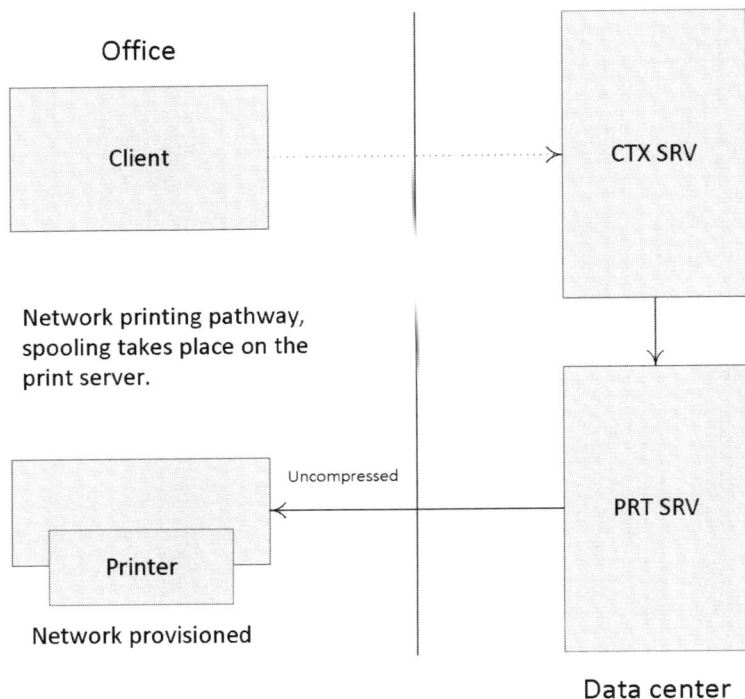

Figure 51: The network printing pathway

FMA fact: So you see that it's not just one thing, it is everything combined that makes or breaks your print architecture: the type of end points you use, policies configured, including the physical placement of your machines, including printers.

Note that it is the same as before only here I say 'try'. This is because with the network printing pathway there are several dependencies before the actual network printing pathway can and will be used. For example, if the Citrix (XenApp) server and the print server are not in the same domain, or are unable to communicate, then, instead of the network printing pathway, the client printing pathway will be used.

So keep in mind, that if this happens and you are using thin client devices, chances are that printing won't be possible at all.

FMA fact: If for whatever reason the Citrix (XenApp) server and the print server are unable to communicate with each other, again the client printing pathway will be used (forced) instead.

So now you may think, well, that's not so bad because when the client printing pathway is used my print traffic will be compressed since it will leverage the ICA protocol. And, although that might be true, this approach can also work against you, as you will soon find out.

Forcing the client printing pathway

As we've seen, when Citrix is involved and you are using network-provisioned printers, it will always try to use the network printing pathway first. However, there might be situations where, although a print server is involved, you would prefer to use the client printing pathway instead.

Let's assume that your Citrix (XenApp) server is located back in the data centre and that the print server is located near your users, as I've already specifically mentioned a few times. Since traffic sent between the two will be unmanaged / uncompressed you want to be careful with this type of set-up, especially when the branch office and the data centre are geographically separated. See the next page voor a visual overview.

Data center

Office

Client

CTX SRV

Network printing pathway,
spooling takes place on the
print server.

PRT SRV

Printer

Uncompressed

Network provisioned

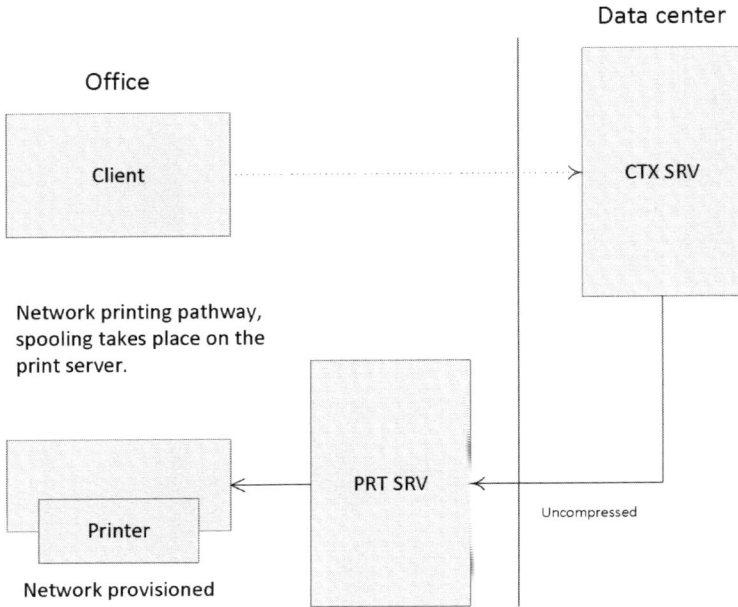

Figure 52: Print server near user

What we can do here is force the system to leverage the client
printing pathway instead of the network printing pathway by
disabling the 'Direct connection to print server' policy. By
disabling this policy all traffic will be routed through the client
printing pathway by default. Interesting, right?

Direct connections to print servers

Applies to: Virtual Delivery Agent: 5.6 Feature Pack 1, 7.0 Server OS, 7.0 Desktop OS, 7.1 Server OS, 7.1 Desktop OS, 7.5 Server OS, 7.5 Desktop OS, 7.6 Server OS, 7.6 Desktop OS, 7.7 Server OS, 7.7 Desktop OS, 7.8 Server OS, 7.8 Desktop OS

○ Enabled
  Make direct connections from host to print server for client printers hosed on an accessible network share

◉ Disabled
  Do not make direction connections

Figure 53: Direct connections to print server policy

So now, instead of sending the application print output over to the print server it will first be sent back to the client device over the ICA channel and thus manageable (compressed) from where it will be handed over to the print server, which will take over from there. And since those three, the client, the print server and the physical print device, are all close together, this will work like a charm.

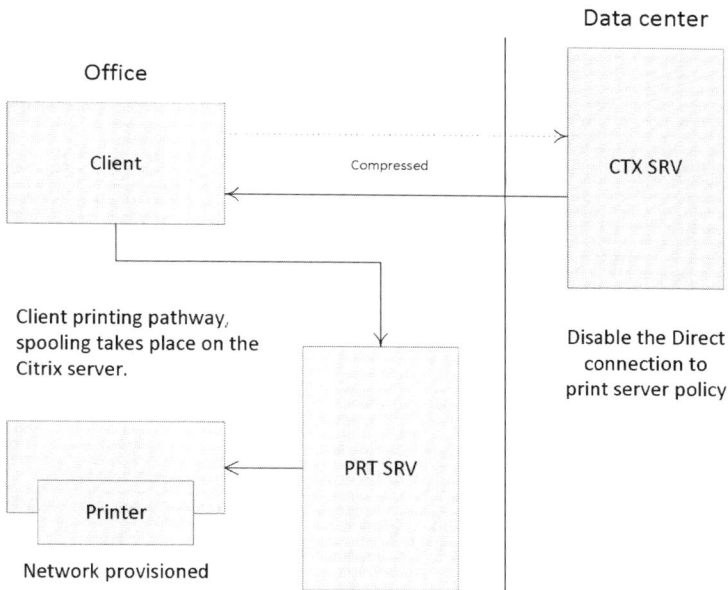

Figure 54: Forcing the client printing pathway

Exception to the rule...

And there always is. When the print server is back in the data centre, as mentioned and shown in one of my previous examples, this set-up, using the client printing pathway I mean, will only make things worse. Have a look at the image on the next page.

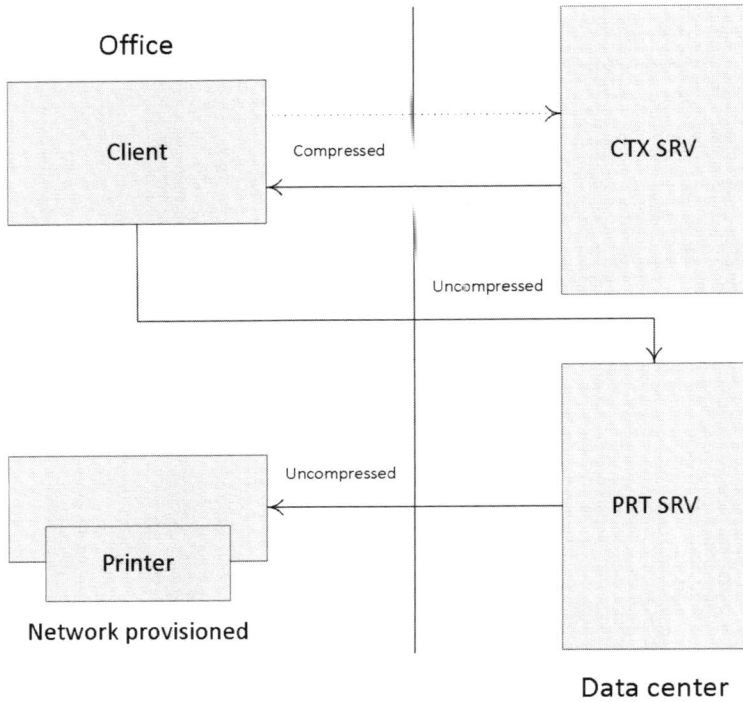

Figure 55: Client printing pathway gone wrong

Here we go again... Imagine you have a session on the Citrix (XenApp) server. You click 'print'. First the print output will be sent back to the client device, over ICA, compressed and so on. From there it needs to find its way over to the print server, and since it is located way back in the data centre: it will again need to traverse the WAN. And even more importantly, it will do so in an uncompressed state. And finally, when rendered etc., the print job needs to be sent to the actual physical print device back in the branch office. Again generating uncompressed traffic over the line. So you can see the inefficiency, right? Try to avoid this set-up at all times.

The Universal portfolio

This consists of the Universal Print Server, the Universal Print Driver and the perhaps lesser-known Universal Printer. Let's start with Universal Print Server. If you think back to my network printing pathway example where the print server was located in the branch office and the Citrix (XenApp) server in the data centre, you probably recall that traffic sent from the XenApp server to the print server was in an uncompressed state.

The Universal Print Server can help us to compress that data. Next to compression it is optimised for network printing scenarios and also works with thin client and tablet devices. It also supports both the EMF as well as XPF print file formats and uses the Universal Print Driver by default, which can be paired / combined with any number of native print drivers if and when needed.

The UPS is built up of a server and client component. The server component gets installed on the print server and the client component is installed on the XenApp server. As of FP3 for XenDesktop 7.6 the Universal Print Server is now officially supported on Windows Server 2012 R2 as well.

In simple terms this is what happens. After a user clicks 'print' the application produces some form of print output (EMF / XPS), this will be handed over to the local print subsystem (UPD) on the XenApp server. Since the Universal Print Server does not support any form of client side rendering, the print output will be immediately sent over to the Citrix UPClient component from where it is forwarded to the UPServer component.

372

This is the part where the print data can be controlled /
compressed. Finally the so-called Windows print subsystem on
the print server will handle (render, spool) it from there on.

Citrix server   Print server

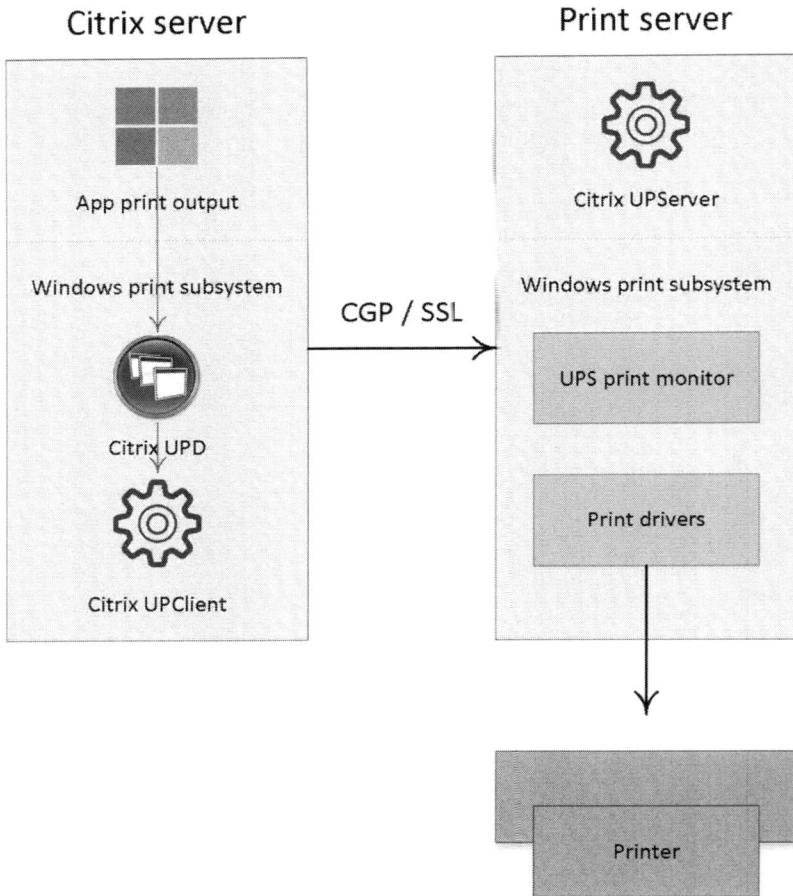

Figure 56: Universal Print Server setup

FMA fact: Proper testing will be necessary to ensure
that (enough) compression takes place.

Additionally, when the Universal Print Server is used you can configure a feature named 'proximity printing', which is based on session (network) printers. With proximity printing, session printer policies are filtered on IP address or subnet: based on your IP address or the subnet that you are in specific printers can be assigned. This way you will always have the printer that is closest mapped within your session.

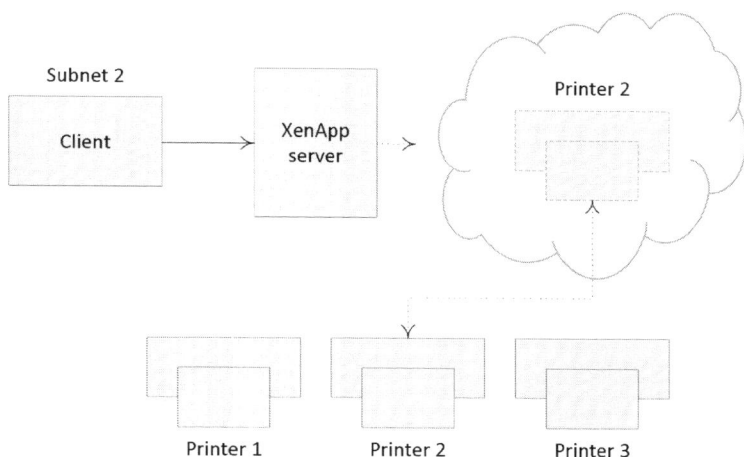

Figure 57: Proximity printing

The Universal Print Driver

This one is well known and has been around for a while now. It's basically meant as a one driver to rule them all kind of scenario, but we all know that is near to impossible. It does do a good enough job in most cases, though. One of the biggest things missing, and the main reason why we use it combined with other native drivers is the lack of enhanced printing capabilities.

As it stands today, it only supports stapling and sorting, that's about it. It is available in both EMF (default) as well as XPS and comes installed as part of the VDA installation. All you need to do is enable it since it will be disabled by default.

> **FMA fact**: Once enabled you might want to have a look at the 'Universal print driver usage and preference' policies. You have a bunch of options to select from.

The Universal Printer

Normally, when a user logs in and successfully establishes a session on the Citrix (XenApp) server, no default printers, or all printers known to the client, will be mapped into the session (default behaviour).

When you enable and configure the use of a Universal Printer, instead it will create a generic, or logical, print object at the beginning of the session. This means that no printer mapping or enumeration will take place at all, which will speed up the actual user login process.

This logical object is then virtually mapped to the client's default configured printer, although this can be configured to any printer known to the client device. As a side note, this will only work for Windows-based clients.

Let's speed things up a little

There are a couple of ways to speed up or improve Citrix printing. Some are reasonably simple and obvious, while others might need some additional consideration and planning:

- Configure and apply true QoS through Multi Stream ICA.
- Give the ICA virtual print channel a higher priority (be carefull with this).
- We can allocate, limit and control print traffic through policies, which can then be applied per user, server or for the whole Site.
- We can configure session (network) printers on fast(er) networks. Here you basically specify a bunch of specific network printers (could be only one just as easily) to be mapped within a session and assign them to users etc.
- Use the Universal Print Server for additional compression and QoS options.

FMA fact: Is printing slow? Remember that it isn't just about the bandwidth exclusively. Make sure to check for congestion and latency.

Key takeaways (warning... it's a big list)

- There are two main (Microsoft) print file formats, EMF and XPS.
- EMF print output is first rendered by the GDI – Graphics Device Interface – before being handed over to the spooler service.
- XPS was introduced as of Windows Vista. EMF development ended with Windows XP and Server 2003.
- EMF data is not compressed. XPS data does get compressed.
- With EMF, each image needs to be redrawn over and over again, even if the same image is used multiple times. XPS can reference a single image multiple times: think company logos, watermarks etc.
- To be able to use XPS, both your print device and the print driver need to support the XPS print file format. If not, it will fall back to EMF.
- High-level Print Spooling: Print output is received by the spooler service, print driver renders Metafile into raw data readable by print device (the actual print job), spooler service sends print job to physical print device.
- When spooled locally, local resources (CPU, memory) are leveraged. No network traffic is generated.
- When spooled remotely (print server) remote resources are leveraged. This will also produce additional network traffic between the XenApp and print server. Might be something to consider depending on your print architecture.
- Most print issues can be led back to badly written drivers. Not tested and/or optimised for multi-user environments.

- Main problems used to be (or still are): Spooler service crashes, CTX print manager service crashes, blue screens, auto-print creation failures, high CPU loads.
- Do NOT make use of kernel mode (version 2) print drivers.
- Use user mode (version 3 and 4) print drivers exclusively.
- Consider isolating your print drivers a.k.a. Print Driver Isolation introduced with Windows Server 2008 R2. But... only apply Print Driver Isolation where it makes sense.
- Version 4 modes print drivers: Designed for Metro-style applications (XPS), enhanced printer sharing, easier to install, maintain, manage etc.
- When a Citrix session starts, after the user logs in, it will, by default, try to map all printers known to the client device within the session.
- Change this behaviour to: map the client's default printer only. Configure the 'Auto-create client printers' policy for this. Of course you have multiple options to choose from.
- Tthe XenApp server will try to match the print driver (s) found on the client device. If the print driver cannot be found, the system attempts to install the driver from the Windows operating system. If the driver is not available in Windows it will (try and) use the Citrix Universal Print Driver (it will need to be enabled for this to work).
- Configure the 'Automatic installation of inbox printer drivers' to change this behaviour.
- Think about implementing 'printer driver mapping compatibility'. Print driver mapping is useful in situations where the print driver on the client is named

differently than the print driver on the server (these need to match), but offer the exact same functionality. It can also be configured to create a whitelist: this way you can tell the XenApp server that it is ok to auto-install print drivers when not found on the system, but only if those drivers are on the (white) list.

- Use 'signed' drivers exclusively and always thoroughly test your print architecture set-up, no matter how convinced you may be that it will work.
- Limit the number of print drivers installed: less is more!
- Avoid upgrading print drivers. Always uninstall the old driver and install the new one.
- Always match the print server OS to that of the XenApp server OS.
- The Citrix Print Management Service communicates with the spooler service and the local ICA Client, it compresses print data before sending it over the ICA channel, and also manages the ICA virtual channel for client print mapping.
- Printing preferences (user) and properties will be stored on the client device by default. If this is not supported, they will be stored in the user profile within the server Operating System.
- Configure the 'Printer properties retention' policy to change this. Again, you have multiple options.
- A printing pathway defines how print traffic can or will be routed throughout your environment. It also tells us where a job gets processed, spooled, rendered etc.
- There are two Citrix printing pathways: the client printing pathway and the network printing pathway.

- Besides these pathways there is also a set-up named 'Server local printers', which is basically a physical print device directly attached to a XenApp server.
- When using the client printing pathway, application print output is spooled / rendered on the XenApp server (local from a client perspective) before it is sent back to the client device.
- With the client printing pathway the traffic between the XenApp server and the client device is sent through the ICA protocol, meaning it can be managed / compressed.
- When a (fat) client device has a local printer attached, the client printing pathway will always be used.
- When TCP/IP direct printers are added manually or by using / applying Group Policy Preferences, the printer is seen and treated as a locally attached printer. As such, print traffic will flow through the client printing pathway.
- Thin client devices (Linux-based) do not support the client printing pathway. They lack local printing capabilities. The network printing pathway (session printers) will need to be used instead.
- The network printing pathway will send the application print output from the XenApp server to the print server where it will be spooled / rendered. Spooling takes place remotely. From there it will send the print job to the physical print device.
- Using the network printing pathway all traffic sent between the XenApp server and the print server will be uncompressed / unmanaged, non-ICA.

- The Universal Print Server can help compress / manage traffic sent between the XenApp server and the print server.
- When a client device has a network-provisioned (print server) printer, Citrix will always try and route print traffic over the network printing pathway.
- I say 'try', because if the print server and the XenApp server are in different domains and they are unable to communicate, the client printing pathway will be used instead. The same applies when both machines are unable to communicate for other reasons.
- By disabling the 'Direct connection to print servers' policy, we can force the client printing pathway to be used, even when network-provisioned printers are leveraged.
- There is no 'one size fits all', period!
- Keeping the XenApp and print server close together isn't always the best solution.
- All this applies to XenApp as well as XenDesktop, and isn't IMA- or FMA-specific.
- The Universal Print Driver (UPD) is disabled by default.
- The UPD is installed as part of the VDA.
- There is an EMF as well as an XPS print file format UPD.
- The EMF UPD will be used by default. This can be changed through policy.
- Both the Universal Print Server and the Universal Printer use the Universal Print Driver by default.
- The Universal Printer is a logical / generic object created at the beginning of a session. It will be mapped to the client's default printer but this can be changed to any printer known to the client device.

- When using the Universal Printer, no print mapping / enumeration takes place, speeding up the logon / login process.
- The Universal Printer only works for Windows devices.
- It is potentially useful when the 'Wait for printer to be created' policy is used or when you need access to multiple printers, local & network.
- The Universal Print Server (UPS) consists of a client (UPClient) and server (UPServer) component.
- It uses the UPD by default but can be paired with Windows Native print drivers, again, for more enhanced printing capabilities.
- It's optimised for network printers and offers additional compression and QoS options.
- It supports both EMF and XPS-based print drivers.
- It also works for thin client devices and tablets, based on network (session) printers.
- The UPS does not support client side rendering / spooling, meaning that all application print output will be sent over to the print server (which has the UPServer component installed) right away.
- All traffic sent between the XenApp (UPClient component) and print server (UPServer component) can be managed / compressed when enabling the UPS.
- Network printers will leverage the UPS automatically through a process called auto-discovery.
- It can handle up to 50 print jobs per minute.
- Recommended for remote office scenarios. Please note that testing will be necessary to see if adequate compression ratios are achieved.
- Helps in managing a large number of network printers.

- Can be used for proximity printing. The UPS is a prerequisite.
- Use session (network) printers on fast(er) networks.
- Session printers are network printers that can be assigned and mapped to a specific user or user groups.
- With proximity printing, sessions are filtered based on IP addresses or subnets (there are some more options). This way a user will always connect to the closest printer (UPS is needed).
- When dealing with slow printing remember that it's not all about network bandwidth. Also check for congestion and latency.
- The 'simpler' the print driver, the less traffic will be generated. Use vendor drivers only when specific functionality is needed.
- Last-minute addition from the E-docs pages: XenApp and XenDesktop 7.6 FP3 include an Always-On logging feature for the print server and printing subsystem on the VDA. In order to collate the logs as a ZIP for emailing, or to automatically upload to Citrix Insight Services, use the PowerShell cmdlet (Start-TelemetryUpload) supplied with the VDA installer in 7.6 FP3.
- Citrix Printing Tool 3.1 helps configuring and troubleshooting the Citrix Printing subsystem on XenApp, XenApp Online Plug-in and XenDesktop.
- Print Detective is an information-gathering utility that can be used for troubleshooting problems related to print drivers. It enumerates all printer drivers from the specified Windows machine, including driver-specific information. It can also be used to delete specified print

drivers. It allows for log file capabilities and provides a command-line interface as well.

- All-purpose troubleshooting tool – Run Citrix Scout from a single XenDesktop controller (DDC) or XenApp server to capture key data points and CDF traces for selected computers followed by a secure and reliable upload of the data package to Citrix Technical Support.
- The Citrix UPS Print Driver Certification Tool can be used to test the compatibility of a print driver with the Citrix Universal Print Server.
- Not sure? Test your print drivers thoroughly using StressPrinters.
- Check out Microsoft's (MSDN) web page to find out more about Print Driver Isolation.
- Release data: February 2012, primarily focused on XenApp 6.5: XenApp Printer Driver Manager. Manage your XenApp print drivers. Update the Automatic Printer Replication List with a GUI.
- A collection of Citrix troubleshooting and diagnostic tools: CtxAdmTools.

Troubleshooting the FlexCast Management Architecture

Troubleshooting the FMA

When it comes to troubleshooting our XenDesktop and/or XenApp environments there are a lot of (free) tools that can be of assistance. Some are aimed at solving a specific issues, while other tools are more generic and can be helpful in multiple ways. However, while this is all great, I do think that a lot of IT administrators forget about the basics: you need to know and understand the products that you are working with before anything else, here's my list of things to think about when it comes troubleshooting, and note that these bullets apply to all sorts of technologies / products, not just Citrix:

- You need to understand the architecture you are dealing with, the FMA in our case. Its main components and services, communication paths, and so on.
- Expected behaviour and interaction: how does it all work under 'normal' circumstances?
- Traffic flow throughout the infrastructure and its components: this helps to identify potential bottlenecks.
- Assemble a personal tool kit. As mentioned, we have a lot of tools at our disposal: sometimes it can be hard to find out what the exact purpose of a tool is or how it should be operated. By doing some research beforehand this will potentially save you valuable time when things do go wrong. And we all know this is going to happen sooner or later, right?
- Only when you apply the first three steps you will be able to know where and when to apply which tool.
- Know where to find information. This may sound a bit silly, but it doesn't hurt to go over some of the options you have when it comes to finding useful information. Which forums do you visit? Think about (ex-)colleagues

or community folks you can contact. Perhaps make yourself a top 10 of blog authors and so on. Give this some thought. And don't forget about social media.

Efficiency and general tips

When troubleshooting, it is all about efficiency: fixing an issue should take as little time as possible. This calls for a structured approach or methodology: Investigate, Analyse and Implement.

First of all it needs to be acknowledged that there actually is a problem. Who is your source? The helpdesk, the company's CEO, a user who always has something to complain about? I think you know where I am going with this, right?

Secondly, you need to know, or find out what is going on, what the actual issue is. How many users or departments etc. are affected? How do they describe what is going on? Talk to your users and the Helpdesk.

What is the overall impact to the business and beyond? Are there any business critical systems and/or processes involved? If you are dealing with a potential major outage, try to estimate the amount of time and resources needed to come up with a potential fix, even if it is just temporary. Can the problem be reproduced? Whom do we need to talk to?

As mentioned, try to isolate the issue: which components and/or services are actually affected? Plan accordingly.

What do the event logs tell us? A Doctor Watson log perhaps. Is there any monitoring software in use? What does it tell us? Were there any changes made to the environment during the last couple of days or hours even? Maybe Studio and/or Director can help, see previous chapters on this as well. A simple PING or Tracert might tell us something more.

My point is: start small and take the relatively 'easy' steps first, try to make some progress. Are there any quick fixes you can try or implement? Is there a workaround available?

All this is exactly why those first few bullets are so important.

By preparing yourself in times of 'peace' you can and will save yourself valuable time when things start to go wrong. Once you have familiarised yourself with the basics as mentioned previously, you are good to go. Here are some more general troubleshooting tips I picked up along the way:

- Never try to guess the solution: always base your actions on facts.
- Don't assume anything, no matter how obvious it may seem. You know what they say about assumptions, right?
- Try to isolate the issue, make it smaller and take it step by step.
- Make sure to inventorise all information found.
- Categorise and prioritise information. Once you have an idea of what some of your next steps might be, and a lot of the time you will have multiple options, think about what to do first, second etc. For example, you might want to try the option with the least impact first. List your options and prioritise them; always have a plan B, though.

- Come up with a morning ritual. We have all been there: an issue that seemed obvious to solve, which two weeks later is still giving you grey hairs. In most cases a lot of the same people will be involved on a daily basis. By getting together at the start of the day, only if it is for five to ten minutes, everybody knows what the (attack) plan for the day is and what he or she needs to be doing. Any progress and/or setbacks can also be discussed, including any actions that need to be taken etc.
- Make sure to assign a specific issue or problem to a person. This way you have a single point of reference, which also helps during the earlier-mentioned morning ritual.
- Keep track of what you have been doing individually, and as a team when applicable. You don't want to run the same tests over and over, or install a certain hotfix for the third time without even knowing about it, do you? I think this particular point is often underestimated. It can save you a serious amount of time and effort.
- Think out loud and share information. I don't think I have to explain what I mean with this one.
- Do not forget about social media. The potential 'reach' you have on Twitter, to name one, is amazing. Even if you do not have hundreds or thousands of followers, a single retweet might do the trick.
- And finally, another BIG one: Ask for help! Don't think you know it all, because you don't. When in doubt, ask! You do not want to be the one responsible for making a big problem even worse, just because you were not 100% sure of what to do.

Troubleshooting in action

Throughout this next section I will list several issues, solutions, troubleshooting steps, tips and tricks, troubleshooting tools, articles and other potential, hopefully helpful material.

XDDBDiag

The XenDesktop Database Diagnostic tool. It was first designed with XenDesktop version 5 but can be used with all new 7.x editions as well. This command-line support tool performs a consistency data check on the data and connectivity verification in a XenDesktop database. A great tool to do some proactive administrating as well. Diagnostic output can be saved in the form of a comma-separated value (.CSV) file located in a compressed file (.zip) named:

Computername_XDDBDiag_Output.zip to the same directory in which the programme is located. It provides the following information:

- Site information
- Virtual Desktop Agent information
- Current connections / Connection log
- Hypervisor connections
- Policy information
- Desktop group
- Controller information
- SQL information, and more.

It will automatically search for new updates when launched, but this is something that can easily be turned off as well. Check out the following CTX article for some more details on how to use it: CTX128075.

XDPing

Another command-line tool originating back to XenDesktop version 5 and commonly used to trace and track down connectivity issues. As of version 2.2 the XDPing tool also supports all current XenDesktop 7.x editions. It automates the process of checking for the causes of common configuration issues in a XenDesktop environment. The tool can be used to verify configuration settings on both the XenDesktop Broker and VDA machines, both from the console and remotely. Read through this CTX article to see which command-line options you have when executing the tool; it also includes a short video on how to use it: CTX123278. It can also monitor and check certain XenDesktop services information and query the local event log to check for known events that are related to XenDesktop. All in all a great tool to handle some of those more common proactive admin tasks as well.

Services and logs overview

With both XenDesktop & XenApp, it is important to understand what is taking place under the covers, which processes and services are involved when enumerating applications, connecting and disconnecting users, provisioning new machines etc. Having said that, with XenDesktop we can enable something called service logging.

Service logging can be enabled either from the command-line or through Citrix Scout (installed by default on XenDesktop and XenApp Delivery Controllers) using a Graphical User Interface. Just keep in mind that Scout still lacks the ability to log data for certain services like the Broker Agent: this is part of the VDA as of version 7.x (an important one). When you enable service logging using the command-line, all services will be available. Other services that can be monitored using Scout include, the

ADIdentity, Broker, Configuration, Host, Machine Identity and Machine Creation services. This is what a manual command-line may look like:

Citrix.MachineCreation.SdkWcfEndpoint.exe-LogFile C:\XDLogs\Name.log

Next to the Delivery Controller (Broker Service log) and the VDA (VDA Broker Agent log) the PortICA service a.k.a. the ICA Service is probably one of the most important ones to keep an eye on (and log information on) when troubleshooting connectivity issues. It handles just about everything from an ICA / HDX perspectice except for direct communication with the Delivery Controller.

Read this CTX article for more information on VDA Broker Agent logging: CTX117452.

PortICA logging, in addition to enabling the VDA Broker Agent log, can also be (very) useful when troubleshooting issues regarding the Desktop Virtual Desktop Agent (VDA). PortICA logging is not enabled by default on the VDA. Check out: CTX118837. More on this as we progress.

HDX Monitor

This tool will provide you with detailed diagnostics information on all HDX technologies known today. HDX Monitor version 3.x has been upgraded to also support version XenDesktop version 7.x, as well as XenApp 6.5. This CTX article will tell you all you need to know: CTX135817. Note that HDX Monitor is built into Director as well.

Scout

As of XenDesktop and XenApp 7.5, Citrix Scout is installed on your Delivery Controllers by default. It is a powerful tool that combines, or aggregates, a bunch of the individual tools discussed throughout this chapter. In fact, if you have a quick peek in the Scout installation directory, the Utilities folder to be exact, you'll see that there are several applications listed, CDF control being one of them.

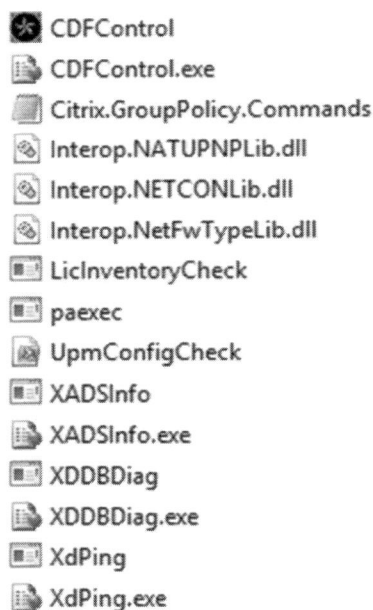

- CDFControl
- CDFControl.exe
- Citrix.GroupPolicy.Commands
- Interop.NATUPNPLib.dll
- Interop.NETCONLib.dll
- Interop.NetFwTypeLib.dll
- LicInventoryCheck
- paexec
- UpmConfigCheck
- XADSInfo
- XADSInfo.exe
- XDDBDiag
- XDDBDiag.exe
- XdPing
- XdPing.exe

Figure 58: Scout utilities folder

These applications can be started just as if they were downloaded separately and will include all features and functionality that you might be used to no exceptions. CDF control is an important one; it is used by Scout to perform the actual CDF tracing locally or on the remote machine.
After clicking the 'Start CDF Trace' button, one of the first

things you'll do is select the machines to run the actual CDF trace on. The Delivery Controller from where Scout is started will be selected by default.

Prerequisites

You won't be able to actually perform a CDF trace, or much else for that matter, until you have made sure that certain prerequisites are met. This is what needs to be in place:

- Local administrative privileges on the Delivery Controller
- Local administrative privileges on the remote machines
- WinRM needs to be enabled / configured on the remote machine
- Remote Registry needs to be enabled on the remote machines
- File and print sharing needs to be enabled on the remote machines
- All machines need to share the same domain
- .NET Framework 3.5 with SP1 or .NET 4.0
- Microsoft PowerShell 2.0.

If the selection will include any remote machines, Scout will immediately check if it is able to communicate with these machines: this is where some of the earlier mentioned prerequisites come into play. If it runs into any issues while trying to connect it will tell you what is wrong. File and print sharing, WinRM or perhaps Remote Registry, needs to be enabled on the remote machine.

Collecting data

The second big feature of Scout. It enables you to collect data (referred to as Data points) related to the systems BIOS, the OS installed, memory information and drivers; it also reads certain registry keys, system and application event logs, Site and Farm information, WinRM settings, and a lot more!

Data needs to be collected before it can be automatically uploaded to Citrix. First you need to select a certain number of machines from where data will be collected, reviewed and eventually uploaded (this is also where Citrix Insight Services comes into play). You can select up to 10 machines in total. Once collected the data will first be analysed, and if any possible corrective actions are found they will be shown on-screen, giving you the option to execute them. Next you will be asked to choose a location where you would like to store the data in a .zip format.

Once the data is saved you will be presented with a dialogue explaining the upload & analysis process. Click Continue on this to proceed. Then the Upload to Insight Services dialogue appears: enter your My Citrix Username, password etc. and click Upload. The status report is sent directly to Citrix Technical Support. An MD5 checksum test is performed to ensure your upload was successful. Also see Insigth Services on page 402.

PortICA / picaSvc2.exe logging

When performing a CDF trace, by default, all main FMA services will be included (although you are able to manually exclude services: more on this in a bit) during a CDF trace: all except for one, the PortICA service. Before I continue, it's important to understand that the PortICA service, renamed as picaSvc2.exe as of XenDesktop 7.x and also known or referred to as the ICA Service, is one of the most important services when it comes to your virtual desktop infrastructure (VDI). It 'lives' on your desktop OS-based VMs (VDAs) and as mentioned earlier, it takes care of almost everything that is going on the machine except for direct communication with the Delivery Controller (Desktop service). If you have a closer look at the involvement of the PicaSvc2 service during the initial user connection phase, I think it goes without saying that you want to always include the PortICA service, when running a CDF trace, for example. The same goes for any clear text / verbose logging that you might enable. Fortunately we can enable the PortICA service by hand to be included in these kinds of traces / logs.

Enable logging

PortICA logging can be enabled in two ways; the first one is by hand. CTX118837 will tell and show you exactly what needs to be done. You will first need to create an XML file (PortICAConfig): copy and paste the content listed in the abovementioned CTX document, save it etc. Just follow the steps in the CTX doc and you will be fine. I probably make it sound harder than it actually is. The second method is by using Scout. This will basically automate the above steps for you.

There is no difference between the two except that Scout offers you a GUI and you won't have to manually create, or copy and paste anything. Again, it will depend on the type of issue you are troubleshooting whether this will work for you, you might want to enable PortICA logging by hand on one of your base images, for example. That would be a judgement call.

Anyway, this is how it's done using Scout. First you go into the Collect & Upload window, find the remote machine where you want to enable PortICA logging, and click on the settings icon. After that the 'WinRM/Service Log Settings' screen will appear and all you have to do is swipe the PortICA Service button to the right (On).

It is CDF in the background

Remember how I explained that Scout actually uses CDF control to run the CDF traces? What happens is that as soon as you click continue to start the trace, CDF control is copied over from the installation / utilities folder to the remote machine and is executed remotely. Once you click stop, CDF control will be deleted from the remote machine and all collected data will be copied over to the Delivery Controller from where Scout was originally started.

Read the following CTX article for more information on how to use Scout: CTX130147

CDF Control

CDF stands for Citrix Diagnostic Facility: it has been around for over eight years and is still one of the most used diagnostic tool kits used today! While built into Citrix Scout it's also available as a stand-alone download and fully supports all new XenDesktop editions. It is an event tracing controller/consumer, geared towards capturing Citrix Diagnostic Facility (CDF) trace messages that are output from the various Citrix tracing providers (will be explained the next section). Note that you will need to have local administrative permissions to be able to start tracing. Here's where to get it and how to use it: CTX111961.

Consider it to be good practice to try and collect some CDF traces prior to opening up a support case with Citrix, since this is probably one of the first things they'll have you do, unless you are in doubt on where to start, of course.

Where does the information come from?

Every Citrix component (like a Delivery Controller) is split into a certain amount categories a.k.a. trace providers. A category can be everything related to USB, or ICA traffic, printing, FMA services, profile management, provision services, and so on and so forth: there are a few dozen in total. These categories are divided into several modules, and these modules consist of various so-called trace messages.

Now, when a CDF trace is run again, using Scout or CDF control, diagnostics information is collected by reading the trace messages from the various modules, and this is what actually gets logged as part of the trace. When a trace message gets called upon or is read, it will respond with its current state, which could be an error code telling us what's wrong.

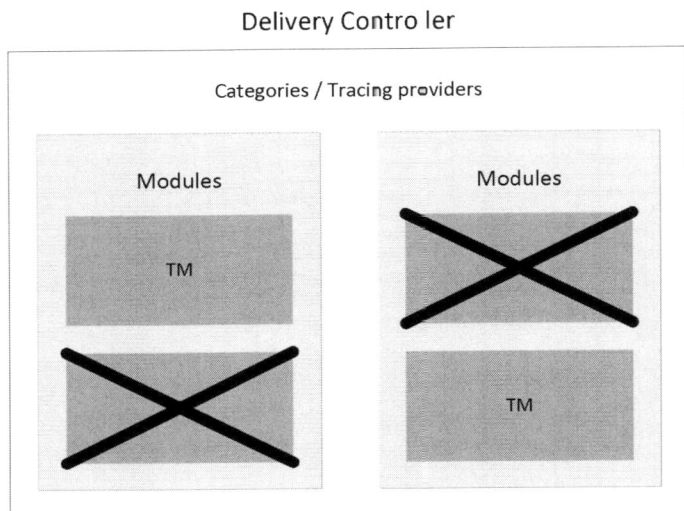

Figure 59: CDF tracing modules

The number of modules, and thus trace messages, per Citrix component will differ. A Delivery Controller will hold a lot more modules / trace messages than a virtual machine as part of your VDI deployment, for example. If you open up CDF control on a Delivery Controller you'll see exactly what I mean.

Trace Message Format files

Once you have stopped the trace, either using the stand-alone CDF Trace tool or from within Scout, the collected information will be saved in the following folder:

AppData\Local\Temp\Scout\ of the logged-on user executing the trace.

All CDF traces will be saved with the .etl extension. At this time you could just grab the data, zip it, and send it over to CTX Support as (perhaps) requested.

Or maybe CTX isn't involved (yet) and you want to have a look
for yourself; or both. As soon as you open the .etl file, perhaps
using a tool like WordPad, you'll notice that the letters, numbers
and other characters displayed won't make much sense to the
human eye.

When a CDF trace is started and the trace messages are read
from the modules, the information that gets logged is partly in
the form of GUIDs. Which means that these (.etl) files will first
need to be parsed, or translated if you will, before they will make
any sense at all.

As mentioned, the .etl files first need to be parsed before they
become readable. To be able to this you'll need at least two
things: first, a tool that is able to do the parsing for you; and
secondly, TMF files which hold the instructions for parsing and
formatting the binary trace messages generated by Scout and/or
CDF control. As you can read in the below statement / quote,
TMF files aren't thought up by Citrix, it's more of a general
approach: The trace message format (TMF) file is a structured
text file that contains instructions for parsing and formatting the
binary trace messages that a trace provider generates.

The formatting instructions are included in the trace provider's
source code and are added to the trace provider's PDB symbol
file by the WPP preprocessor. Some tools that log and display
formatted trace messages require a TMF file. Tracefmt and
TraceView, WDK tools that format and display trace messages,
can use a TMF file or they can extract the formatting
information directly from a PDB symbol file. In the Citrix world
we would use CDF control and/or CDF Monitor for this.

There are two types of TMF files available, public and private. Public TMF files are the ones we use for personal file parsing. The private TMF files are for CTX Support eyes only, something to keep in mind. Public TMF files can be acquired in two ways, you can download them directly from the Internet by using CDF control, or you can contact an online TMF server, live parsing your .etl files.

I would advice to always try and download the TMF files whenever possible. When you try to parse large files directly from the Internet using an online TMF server and the connection fails, or perhaps you are on a high-latency line, or the TMF servers are, or go, offline at some point (which isn't unusual, by the way) you will have to start all over again. Of course you will first have to wait until the TMF servers are reachable again. Next to that, if you need to parse large traces: this could take a long time when applying the online parse method.

It also has to be noted that parsing, and especially reading CDF traces (.etl files), is something not to be taken lightly. With this I mean that, although the parsing of .etl files is a relatively easy process, the reading of these files, once they are parsed, is something else. You'll need some special skills to be able to actually find the error or fault causing your issue. Then again, it could be something you're into, or perhaps you're curious and just want to have a look to see what's in there: all are valid reasons to go and have a peek.

Citrix Support

Imagine yourself digging deep into a CDF trace: you have narrowed it down to just a few specific modules and you know exactly what to look for and what is most likely causing your issue, whatever it may be. It could happen that the publicly available TMF files are not sufficient and that you need some of the private TMF files to parse a specific part of the trace that will expose your issue. What to do? That's right, you need to contact Citrix Support. Of course in a scenario like this you will probably be finished quickly since you will be able to pinpoint what needs to be parsed to find out what's wrong. But still, you'll need a support contract for this to happen.

Citrix Print Detective

This tool has been around for a few years now and as of version 1.2.1.5 it also supports XenDesktop 7. Print Detective is an information-gathering utility that can be used for troubleshooting problems related to print drivers. It enumerates all printer drivers from the specified Windows machine, including driver-specific information. It can also be used to delete specified print drivers. It allows for log file capabilities and provides a command-line interface as well. It supports all of Microsoft's desktop and server platforms. How to use Print Detective? Go to: CTX116474.

Insight Services

Insight Services is the glue binding it all together: here you can upload your log and trace files and link them to any support cases you might have registered earlier. Once you upload a file, Insight Services will automatically analyse your log files and scan them for hundreds of known issues. From their website: Citrix Insight Services reads log files from XenDesktop, XenServer, XenApp, NetScaler, PVS, ByteMobile, XenMobile, CloudBridge, CPBM and XD/XA Connector, and we'll be adding products to it over time. We're adding new plug-ins that capture known issues for these products all the time. So Citrix Insight Services will keep getting better.

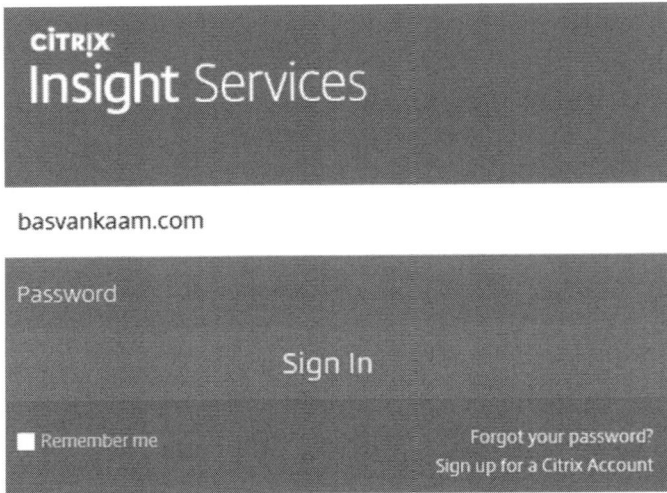

Figure 60: Insight Services login

When Citrix Insight Services discovers any known issues in your environment, it suggests hotfixes, patches and updates with red/yellow/green prioritisation. It will also analyse your configuration and give you best-practice advice, with links to relevant articles or white papers.

Citrix Insight Services isn't just for troubleshooting. It's also a great way to give your infrastructure a quick Health Check, so you can spot any issues before they become real problems. Got to https://cis.citrix.com and make sure to read through CTX131233 for more information around Insight Services.

Call Home and CIS in Director

As it did before, Citrix Call Home performs periodic collections of your system and product configuration, plus performance, error, and other information. As of XenDesktop version 7.8 this information can now be automatically (this can be scheduled to your needs and/or preferences) sent to Citrix Insight Services for proactive analysis and resolution.

Also new in version 7.8 is the ability to access Citrix Insight Services instantly from Director by means of a drop-down menu. This way you can easily access all information collected through Call Home and Scout combined.

PowerShell

While PowerShell can be used in many ways to configure and troubleshoot XenDesktop and/or XenApp architectures, here I would like to focus on the main infrastructural services that make up the FMA. The states of your FMA services are best checked using PowerShell.

Using some of the PowerShell Get- commandlets when checking up on your FMA services will show you exactly what is going on, when and if something is wrong. It's much more detailed and reliable than using the Windows services.msc console.

If you have a central management server, or multiple I suggest you create a personal PowerShell profile and include some of the basic Get- FMA service checks in it. This way, every time you open PowerShell these basic checks will be done automatically before you continue. If you look at Director, on the main dashboard, there you also see your Delivery Controllers listed at the bottom of the screen. If all is well, green checkmarks pop up next to them. This is also PowerShell issuing Get-Commands in the background.

Here are a few examples to check some of the more important FMA services:

- Get-BrokerServiceStatus
- Get-ConfigServiceStatus

- Get-HypServiceStatus
- Get-AcctServiceStatus
- Get-ProvServiceStatus

Another thing to mention is that both Studio and Director run on top of the PowerShell SDK as well. Everything you can do within Studio can also be done through PowerShell, including a whole bunch of configuration options and tweaks that are not possible using 'just' Studio. When you check your Delivery Controllers in Studio, you'll see a number in minutes next to each Controller that indicates when the Delivery Controller has last registered itself with the Central Site database. This number should always be 0. By default, the Controller checks in every 20 seconds (they exchange heartbeat messages) which will then be valid (TTL) for another 40 seconds.

Old school

It's great that we have such an extensive toolset at our disposal, but let's not forget about the basics. A simple NetStat and/or firewall port check, a Ping to check network connectivity perhaps, Tracert, Telnet etc. Are all our services up and running, no errors or warnings, no time or sync issues, a quick and dirty manual event log check, and when you do, remember to check all components that might be involved, your Controller, StoreFront, Web Interface, VDA etc. You get my point, right? Of course this kind of functionality is built into most of the tools as well, but sometimes all you need is a simple DOS Prompt and you're good to go. No separate install or configuration steps needed.

Toolset collections

I could probably fill another 5 pages or so with separate troubleshooting tool descriptions, but in practice you will probably only use a handful, especially with tools like Scout, aggregating multiple into one.

However, to make sure I do not leave any potentially important tools out of scope, I will also include links to the Citrix Diagnostic Toolkit and the Citrix Supportability Pack. Both contain an enormous amount of Citrix (-related) tool sets, free for you to use. You will find that both will have an overlap, as do I in my troubleshooting tools mentioned throughout this chapter. The Citrix Supportability Pack has just been updated (April 2016) with a whole bunch of (very) usefull and new tools like: The AppDisks diagnostics tool, Audio Volume Persistence Tool, Database Sizing Tool, Foreground Lock Timeout Tool, SmartHub, VDA Cleanup Utility, PreSCAN and more!

- You will find the Citrix Supportability Pack over at: CTX203082.
- The Citrix Diagnostic Toolkit is located at: CTX135075.

Troubleshooting VDA registration process

Within the FMA VDAs need to register themselves with a Delivery Controller, otherwise they won't be of much use. Follow the steps outlined in the CTX document below and/or have a look at the visual overview over at the next page to successfully troubleshoot the VDA registration process. CTX136668.

```
Start → VDA not registered with controller

1. Check if the Desktop service is running

2. Ping FQDN of VDA from controller
   → Use Citrix port check utility to IP of VDA

3. Ping FQDN of controller from VDA
   → Use Citrix port check utility to IP of DC

   → NetStat to check process using port
     Temporarily disable firewalls
     Check if all controller services are running

4. Confirm time difference on controller and VDA < 5 Min.

5. Confirm controller configuration on VDA
   → Enable auto update of controllers policy
     ListofDDCs at: HKLM\Software\Citrix\etc.
     OU base via FarmGUID (backward compatibility only)
     C:\Personality.ini (if MCS is used to provision machines)

6. Enable logging on controller CTX117425
   → Look for any logged errors

End
```

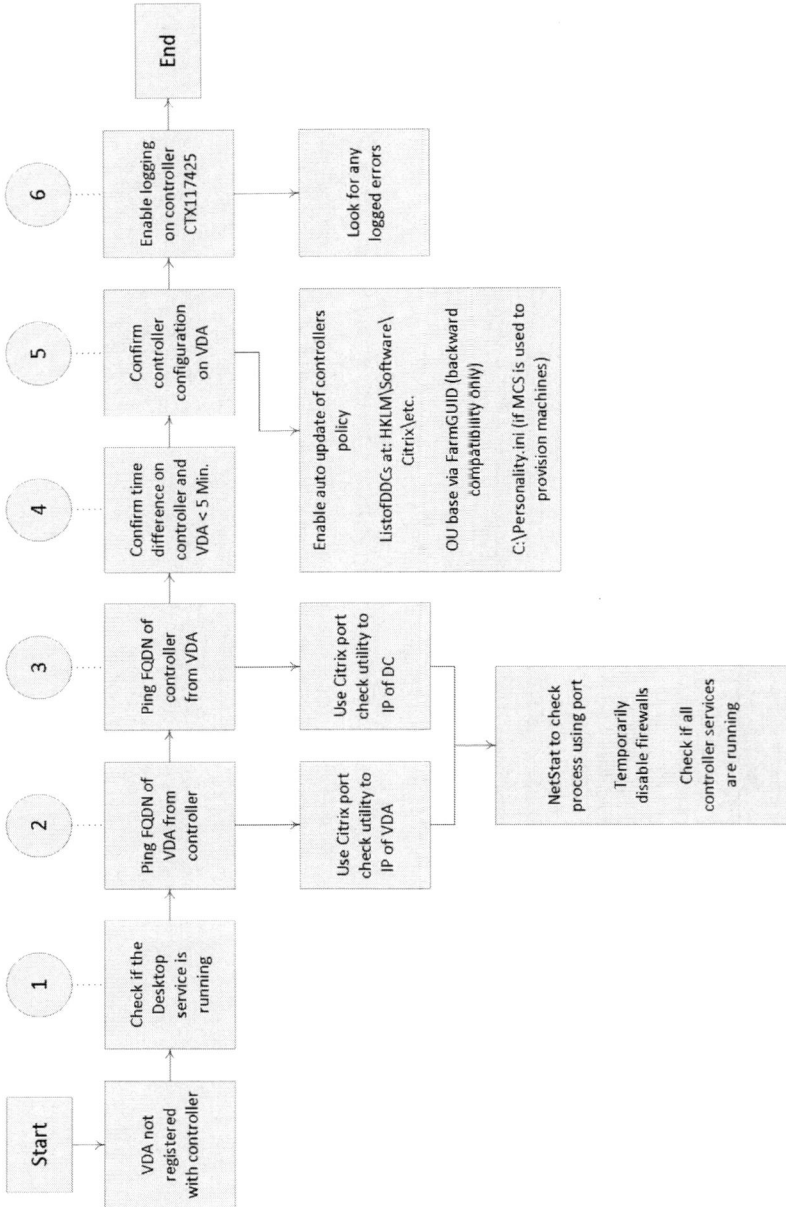

Figure 61: VDA registration troubleshooting steps

Citrix Heatlh Assistant

Version one (multiple will follow) of the Citrix Health Assistant focuses on VDA registration issues for both XenDesktop and XenApp. A series of health checks will be run in an automated fashion to identify any potential root causes for common VDA registration issues. It is a GUI based tool but also supports the use of command line commands. The following health checks are included:

1. VDA Machine Domain membership verification
2. VDA software installation and relevant services status verification
3. VDA communication ports status
4. VDA services status
5. Windows firewall configuration
6. VDA communication with Desktop Delivery Controllers (DDC)
7. VDA time sync with each DDC

Look up the following CTX document for some additional information and the actual Health Assistant download: CTX207624.

UPS print device certification tool

The Citrix UPS Print Driver Certification Tool can be used to test the compatibility of a print driver with the Citrix Universal Print Server. The tool checks for compatibility by using the print driver to simulate load, allowing a network administrator or print driver manufacturer to determine the following:

- Print driver is capable of handling the load normally seen with a Citrix Universal Print Server.

- Print driver meets the Citrix Universal Print Server performance requirement.
- Identifies potential print driver issues, allowing a network administrator or print driver manufacturer to further troubleshoot problem areas.

See the following CTX document for more detailed information: CTX142119.

StressPrinters

This tool can be used to compare various print drivers (CPU load, time required to successfully create a printer) as well as simulate multiple sessions' auto-creating printers using the same print driver. Have a look at the CTX document for an instruction video on how to use the StressPrinters tool: CTX129574.

Receiver Clean-Up tool

The Receiver Clean-Up utility is designed to assist with the following scenarios:

- When errors occur during upgrade from an earlier version of Receiver or Online Plug-in.
- When unexpected behaviour or performance is experienced after upgrade from an earlier Receiver or Online Plug-in.
- If Receiver upgrade is not possible due to feature incompatibility and/or a clean uninstall is required.

The Receiver Clean-Up Utility removes components, files, and registry values of Online Plug-in 11.x, 12.x, and Receiver for Windows 3.x, 4.x (Online Plug-in 13.x, 14.x). This includes the Offline Plug-in component if installed. See the accompanying

CTX document for more information and to download the actual tool: CTX137494.

The Remote Display Analyzer

This is a tool for and by the community. It is developed and thought up by Bram Wolfs and Barry Schiffer and has been very well received. Although the concept behind it might sound simple, I can assure you the technology is not. The tool is somewhat special; first of all it will show you which HDX codec is being used, including all related and relevant information. Best thing is, it will only take you two mouse clicks (one double-click, actually) literally. No command prompts, no WMI queries, HDX Monitor or Director etc.

Secondly, and this is huge, it will let you change display settings on the fly and LIVE switch between the different codecs available, without needing to log out, reconfigure, reboot etc. Framehawk included. You could say it's an industry first, since even Citrix themselves have not been able to come up with something similar. All real-time statistics and related information can be viewed using a 'normal' user account, no admin permissions needed.

Below you will find a short but impressive list of what you as an admin can expect from the Remote Display Analyzer:

- It is meant as a tool for admins, not users. You don't always need admin permissions, though.
- It will give you a (real-time) indication of what the resource consumption is for a specific workload, which might come in handy for troubleshooting.
- It will show you the configured display mode right away, only seconds after launching the tool.

- It will only show you information that matters for the detected display mode, clear and crisp so no (more) confusion whatsoever.
- You can change display settings on the fly, see what works best under which circumstances.
- It is possible to switch between encoders by changing the settings and also possible to switch between DCR and ThinWire.

Make sure to check out their website at www.rdanalyzer.com and follow them on Twitter at @rdanalyzer.

Conclusion

This chapter should give you a good indication of what is out there. Of course I will never be able to list and highlight all the tools available today, but I am pretty sure that I have covered the most popular ones including all accompanying CTX articles, leading you to even more useful information and downloads.

Key takeaways

- Successful troubleshooting starts with understanding the environment, architecture and components you're working with.

- In times of 'peace' make sure you spend some time getting to know the various troubleshooting tools and methodologies out there. Assemble your own tool kit and/or come up with your own troubleshooting methodology /approach.

- Make sure to go over some of the tips I gave you at the beginning of this chapter: there are some useful pointers in there. Not much use in repeating them all here, the same applies to all the tools listed.

General sizing guidelines and Citrix Workspace Cloud

Sizing and storage considerations

With XenApp, sizing is all about how many users we can fit onto a single machine, physical or virtual, without compromising, or affecting the overall user experience. With a XenDesktop VDI it is always one user per desktop and and preferably it needs to perform as close to a physical PC as possible, or better (although this applies to RDSH as well, of course). Unfortunately there is no 'one size fits all' when it comes to sizing your RDSH and/or VDI machines; since there are multiple factors to consider. It will greatly depend on the type of applications used (video, audio, number crunching etc.), the intensity with which your users will use them, the server and/or desktop Operating System used and so on.

The underlying storage infrastructure also plays an important role in all this. While your server and desktop machines can have all the CPUs, GPUs and memory in the world, if your storage platform does not deliver the requested amount and types of IOPS (which can be very workload-specific) and/or storage throughput needed (never mind the GBs needed to actually build your machines) you are set up for failure. The types of machines you deploy (non-persistent and persistent) and the provisioning mechanism used will need to be taken into consideration as well.

This is why it is very important to understand the different types of workloads you have to deal with and the different forms of provisioning at your disposal. As we have seen in some of the previous chapters, there are some distinct differences between MCS and PVS, for example, and they both impact storage in different ways (write cache considerations, differencing disks). This is also where things like application and baseline

performance statistics come into play to help you better
understand what is expected and needed within your newly built
XenDesktop / XenApp Site. Perhaps this is data you already
have or it's something your customer can provide and of course
talking to certain applications vendors might help as well.
However, in most cases it will come down to real-world testing,
and then test some more.

Do not overdo it

Although calculating storage needs (free space, IOPS,
throughput, latency included etc.) and defining application
performance profiles (CPU, GPU, memory etc.) can take up
quite some time and effort, be careful when doing so. Users can
be very unpredictable and even if you spend weeks on
calculating your potential storage and compute needs it won't
guarantee anything. The same applies to load testing, by the way.
It is an indication and nothing more. Real-world testing, as
highlighted earlier, is the only true way of validating what you
have built. See what happens and talk to your users.

Some help

Luckily, when it comes to sizing your XenDesktop / XenApp
compute and storage needs, we can use multiple resources to
draw inspiration from. For one we can learn from others: what
was their approach in the past? Did they run into any 'specials',
and if so, how did they handle them? I'll include some helpful
links at the end of this chapter. I can also recommend having a
look at the Citrix XenDesktop Design Handbook, and, although
it is a bit outdated (it is based on version 7.6), it does offer a
whole bunch of best practices with regard to building and
configuring your Site, including compute and storage sizing
considerations for building up your Delivery Controllers,
StoreFront servers, database server, VDAs and more.

Also, next to one or two community-powered sizing calculators, Citrix also offers us Project Accelerator.

Citrix Project Accelerator

I won't go over Project Accelerator from start to finish since it is still, and will continue to be, a work in progress. However, the basics and concepts remain the same, as they often do. Project Accelerator is a web-based application (project.citrix.com) that guides you through various questions, requirements, and common design choices. It is founded on the practices used by the experts within Citrix Consulting and it is regularly updated with new information from the Citrix consultancy and lab guys keeping it fresh and current, although at the time of writing it currently supports up to XenDesktop / XenApp version 7.5. But don't let that hold you back from giving it a try.

Once you have signed up and started a project you will first enter the Assess Phase. Here you will need to define your organisation: which is a five-step process. First you provide information on your business, the type of project, user groups and applications, and finally you will need to link those applications to your user groups. This phase will include questions on topics like the type of industry that you are in, how many users this particular solution will need to support, primary business priorities like BYOD, being able to work from anywhere, reducing costs, better desktop management and so on. They will ask you for any existing (Citrix) skill sets (XenApp, XenDesktop, NetScaler, XenServer, XenMobile, App-V, Hyper-V, VMware and so on: it's a pretty long list) within the team responsible for building and configuring the new Site. Take your time and fill in all the fields as detailed as possible: this is by far the most important step / phase.

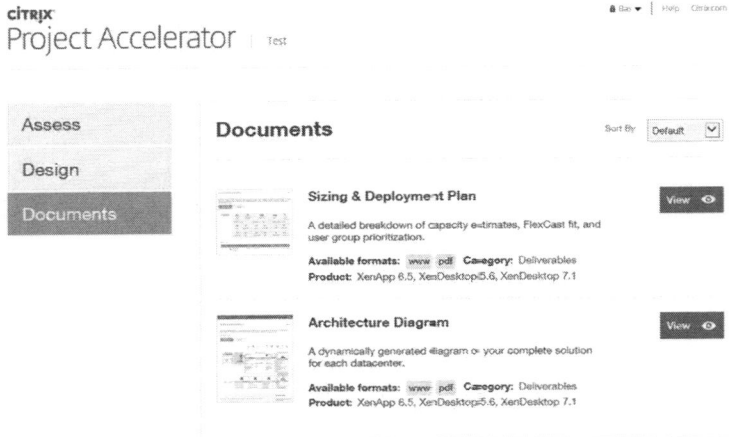

Figure 62: Citrix Project Accelerator

FMA fact: When thought through beforehand this phase wil probably take you somewhere between 30 to 60 minutes, depending on the number of users and user groups, including the number and the type of applications involved.

Based on the information entered during the Assess Phase, the second phase, Design, will make certain technical recommendations with regard to the products used to actually build the solution, the FlexCast delivery model, hardware and sizing recommendations (compute resources in general, including suggestions arround CPU overcommitting and so on), IOPS and more. Do note that you will be able to manually adjust all suggestions made by Citrix, based on personal experience.

This phase also includes recommendations around image provisioning and management like PVS and MCS, including the preferred types of storage.

As soon as you are satisfied you can safe your work and skip to the Documents sections where you will find an Architecture diagram and a Sizing and deployment plan based on the information you entered during the first two phases. Use it to your advantage.

IOPS and general storage considerations

It is, or at least can be important to understand what an IOPS actually is, why they (multiple) are important, how they are measured, the different types of IOPS, which factors influence performance, either negatively or positively etc. Being familiar with the IOPS fundamentals will give you a better insight into what is actually going on under the hood and how things interact and rely on each other.

Nowadays infrastructures are being virtualised almost without exception, and as we all know, the success of our projects greatly depends on the end-user acceptance. Ultimately they expect to experience the same snappiness as they do on their physical desktops or even better. Of course this is what we as consultants and system administrators aim for as well, but unfortunately it isn't always that straightforward. The bottom line is, we need speed! If we drill down just a bit further speed closely relates to IOPS, you'll read why in a minute. Bottom line: we need as much (low latency) IOPS as we can get our hands on to drive our VDI and/or RDSH-based infrastructures to their full potential.

Let's start at the beginning, IOPS stands for: Input / Output Operations Per Second, which in general is either a read or write operation. Simply put, if you have a disk that is capable of doing 100 IOPS, it means that it is theoretically capable of issuing 100 read and/or write operations per second. However, being able to issue 100 read and/or write operations isn't the same as actually processing them: reading and writing data takes time. This is where latency comes in. If our disk subsystem can handle, or issue, 100 IOPS but they are processed at around 20 milliseconds per operation (which is slow, by the way), then it will only be able to actually handle 50 operations per second, as opposed to the issued 100.

In the above example, 20 milliseconds is what we would refer to as the latency involved. It tells us how long it will take for a single IO request to take place or be processed.

There is a lot more to it

Remember that a random IOPS number, on its own, doesn't say anything. We can do a million IOPS! Well, ok, that's nice, but how did you test? Were they read or write operations? If mixed, what was the percentage reads vs. writes? Writes are more resource-intensive. Did you read from cache? What was the data block size? How many host and disk controllers were involved? What type of storage did you use? Was there RAID involved? Using RAID will probably negatively impact the IOPS number, but still. The same applies to data tiering. Physical disks? Probably. If so, are we dealing with sequential or random reads and writes? In addition, and this is probably the most important one, how much latency is involved in milliseconds? This will range from around 2 milliseconds, which is comparable to a locally installed physical disk, to 20+ milliseconds at which performance, if any, will be highly impacted. An overview:

- 0 – 12 milliseconds – Looking good: the lower the number, the better off you are.
- 10 – 15 milliseconds – Still acceptable in most cases: users might notice a small delay.

- 15 – 20 milliseconds – Step up and take action: most of your users won't be happy.
- 20 – 25 milliseconds – Get your pen and paper out and shut it all down.

FMA fact: A high number of IOPS is useless unless latency is low! Even with SSDs which are capable of providing a huge number of IOPS compared to traditional HDDs, latency matters. Latency tells us how long it takes to process a single read or write I/O request.

With 'legacy' physical disks, overall speed and latency greatly depend on the rotations, or revolutions, per minute (RPM) a certain disk is capable of: the laws of physics apply. Today we can classify hard disk speeds (HDD) as follows: 5400 rpm, 7200 rpm, 10,000 rpm and 15,000 rpm. A higher rpm equals higher read and write speeds. Another factor impacting performance is disk density. The higher the density, the more data a disk is able to store on its 'platter'; data will be written closer together on the disk, and as a result the disk's read/write head will have to travel shorter distances to access the data, resulting in higher read and write speeds.

This may sound like a small note to some, but imagine having a SAN or Filer holding hundreds of disks: having 15,000 rpm and high-density disks makes a real difference! So when a random vendor tells you that their storage appliance is capable of doing a crazy high number of IOPS, you probably have a few questions to ask them, right?! I think it's also clear that the more IOPS we can actually process, as opposed to issue, per second, the better our overall performance will be!

> **FMA fact**: Latency is king: the less you have, the faster
> your infrastructure will be! Also, there is no standard
> when it comes to measuring IOPS! There are too many
> factors influencing overall performance and thus the
> number of IOPS.

They are not the same

Not all IOPS are the same: sure, you could boil it down to it
being either a read or a write, but that's not the whole truth
now, is it? First of all, reads and writes can be random or
sequential, reads can be reread and writes can be rewritten,
single and multiple threads, reads and writes taking place at the
same time, random writes directly followed by sequential reads
of the same data, different block sizes of data that get read or
written, ranging from bytes to megabytes and all that's in
between, or a combination of the above.

As mentioned earlier, it is important to understand your
application workloads and their characteristics with regard to the
IOPS they need. This can be a very tricky process.

Take block size (just one of many examples): having a huge
number of smaller data blocks as opposed to having a relatively
small number of larger data blocks can make a huge difference.
Having said all that, remember, don't go nuts; you do not have
to get to the bottom of it all, all the time.

Ask your storage providers for detailed test procedures, how did
they test and what did they use. In addition, at a minimum you
will want to know these three 'golden' parameters:

- The latency, in MS, involved
- The read vs. write ratio
- Data block sizes used.

Steady state, boot and logon

We have already highlighted read and write IOPS: both will be part of your workload profile. However, a lot of application vendors will refer to an average amount of IOPS that is needed by their workload to guarantee acceptable performance. This is also referred to as Steady State IOPS, a term also used by Citrix when they refer to their VDI workloads.

After a virtual Windows machine boots up, users log in and applications are launched, and your users will start their daily routines. Seen from an IOPS perspective, this is the Steady State. It is the average amount of read and write IOPS processed during a longer period of time, usually a few hours at least.

FMA fact: Although the average amount of IOPS, or the Steady State, does tell us something, it isn't sufficient. We also need to focus on the peak activity measured between the boot and the Steady State phases and size accordingly.

When we mention the 20:80 read/write ratio we are usually referring to the Steady State. Something you may have heard of during one of the many MCS vs. PVS discussions. As you can see, the Steady State consists mainly of write I/O; however, the (read) peaks that occur as part of the boot and/or logon process will be much higher. Again, these rules primarily apply to VDI-type workloads like Windows 7 & 8.

There are several tools available helping us to measure the IOPS needed by Windows and the applications installed on top. By using these tools we can get an idea of the IOPS needed during the boot, logon and Steady State phases as mentioned earlier, as well as application startup. We can use Performance Monitor: using certain PerfMon counters it will tell us something about the reads and writes taking place, as well as the total amount of IOPS and the Disk queue length, also telling us how many IOPS are getting queued by Windows. Have a look at these counters:

- Disk reads/sec – read IOPS
- Disk writes/sec – write IOPS
- Disk transfers/sec – total amount of IOPS
- Current Disk Queue length – IOPS being queued by Windows.

Here are some interesting tools for you to have a look at: they will either calculate your current IOPS load or help you predict the configuration and IOPS needed based on your needs and wishes.

1. Iometer – measures IOPS for a certain workload: iometer.org/doc/downloads.html
2. ESXTOP – specific to ESX, provides certain disk states, totals, reads and writes: yellow-bricks.com/esxtop/
3. WMAROW – web interface, used to calculate performance, capacity, random IOPS: wmarow.com/strcalc/
4. The Cloud Calculator – web interface, disk RAID and IOPS calculator: thecloudcalculator.com/calculators/disk-raid-and-iops.html
5. Process Monitor – general analyses of IOPS:

http://technet.microsoft.com/en-us/sysinternals/bb896645.aspx

6. Login VSI – VDI workload generator, simulate user activity on your infrastructure: loginvsi.com/

As we will see shortly, there is a distinct difference between the boot and logon phase. Both (can) create so-called 'storms', also referred to as a boot storm and/or a logon storm, potentially impacting overall performance. This is where the read IOPS peaks mentioned earlier come in.

FMA fact: Storage throughput isn't the same as IOPS. When we need to be able to process large amounts of data, bandwidth becomes important: the number of GB/sec that can be processed. Although they do have an overlap, there is a clear difference between the two.

Be aware that RAID configurations bring a write penalty; this is because of the parity bit that needs to be written as well. A write can't be fully completed until both the data and the parity information are written to disk. The time it takes for the parity bit to be written to disk is what we refer to as the write penalty. Of course this does not apply to reads.

When looking at VDI workloads, we can break it down into five separate phases: boot, user logon, application launch, the Steady State, and logoff / shutdown. During the boot process, especially in large environments, dozens of virtual machines might be booted simultaneously, creating the earlier highlighted boot storm. Booting a machine creates a huge spike in read I/O, as such, and depending on the IOPS available, booting multiple machines at once might negatively impact overall performance.

> **FMA fact**: If IOPS are limited, try (pre-)booting your
> machines at night. Also, make sure your users can't
> reboot the machines themselves.

Using this method will only get you so far; there might be
several reasons why you may need to reboot multiple, if not all,
machines during daytime. Something to think about as your
VDI environment might not be available for a certain period of
time.

Logon storms are a bit different in that they will always take
place during the morning / day. It isn't something we can
schedule during the night, users will always first need to logon
before they can start working. Although this may sound
obvious, it's still something to be aware of. Logons generate
high reads (not as high as during the boot process) and less
writes, although it's near to equal. This is primarily due to
software that starts during the logon phase and the way that user
profiles are loaded. Using application virtualisation, layering,
folder redirection, Flex Profiles etc. will greatly enhance overall
performance.

As you can see, especially during the first few phases, there will
be a lot of read traffic going on. Fortunately reads are a bit less
demanding than writes and can be cached quite simple so they
can be read from memory when the same data is requested
multiple times.

The way this happens differs per vendor / product. Just be
aware that, although caching might be in place, it won't solve all
your problems by default. You will still need to calculate your
needs and size accordingly. It does make life a little easier,
though.

Although we are primarily focusing on IOPS here, note that the underlying disk subsystem isn't the only bottleneck per se. Don't rule out the storage controllers, for example: they can only handle so much; CPU, memory and network might be a potential bottleneck as well. RAID penalties, huge amount of writes for a particular workload, data compression and/or de-duplication taking place, and so on.

FMA fact: Launching applications will generate high read I/O peaks and initial low writes. Chances are that after users log on they will start, either automatically or manually, their main applications. Again, this is something to take into account, as this will probably cause an application launch storm, although it's usually not recognised as such.

Steady State we already discussed earlier: this is where write I/O will take over from read I/O, on average this will be around the earlier mentioned 20:80 read/write ratio. So if we scale for the peaks, read as well as write, we can't go wrong – at least that's the theory.

What else?

Today the market is full of solutions and products helping us to overcome the everlasting battle against IOPS. Some are 'patch' like solutions, which help speed up our 'legacy' SAN and NAS environments using SSDs and Flash-orientated storage in combination with smart and flexible caching technologies, while others focus on converged-like infrastructures and in-memory caching.

These in-memory solutions are somewhat special: they don't necessarily increase the number of IOPS available, but instead they decrease the number of IOPS needed by the workload because writes go to RAM instead of disk, ultimately achieving the same or even better result(s).

Using any of these types of products will greatly increase the number of IOPS available (or decrease the number of IOPS needed) and decrease the latency that comes with it. Just know that no matter which solution you pick, you will still have to determine the number of IOPS needed and scale accordingly.

Even when using the most enhanced IOPS accelerator today won't guarantee that you will be able to boot your entire VDI infrastructure during daytime and won't run into any issues.

FMA fact: By leveraging RAM for writes, a.k.a. RAM Cache with Overflow to Disk in terms of Citrix PVS write cache, we can significantly reduce the number of IOPS needed. In fact, Citrix claims to only need 1 to 2 IOPS per user on a XenApp environment without any complex configurations or hardware replacement.

Give your antivirus solution some extra attention, especially with regard to VDI. You will be glad that you did. I suggest you start here:

brianmadden.com/blogs/rubenspruijt/archive/2013/01/15/project-vrc-antivirus-impact-and-best-practices-on-vdi.aspx

Last but not least, during logoff and shutdown we will see a large write peak and very little read activity. Just as we need to plan for peak reads at the time of boot and logon, the same applies for write peaks during logoff. Again I'd like to emphasise that, although there might be a ton of IOPS available, it's the speed with which they are handled that counts! Less latency equals higher speeds.

To over-commit, or not to over-commit...

While I could advice you to never over-commit a hosts physical CPU / Core more then 3: 1, or 4: 1, and to always configure at least 4, or perhaps 8 vCPUs when it comes to sizing virtual XenApp servers, for example, I won't. I won't, because it doesn't make much sense, at least not without some more background information.

First you would need to answer questions like; what types of workload (s) will I be supporting, are there any specific characteristics that I need to take into consideration (CPU, GPU and/or RAM intensive)? How many users do we want to 'cram' onto a single machine, what is the underlying Operating System used and what about any anti virus and monitoring software? They both have an impact on density / performance as well. What type of hardware are we going to use?

And while some application (and hardware) vendors can give you specific information on what to look out for, unfortunately in most cases you will have to find out for yourself, meaning trial and error in most cases.

Having said all that, throughout the years certain (performance) baselines have been established (based on specific hard and software configurations / profiles) and users have been categorized as lightweight, medium or heavy depending on the types of workloads they use and the intensity with which they use them. These 'baselines' advice us on the number of users per CPU / core, the amount of RAM needed, including the number of (steady state) IOPS, again, on a per user basis. Here the medium type user is by far the most popular one.

He or she will use applications like Office, Acrobat Reader, one or two Internet Browsers using multiple tabs at any given time, e-mail in the form of Outlook, Gmail etc. and of a course a YouTube movie will be played every now and again, in short, a typical office worker.

Having this type of information on your users makes it (a lot) easier to start from scratch when it comes to sizing your XenApp machines and/or VDI based VM's. Here my statement made earlier, where I mention that it doesn't make much sense to advice starting out with 4 or perhaps 8 vCPUs for a XenApp server, doesn't really apply.

Although, the number of preferred users, including their intensity levels etc. but also the type of hardware used (are there GPUs in play as well? CPU speed, underlying storage platform etc.) will most certainly influence the total number of compute resources needed, you will have to start somewhere, right? So starting out with lets say 8 vCPUs and 16 / 32 GBs of RAM, for example, on a Server 2012R2 virtual XenApp server might not be such a bad idea. In the end we probably all have our own approach, although most will not differ too much is my guess.

If you go through the XenDesktop Design Handbook it will show you a couple of specific formula's enabling you to get a (ballpark) figure regarding the number of physical CPU cores needed, depending on a certain amount and type of users, including the underlying Operating System used, the same goes for physical RAM, nice to help you on your way. Have a look at the following list of links; it includes the XenDesktop Handbook and Project Accelerator as well.

- The XenDesktop 7.5 sizing calculator by Andrzej Gołębiowski http://blog.citrix24.com/xendesktop-7-sizing-calculator/
- Have a look at this post from Thomas Gamull. It is on sizing (real world) Citrix environments with a specific focus on XenApp 7.x: https://www.citrix.com/blogs/2014/04/01/quick-server-sizing-for-xenapp-7/
- The XenDesktop Design Handbook (direct link to the .PDF document): http://support.citrix.com/servlet/KbServlet/download/35949-102-713877/Citrix
- Sign up and log into mycugc.org and do a search for server / machine sizing. You will come across multiple threads discussing the subject.
- Citrix project Accelerator: https://project.citrix.com

Key takeaways

- When it comes to sizing your XenDesktop / XenApp infrastructures: there is no 'one size fits all'.
- You need to understand the workloads you have to deal with and size accordingly.
- There is more to it than 'just' compute resources: don't forget about your underlying storage platform.
- While sizing is important, try not to overdo it. Real-world testing will always be needed.
- Ask peers for help and/or advice, consult the Citrix XenDesktop Design Handbook, use Project Accelerator and test, test and test some more.
- Load testing can give us an indication of what might be possible, but remember that your users can be (very) unpredictable.
- When conducting load tests, always try to incorporate any exotic applications that you might have. These are the ones you should be most curious about.
- IOPS fundamentals help you in understanding what is going on under the hood. It will also help in understanding what other IT folks might be talking about in other articles / blogs.
- A random IOPS number on its own doesn't mean anything. What type of IOPS are we talking about: reads, writes, random, sequential, rereads and/or writes, single or multiple threads, block sizes and so on. And even more importantly, what is the latency number in MS?
- Storage providers should be able to provide you with at least the latency in MS, the reads vs. writes ratio, and the data block sizes used during testing.

- Remember that there is a big difference between steady state, boot logon, application launch and logoff storms.
- Storage throughput is not the same as IOPS. When dealing with large amounts of data that need to be processed and transmitted, storage throughput becomes more important.
- Reads are less intensive than writes. Also, today we have a lot of options when it comes to caching reads.
- While IOPS are important when it comes to sizing and forming a potential bottleneck, do not forget about CPU, memory and storage controllers. They can only handle so much.

The Citrix Workspace Cloud

Unless you are completely new to working with XenDesktop and/or XenApp products, you must have heard a thing or two about the Citrix Workspace Cloud (CWC) by now. Since it also heavily relies on the FlexCast Management Architecture I couldn't write this book without at least mentioning it. In fact, as soon as Citrix introduces a new feature or functionality that touches the FMA, CWC will have it first. Being a cloud platform / service it has the added advantage of getting new code out to customers relatively quickly. For this they apply a so-called phased 'bucket' approach, which unfortunately, is still under NDA at this time.

Since CWC is still a relatively new offering / product, and evolving as we speak, I wouldn't be surprised if the current subscription model, the services involved and perhaps even its name will change before the end of 2016.

Citrix Workspace Cloud is actually more of a managed or management platform than anything else. It offers us several different services; these are Apps and Desktops (XenDesktop and XenApp), Mobility Management (XenMobile), Secure Documents (ShareFile) and Life Cycle Management, which is sort of new. For the purpose of this book I will focus on the Apps and Desktop and Life Cycle Management services.

The CWC control centre, or control plane, is at the top of the stack: it's where all the magic happens, so to speak, and what you as an administrator would use, or interact with, to manage and configure your CWC-based deployments. Below that are the Resource Locations: that is where the XenDesktop / XenDesktop VDAs, data and applications reside, which are managed, controlled and owned by you, the customer or a partner in between – a CSP, for example. These Resource Locations can be located on-premises, within a datacentre or on a public or privately owned cloud: it doesn't really matter, as you are in control. They are connected to the Workspace Cloud services platform through Cloud Connectors.

FMA fact: CWC supports both MCS as well as PVS for machine provisioning.

So how does all this work? Let me walk you through it. Simply put, you take a 'normal' XenDesktop / XenApp deployment and then 'cloudify' the infrastructural or management pieces and components.

Or better said, Citrix has already taken care of that for you. Your Delivery Controllers, SQL database, License Server, Studio, Director and/or StoreFront servers will all live up in the Citrix Workspace Cloud as part of the Apps and Desktops service.

You tell Citrix what you need and they will set it up and configure it for you. From there on they will also take care of any ongoing management and maintenance tasks. Now all you will be left with are your VDAs and NetScaler, from a Citrix infrastructure point of view, that is, and you can host them wherever you like (Resource Location). It is the ultimate hybrid cloud model and the way forward according to most, me included. And if you have a look at the accompanying E-docs page you will find that there currently is an AppDisks Tech Preview for CWC as well!

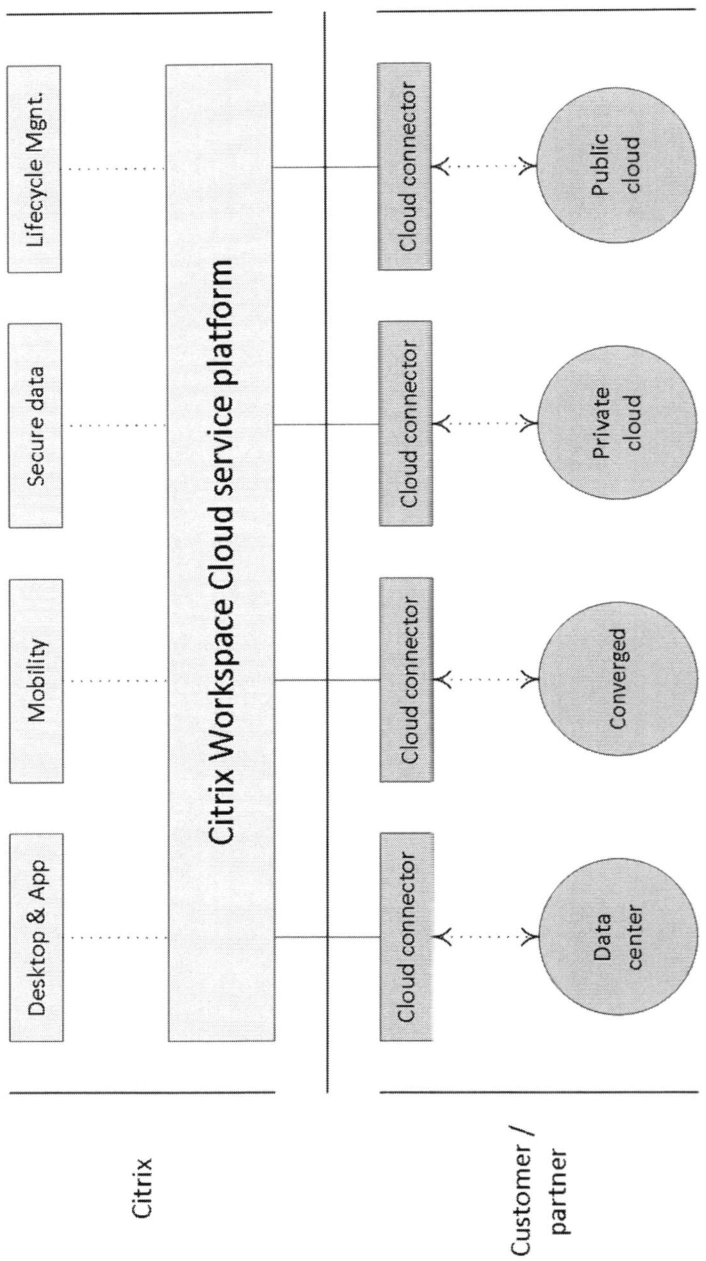

Figure 63: The Citrix Workspace Cloud

FMA fact: Because of Microsoft's licensing restriction with regard to desktop Operating Systems, it is very hard to come up with a true DaaS solution based on an actual desktop OS while keeping costs acceptable. With CWC you can host all of your infrastructural components up in the cloud and leverage your own on-premises VDAs, which can be VDI and 100% desktop OS-based deployments. While not exactly the same, it comes close to a desktop OS-based DaaS (private cloud) offering.

StoreFront options

You may have noticed that I used 'and/or' when mentioning StoreFront: this is because with StoreFront you can choose where to actually host it. This has a lot to do with the ability to customise your own domain names and URLs. Your options are:

- A cloud-hosted StoreFront: The applications and desktops service in Workspace Cloud hosts a StoreFront site for each customer. The benefit of the cloud-hosted StoreFront is that there is zero effort to deploy, and it is kept evergreen by Citrix. Cloud-hosted is recommended for all new customers, previews, and proofs-of-concept (PoCs).

- An on-premises StoreFront: Customers may also use an existing StoreFront to aggregate applications and desktops in Workspace Cloud. This offers greater security, including support for two-factor authentication and prevents users from entering their password into the cloud service. It also allows customers to customise their domain names and URLs. This is recommended for any existing XenApp and XenDesktop customers that

already have StoreFront deployed.
- A combination of on-premises StoreFront and cloud-hosted StoreFront.

Source: Citrix E-docs website

The Cloud Connector

This is the component that connects your VDA resources to, in this case, the Apps and Desktop Workspace Cloud Services. The Cloud Connector is made up of several providers or services, which in turn take care of things like registering VDAs and the ability to connect into your on-premises Hypervisor or public cloud platform of choice.

> **FMA fact**: The Cloud Connector is what your VDAs will point to and use as a broker, instead of a Delivery Controller when compared to an on-premises deployment.

The Cloud Connector is installed on a Windows Server 2012 R2, domain-joined (within your own Resource Location) machine. Although installed on-premises, or at least within one of your own Resource Locations, which can be cloud-based as well, as a component it is fully managed from and by CWC.

It consists of a fairly light touch installation, and since it will be managed from CWC it will always be up to date with the latest patches and so on. It will allow secure communications only through port 443 (outbound), and if needed or desired it can be placed behind NAT and Web proxy services as well.

> **FMA fact**: You will need to set up at least two Cloud Connectors per Resource Location to achieve HA. You won't have to configure load balancing in any way for these two Cloud Connectors. CWC will send requests and data to one of the two Connectors, and if it gets too busy or stops responding, the data will be sent over to the idle Connector, or the load will be spread amongst the two.

Authentication and credential handling

Security is top of mind when discussing cloud-based solutions, and it is no different with the CWC offering. Here are some security facts to hopefully give you some peace of mind.

- When an Administrator authenticates to CWC, he or she will do so using the sign-on system from Citrix online. During the authentication process a one-time signed JSON Web Token will be generated, which will give the Administrator access to the apps and desktop service within CWC.
- All user credentials will be encrypted by the Cloud Connector component using AES-256 encryption combined with a random one-time key, which will be generated for each launch. This key will be forwarded to the Citrix Receiver (it doesn't go into the cloud, ever) from where it will be passed over to the VDA so it will be able to decrypt the user password when a session is launched, creating a single sign-on experience.
- When Machine Creation Services creates machine accounts in the customer's AD through the Cloud Connector, the Administrator will be prompted for each operation that will need to take place. This is because

the machine account of the Cloud Connector only has read permissions within the Active Directory.

- Hypervisor passwords needed for authentication will be generated by the Administrator, encrypted and stored in the cloud-based SQL database

FMA fact: The customer's metadata will always be stored separately for each tenant, and secured with unique credentials.

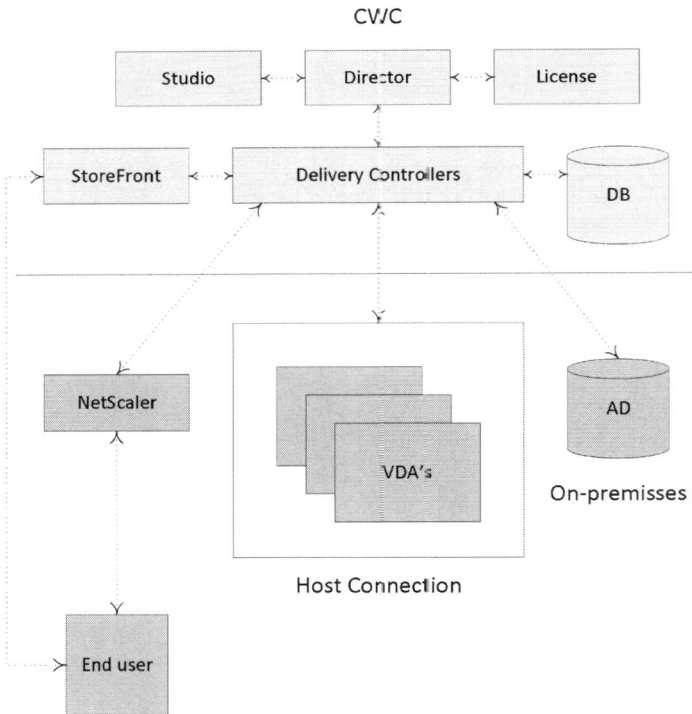

Figure 64: CWC simplified

Life Cycle Management Services

Citrix Lifecycle Management is a CWC cloud-based service life cycle management solution used to accelerate, automate and simplify the design, deployment and ongoing management of Citrix workloads including Enterprise applications. Using predefined and Citrix-certified blueprints, customers can roll-out complete Citrix-based environments fully automated onto their Hypervisor or cloud platform of choice, which are also referred to as Resource Locations as highlighted earlier.

Depending on your Life Cycle package subscription / license (Deploy, Design and Deploy, Design, Deploy and Manage) you will be able to design your own blueprints and edit existing ones, and of course you will have access to the Citrix library holding all Citrix-certified and predefined blueprints, made by either Citrix or third-party partners.

Next to that you have several options with regard to alerting, monitoring, disaster recovery, a fully automated upgrade from XenApp 6.5 (including application and policy configurations) and a bunch more. All you have to do is select your deployment of choice, configure the size and scale and Citrix, or CWC will take care of the rest!

FMA fact: Citrix offers out-of-the-box blueprints for XenDesktop, XenApp, XenMobile, NetScaler and the Workspace Suite.

Ongoing management is something that will still take some work from your side but by leveraging some of the robust and automated monitoring capabilities together with the ability to specify recovery of specific service components or entire services, including multiple recovery destinations, it will make your life a whole lot easier.

To finalise, the earlier highlighted Cloud Connector is used to connect to your on-premises or cloud-based Resource Location, including Active Directory. The provisioning and configuration of the blueprint-based machines will also leverage the Connector.

Key takeaways

- CWC offers customers the ultimate hybrid model and an easy way to get used to and migrate to the cloud.
- All the latest and greatest FMA features will first be made available to CWC before being built into the on-premises XenApp and XenDesktop products. And this also applies to both ShareFile as well as XenMobile.
- They use a unique, but very simple updating and testing mechanism for this, which unfortunately is still under NDA at the time of writing.
- Although when using the life cycle management service, you will still need to maintain and manage your VDAs, StoreFront and NetScalers to some extent, it will make life a lot easier. Take it for a test-drive.
- Resource Locations include: on-premises / your own datacentres, Azure, AWS and/or the Citrix CloudPlatform, and more will follow I'm sure.
- Ongoing management and monitoring are done from the CWC consoles; they have the exact same look and feel as the on-premises Studio and Director consoles.

The community is strong with this one!

The community surrounding Citrix is a powerful one: some of the brightest minds in the IT industry are involved. During the last three years or so I have been privileged to have met quite a few, though far from all of course, while visiting and presenting at various venues around the world. Although I am still fairly new to the scene, it already feels like I have been a part of the 'family' for at least ten years. I guess that is what happens when you mingle with the right kinds of people.

Besides the wealth of knowledge these guys and gals bring to the table (as you wouldn't believe), which is truly inspiring and educational at the same time, you are guaranteed to have a great time if you hang and go out with the Citrix posse, since having fun is their number one rule. Now when I mention the 'Citrix community' I am not talking about 5, 10 or 25 individuals in particular: no way. I am talking about you and thousands of other tech enthusiasts all over the world. And you can like VMware and Microsoft as well if you want, that's ok – with most, anyway.

Everybody I have met up until now has been very kind and most of all helpful. But I guess it's our genes; we all like to share what we know and/or have learned from others, right? Me included. I already have made some great new friends along the way and hopefully many more will follow in the years to come!

myCUGC

Last year Citrix launched their latest community initiative, and with great success, I might add. They named it myCUGC a.k.a. the Citrix User Group Community. Their website www.mycugc.org is their main hub and from there you will be able to connect with all who share the same love for the Citrix portfolio as you do.

There are over 8000 registered members already (since May 2015) and I'm guessing that by the time you are reading this book they will have neared or surpassed the 10,000 mark. The main forum is active all through the week: CTP, Citrix Technology Professionals share their thoughts from time to time, as well as other community members in the form of the community roundtable, blog posts, a SIG (Special Interest Group) or by hosting a webinar (which are plentiful as well) and so on: lots to see and hear.

It is also the place where new CUGs are formed and started. It is as simple as starting a new forum thread (there is a separate 'Group starting' forum section for this, by the way) and ask who is interested in starting and organising a new Citrix User Group.

And I can tell you, in most cases it took just a few weeks to get from a forum post / request to an official first, in-person, meeting with in most cases at least 20 to 25 folks showing up. At the time of writing around 45 new groups have been successfully formed already. They also have a central agenda hosting all upcoming myCUGC events.

And of course there is (a lot) more to it than the above, but I guess you will have to find out for yourself. Go over to myCUGC.com register and learn, help others, state your opinion and have some fun! See you there. To round things up, here are some quotes from the myCUGC team:

We are the new Citrix User Group Community

For users, by users, we are dedicated to helping our members excel. Our members are technology professionals interested in maximising the value of Citrix and partner products. Together we aim to be a source of high-value content and knowledge sharing, an online and in-person hub for professional connections, and a voice of influence with Citrix.

Mission

The Citrix User Group Community (CUGC) is a community of technology professionals. We strive to be the voice of Citrix technology users and managers. We are dedicated to helping our members and their businesses excel through education, knowledge sharing, networking and influence.

Benefits of Membership

We are just getting started, but as CUGC grows we will focus on providing a global network of users and experts who share solutions and insights. We are creating online communities and local groups so you can connect with technology professionals tackling the same challenges you face. We will offer exclusive content, such as recordings of Citrix Synergy Geek Speak sessions, as well as discounts on education and events.

Citrix

Our partnership with Citrix empowers CUGC. It provides us with access to Citrix content and executives. Citrix has provided invaluable support to get us started, and we will work closely with Citrix to plan events and collaborate on technical education and insights.

E2EVC

It stands for Experts-2-Experts Virtualization Conference, and I can tell you it is a special one. To give you an idea of what to expect when attending, as a presenter or in the audience, I'll share a section of one of my reviews that I wrote after attending E2EVC in Barcelona back in 2014.

What to expect

So you registered. First of all you just saved yourself a ton of money: just compare the prices with some of the other IT conferences, it's at least 3 to 400 euros cheaper. And if you are a so-called early bird, they will throw in some extra discounts as well, and believe me, it all adds up! What about the venues? Awesome: During 2014 I have been to both European events, one in Brussels and just recently in Barcelona. Every year they strike down in one, or multiple of Europe's major cities.

As a bonus, and if possible, they also organise a sight-seeing bus tour on Saturday, free of charge of course. And if you're smart you'll book one or two extra nights and go out to see the city on your own, there's always lots to do and see.

Throughout the day you'll be able to get free coffee, sandwiches at lunchtime, and of course sponsored free beers and pizza during Geek Speak near the end of the event. Then there are the sponsors: they always come up with something extra as well, free drinks, food, a good party, never a dull moment, because, as we all know, it's not just about the technology. That's what makes it special as well, it is really community-driven, and it will be hard, near to impossible even, to find a former attendee who isn't taken by the E2E virus. Once it's done: they all keep coming back for more.

> **FMA fact**: As I mentioned earlier, E2E relies heavily on
> sponsors: they are the ones who make it all possible. The
> E2EVC team doesn't make any money from the event:
> everything that comes in is invested right back into the
> event itself.

The presenters

What about them? It could be you onstage. I'm serious: just pick
a subject and let Alex or one of the other E2EVC team
members know that you might be interested in a presentation
slot and they'll get back to you before you know it. That's the
nice thing about E2E, the presenters as well as the content are
very diverse, and the audience is also very forgiving and
thoughtful. Just taking on the podium is an accomplishment in
itself and everybody appreciates that, so there is no need to be
intimidated by whoever might be in the audience. You need
help, just ask! All together, the presentations are of a high
standard no matter how you look at it.

During the rest of the day

All sessions get recorded and will be made accessible a few
weeks or months after the event has taken place. On the first
day all attendees will gather in one big conference room, which
will stay that way for the first three to four sessions after Alex
has done his introduction. After lunch, and for the following
two days as well, the big room will be split up into two smaller
rooms, so that there will be two sessions to choose from at any
given time. After each session there will be a ten-minute break
and during lunchtime, when applicable, Alex will make his
announcements like he did in Barcelona regarding the agenda
for next year. The day usually starts at 9:30 and will last until
around six o'clock. Although with Alex you never know: he

tends to be very flexible when it comes to the daily schedules :-)
From there you are on your own, but normally groups go out
for dinner and drinks and everybody is free to join: good times.

The team and some history

Here's a quote from their website: "The E2EVC Virtualization
Conference is a non-commercial, virtualization community
Event. Our main goal is to bring the best virtualization experts
together to exchange knowledge and to establish new
connections. E2EVC is a weekend crammed with presentations,
Master Classes and discussions delivered by both virtualization
vendors product teams and independent experts. Started in 2003
with just 4 people and after 23 very successful events grown to a
well-recognised event with over 130 attendees. Our conference
has taken place in cities such as Munich, London, Copenhagen,
Amsterdam, Brussels, Berlin, Frankfurt, Dublin, Paris, Los
Angeles, Nice, Lisbon, Rome, Hamburg and Vienna."
Alex Juschin @E2EVC is the event organiser, however, a great
deal of the work is done by the Cooper sisters, Clare
@Clarecoops9 and Orla @Orlacoops. Without the sisters the
event wouldn't be what it is today, according to Alex himself.

Grandfathers

This needs some clarification; E2EVC has done over 30 events
in total already, meaning that there are some E2E veterans
among the audience. People who have attended at least ten or
more events in total are known as the grandfathers of E2EVC.
The active grandfathers – there are passive ones as well – act as
tour guides for new attendees: you can task them anything you
want to know about the event and they'll tell you. During Alex's
introduction he will ask them to raise their hands or stand up so
you know who you can walk up to if you have any questions. A
great idea, if you ask me.

The networking game

Alex is very big on networking, he believes, and I think most will agree that meeting new people and making friends, while having a drink and sharing thoughts, for example, is one of the most important things an event like E2EVC should be about. That's one of the main reasons why he came up with the networking game. Once he's done talking about why meeting new people, sharing and exchanging knowledge, helping each other etc. is so important, he'll step aside and give the audience five minutes to meet up with as many people as possible. Just walk up to somebody you don't know, shake hands and introduce yourself, that's basically it. Once the five minutes are over everybody sits down and Alex steps up again: who knows ten names? he will ask. Ok, nine? Eight? Seven? Until somebody says, yes, I know seven names. He or she will list the names of the people they just met and that's the first prize gone, which usually is a free ticket to the next event, including transportation. The people who were named all receive 50% off registration for next event. It's really good fun!

Some fact and figures

Since the event is already in its eleventh year there are some cool facts and figures I collected, with the help of Alex of course: I used these for one of my own presentations earlier this year. This also gives you a good idea of the knowledge present at any given E2EVC event: it's the place to absorb information and meet some amazing people at the same time, having a drink while you're at it.

As mentioned, it's an extremely social event. The presentations are of a high quality. At any given E2EVC event you'll probably find around 25 to 30 MVPs, vExperts and CTPs: pretty impressive, right? It takes place from Friday till Sunday, so it won't take you too much trouble to get that one day off work. It's non-commercial, meaning cheap! You'll get to visit some amazing cities. There will be (free) beer and sponsored events throughout the conference. Max 150 attendees per event to guarantee quality and to keep networking easy. You'll meet people from around the world, 15 to 20 different countries per event. The combined E2EVC audience has about 65,000 Twitter followers, which take care of around 700,000 customers worldwide, can you say experience? Sight-seeing bus tours. Free shuttle service from the airport. Their own YouTube channel with over 40,000 views already. Loved by all community members! The opportunity to learn about new and existing technologies, meet new people, make friends and grow your professional network. Present a session of your own, and much, much more!

Conclusion

So if you are an IT enthusiast and want to spend some of your time learning, meeting up with some of the IT rockstars, having a good time, drinking a beer, enjoying the city, or maybe your ambition is to present yourself? Then book your ticket to one of the next E2EVC events now: I promise you won't regret it. And did I mention that Alex is an awesome guy? Thanks again, Alex!

The Citrix Technology Professionals

An elite group of technology professionals annually elected by Citrix. This group consists of 50 people max. Again, it's special. Most, if not all, of the CTPs are real community tigers and as such have shared tons of valuable information throughout the years: their level of knowledge, especially as a group is almost endless. Needless to say, I am very proud to be part of this amazing group of people as of February 2016. If you would like to know more about the CTP programme in general, how to apply for the programme, or perhaps have a look at the list of current awardees, go here:

https://www.citrix.com/blogs/2016/02/04/welcome-ctp-class-of-2016/

It includes all the proper links.

Community references

Presenters (and presentations), bloggers and book authors, forums and webcasts, podcasts, webinars and videos etc. the Citrix community has it all. And while the Citrix community consists of thousands of IT enthusiasts: there is always a group that will lead the pack when it comes to sharing information. Here I would like to share a list of publicly available resources that I have come to learn and love over the years: hopefully you guys will benefit from it in the same way as I have done in the past and present. Please forgive me if I have left one or two out.

Podcasts

Ask Eric: Eric (www.xenappblog.com/askeric) gets a lot of questions by email, which can be hard to cope with, especially since a lot of the questions are the same. Here he came up with the concept where people can verbally record a question, which will then be answered by Eric himself or another field expert on the matter. Eric also offers a whole bunch of CBT training videos (free and paid services) on his website www.xenappblog.com.

FronlineChatter: Frontline Chatter (www.frontlinechatter.com) is a community podcast focusing on the End User Computing (EUC) market and it's community. Every fortnight, Frontline chatter will bring you the latest news in EUC and interviews with the interesting and (at times) crazy individuals in the EUC community.

EUC podcast: The End User Computing Podcast (www.eucpodcast.com) is a community-driven podcast for IT professionals. The content covered on the EUC Podcast is primarily geared toward community support and enablement for application, desktop, and server virtualisation technologies. Comments and community interactions are strongly encouraged to keep the authors honest and non-biased toward the vendors and technologies being covered.

Community websites

Table 13: Community websites overview

Name	Website
Alex Juschin	E2evc.com
Andrew Morgan	Andrewmorgan.ie
Barry Schiffer	Barryschiffer.com
Bram Wolfs	Bramwolfs.com
Danny van Dam	Citrix-guru.com
Dane Young	Daneyoung.com
Dennis Smith	Gourami.eu
Carl Webster	Carlwebster.com
Eric Trond	Xenappblog.com
Erik van Hurck	Evanhurck.wordpress.com
Esther Barthel	Virtues.it
Frank Denneman	Frankdenneman.nl

George Kuruvilla	Blog.gkuruvilla.org
Hans De Leenheer	Hansdeleenheer.blogspot.com
Helge Klein	Helgeklein.com/blog
Helmer Zandbergen	Helmersblog.nl
Henny Louwers	Hlouwers.wordpress.com
Igor van der Burgh	B-critical.com/blog
Ingmar Verheij	Ingmarverheij.com
Jarian Gibson	Jariangibson.com
Jasper Kraak	Kraak.com
Jeff Rohrer	Citrixxperience.com
Jeroen Tielen	Jeroentielen.nl
Kees Baggerman	Blog.myvirtualvision.com
Marcel Venema	Marcelvenema.com/Blog
Marius Sandbu	Msandbu.wordpress.com
Martijn Hulsman	Martijn2share.wordpress.com
Matthijs van der Berg	B3rg.nl
Neil Spellings	Neil.spellings.net
Pascal Heldoorn	Pascalswereld.nl
Patrick Kaak	Bitsofthoughts.com
Remco Weijnen	Remkoweijnen.nl/blog
Rachel Berry	virtuallyvisual.wordpress.com
Rink Spies	Rink76.wordpress.com
Robin Hobo	Robinhobo.com

Rob Beekmans	VThoughtsofIT.blogspot.nl
Stéphane Thirion	Archy.net
Steve Greenberg	Thinclient.net/blog
Steven Poitras	Stevenpoitras.com
Thomas Poppelgaard	Poppelgaard.com
Timco Hazelaar	Timcohazelaar.com
Wilco van Bragt	Virtualization.vanbragt.net

I made a collection of well-known community bloggers of which I thought they would be worth sharing, also using what I already had on basvankaam.com. It goes without saying that there are probably tons of additional blogs out there worth visiting. It is not my intention to step on anyone's toes. If you feel left out, I'm sorry.

Team RGE

TeamRGE (Remote Graphics Experts) is a community group of industry experts. It consists of Shawn Bass, Ruben Spruijt and Benny Tritsch with focus on remoting graphics for virtual desktops and applications. The goal of this group is to share unbiased and independent knowledge via blog posts, white papers, videos and presentations at local and international events. Visit their website over at www.teamrge.com and download their whitepaper: trust me, you will not regret it.

NetScaler E-Book

Go over to the website of Marius Sandbu (he is a true blogging machine) and make sure to subscribe to his NetScaler E-Book project. Here is what he has to say about it: For a couple of years now I have been writing for Packt Publishing and authored some books on NetScaler which has been fun and a good learning experience. The problem with that is...

These projects take a lot of time! And the problem these days is that the releases are becoming more and more frequent and the same goes for other underlying infrastructures, which makes it cumbersome to have up-to date content available.

This is the first step in an attempt to create a full (free) NetScaler e-Book, for this moment in time I decided to focus on Optimizing NetScaler traffic features. Hopefully other people will tag along as well, since there are so many bright minds in this community! You'll find him on: www.msandbu.wordpress.com.

The Remote Display Analyzer

I already highlighted this one earlier. Go over to www.rdanalyzer.com and try out their free version. It will make you want to user their sponsored version. Use the Remote Display Analyzer to easily analyze the result of your configuration and change settings on the fly to assess the best possible end-user experience for every user, on every device, on every location.

The end

Wow, here I will assume that you have made it all the way through my book: I'm impressed. Hopefully you have found what I had to share of some value and you can use it to your advantage. This is what I know and found out regarding the FMA and related technologies. I know that there is (much) more to tell, but I thought this would make a more then appropriate introduction.

To finalize, I would like to thank you very much for your interest, purchase and reading my book. It took me quite some effort to put together: a special experience, for sure. If you have any questions, suggestions and/or other remarks you would like to share, please do not hesitate and let me know by dropping me a line on basvankaam.com.

Thank you,

Bas.

Appendix

Appendix A – FMA facts

1. There is also a Linux-based VDA
2. Active Directory is required for the authentication and authorisation of users in a Citrix environment. This includes DNS.
3. Your Delivery Controllers can be considered as the heart of your FMA deployment.
4. Your environment is as strong as its weakest link. Make sure to apply the 'one is none' rule wherever and whenever it makes sense.
5. Prior to XenDesktop 7 the VDA was referred to as the Virtual Desktop Agent, while today we know it as the Virtual Delivery Agent, a subtle difference.
6. You can configure multiple Machine Catalogs with different desktop and server Operating Systems within the same environment / Site.
7. If a VDA is unable to register itself with a Delivery Controller or communication between the VDA and the Delivery Controller fails for any reason, the machine will stay in an unregsiterred state and won't be directly accesable or manageble through one of your Delivery Controllers.
8. There is a separate HDX 3D Pro VDA for use with GPU acceleration for example. This type of VDA enables you to make use of hardware acceleration, including 3D professional graphics applications based on OpenGL and DirectX (The standard VDA supports GPU acceleration of DirectX only.). It can be selected during VDA installation. Resources can either be

assigned on a one to one basis (Passtrhough) or shared amongst multiple VMs (vGPU).

9. While XenDesktop and XenApp both support Web Interface (EOL June 2018) Citrix recommends using StoreFront for new as well as existing deployments. It is built for the future and as such has a whole bunch of additional features not available in Web Interface.

10. Note how I mention user authentication and user validation. There is a distinct difference. Authentication is to make sure that somebody is who he or she claims to be. Verification is done to find out which resources are assigned (permissions) to the user.

11. Note that besides the Receiver for Web approach, where users log into StoreFront by means of a web page, you can also configure your Citrix Receiver in self-service mode. This way your users will be able to subscribe to their resources directly form the local Citrix Receiver interface. See the 'The Citrix Receiver' section for some more detailed information.

12. Besides using Keywords, as of Citrix Receiver 4.2.100 you can also integrate application and desktop short cuts into your user's Start menus or put them onto their desktops, with no resource subscription needed.

13. Going forward, StoreFront multi-site configurations will be a lot easier to configure and implement. Most functionality will be built into the Graphical User Interface of StoreFront.

14. A XenApp Farm (6.5) or XenDesktop / XenApp Site (7.x) is also referred to as a 'Deployment' by Citrix. Especially if you spend some time on their E-docs pages you, will see this term a lot.

15. We can use the Optimal NetScaler Gateway routing feature to route the user's ICA traffic through the

NetScaler most applicable (the one connecting them to their XenDesktop Site in the case of a multi-site deployment) to the user, even if the initial connection was made through another NetScaler.

16. By default, StoreFront will use your internal services URL as an internal resolvable Beacon point and it will use Citrix.com as the external Beacon point. But you can change them to whatever you like. Just make sure that your internal Beacon is not resolvable externally.

17. Non-Platinum-licensed customers can keep and store data for up to 7 days, while a Platinum license allows you to store all data for up to a year, with the default being 90 days.

18. Connection Leasing is meant to supplement SQL High Availability set-ups.

19. The Receiver X1 combined with StoreFront will greatly simplify overall management and improve the user experience on multiple levels.

20. HDX is not a replacement for the ICA protocol. It offers a set of capabilities or technologies that offer a high-definition user experience, which are built on top of the ICA remoting protocol.

21. While some think that ThinWire is still a relatively new technique, it is not. ThinWire has always been there. It is a core component of the ICA virtual display channel stack (for over twenty years now). That's why they rebranded their latest addition as ThinWire Plus, although it has had several names along the way.

22. If you want to make use of e-mail-based discovery you will need to use StoreFront.

23. All, or at least most, of these resource short cut management options were already available with Citrix Receiver Enterprise up to version 3.4, when they killed

it. It took up to Citrix Receiver version 4.2 to get this functionality back.

24. By disabling the SelfServiceMode (it is enabled by default) subscribed-to applications can only be accessed through the Start menu and desktop short cuts. This is also referred to as short cut-only mode.

25. By default, Studio communicates with the Controller on TCP port 80.

26. While Studio takes care of most configuration and maintenance tasks, depending on your set-up, it doesn't cover everything. If you are using Provisioning Services, you will still have a second, separate management console. The same applies to Citrix NetScaler.

27. Do not compare FMA-based Zones (7.x) with IMA-based Zones (6.5). There are some distinct differences between the two. Make sure to check out the table on page 101.

28. If the RRT to and from a satellite Zone is near or above 250 ms, a separate Site deployment, including an SQL HA set-up, is advised.

29. If you want to limit the number of brokering requests originating from a satellite Zone there is a Registry Key, which can be configured for this.

30. Make sure to check out CTX139382 for a whole bunch of best practices around Director.

31. As it stands today, the EOL for EdgeSight has been set to 30-June-18, or 24-Aug-2016, depending on if you have a valid software maintenance and/or Subscription Advantage. In that case, the EOM is set to 31-Dec-17 or 24-Feb-2016.

32. As of version 7.7 Director can be configured to make use of integrated Windows authentication so that domain-joined users gain direct access to Director

without re-entering their credentials on the Director
logon page.

33. The actual SCOM web interface can be launched from
within Director as well. You will find it on the 'Alerts'
page.

34. Director can also be used to monitor and troubleshoot
IMA-based architectures in the form of XenApp 6.5.
Features include, but are not limited to: Shadow
sessions, Machine details pane, HDX panel, Delegated
Administration support, and Activity Manager for 6.5.

35. By default, you can only use one type of license within
your XenDesktop Site. You either purchase / upload
user/device or concurrent: they cannot be mixed. If you
require both, you must set up and configure separate
Sites, license servers included.

36. The license server uses tables to track user\device
license (asignment) information (as described above).

37. The process of assigning licenses to users and/or
devices, whether concurrent or not, is also referred to as
the checking in and checking out of license tokens.

38. Both XenDesktop and XenApp product licenses must
be purchased with Subscription Advantage or Software
Maintenance for a minimum of one year from delivery.

39. As soon as a Citrix product enters a grace period, one or
several event messages (Windows Event Viewer) might
appear. Here you can also see the remaining time left
within the grace period.

40. All Session Hosts as part of the IMA are responsible for
the checkout and handling of licenses, and thus need to
be able to communicate with the license server. Within
the FMA this is handled by your Delivery Controller (s).

41. When licenses are allocated they are 'bound' to your license server, which is identified by its local hostname and is CaseSensitive.

42. You can also visit the Citrix Trial Center where you can get limited trial licenses to try out certain products. However, note that some licenses will only be available for registered Citrix partners.

43. Citrix also offers Appliance Maintenance, which provides technical support to diagnose and resolve issues encountered with appliance hardware with the latest upgrades for the software elements of hardware products. Malfunctioning appliances are also replaced under this agreement to minimise customer downtime. Note that all licenses within a programme must be either on call-in support or not – they cannot be mixed! If one desires different support levels, different licensing subscriptions must be used to separate these, as well as separate license servers!

44. Technically speaking, Software Assurance is an upgrade of existing licenses (usually OEM). That's why you cannot have SA on thin clients (there is no existing license to upgrade) and you have to buy VDA license instead.

45. If you are not accessing a Windows desktop OS VM on a server, but from a physical PC, you do not need a Windows VDA license. This also means that VDA licenses do not apply to Citrix XenApp.

46. Software Assurance benefits (either per use or device) allow you to have up to four virtual machines (VDI), or one physical machine running a Windows desktop Operating System.

47. Microsoft RDS licenses are needed in combination with Citrix XenApp, not XenDesktop. And Microsoft VDA

licenses are needed in combination with Citrix
XenDesktop, not XenApp.

48. Another thing to keep in mind when trying to achieve
'true' cloud based VDI, is that customers will have to
provide their own (Windows desktop OS) licenses. A
Service Provider is not allowed to sell these.

49. You might have heard about the Nutanix Acropolis
Hypervisor. It will soon be available as a Host
Connection within XenDesktop as well.

50. Just recently, Citrix introduced the CPX model, which is
Citrix's containerised version of NetScaler; mainly used
for testing and development use cases. It is still in tech
preview at the time of writing.

51. While there is a separate NetScaler Gateway license
available, also know that each 'normal' ADC NetScaler
(Standard, Enterprise or Platinum license) includes the
Gateway functionality by default: no additional licenses
needed.

52. The virtual NetScaler (VPX) can handle up to 1500
concurrent ICA connections (supported by Citrix,
theoretically it can handle more). If you need more, then
you'll have to upgrade and purchase a physical MPX
appliance, which, depending on the model, can handle
anything ranging from 10,000 to 35,000 concurrent ICA
connections at a time.

53. There's a lot of overlap between the two (ADC and
Gateway): it basically all comes down to the license you
purchase and upload, with the NetScaler Gateway
license being the most 'basic' one.

54. A NetScaler SNIP address is probably best compared to
a layer 3 routing table entry. Not only does it tell the
NetScaler that it has a connection to a specific network,

so it is 'known', it also tells it how and where to reach it so that it is able to route network traffic its way.

55. You can also configure a SNIP address as a management IP, instead of, or better said, alongside the NSIP address used to manage your NetScaler.

56. You can configure as many Unified Gateway virtual servers as you like or need.

57. vDisk updates can be automated and scheduled. This feature supports updates detected and delivered from WSUS and SCCM Electronic Software Delivery servers.

58. Be aware that while promoting the version, PVS will actually open up the vDisk and write to it. This it can lead to inconsistencies if you are storing vDisks locally and replication can be complicated. Provisioning Services has its own built-in TFTP server. However, you are free to use whatever you prefer.

59. As an added advantage, using the BDM method will also decrease boot times by around 5 to 10 seconds since we don't have to wait for PXE and TFTP.

60. When vDisks are stored locally on the Provisioning Servers, you will need to implement some sort of replication mechanism so that all PVS servers will be able to offer the exact same vDisks. This can also be done manually from the PVS management console. Recommended automation methods include both DFS-R and Robocopy.

61. The streamed wizard supports the following Hypervisors: XenServer, Hyper-V through SCVMM and ESX through vCenter.

62. Personal vDisks can only be assigned to an desktop Operating System; server OSs are not supported at this time.

63. While I use the term 'provisioning' do not confuse the provisioning of machines with MCS with that of PVS (see previous chapter). In general, provisioning means providing or making something available. A term widley used in a variety of concepts within IT.

64. Today technologies like application layering and containerisation can help us overcome most of these application-related issues; however, the general adoption of these kinds of technologies and products will still take some time.

65. While all services closely interact with and depend on each other, at the same time they are also completely separated from each other. Each service is configured to communicate to the Central Site database using its own individual DB connection string. If one service fails, unless they depend directly on each other, it will not affect any or most of the other services.

66. Keep in mind that if you change something for one specific service, like the D3 connection string for example, you will have to do this for all of the other FMA services as well.

67. All FMA services run under the NT AUTHORITY\Network service account. Also, when authenticating to the Central Site database (this is where the Configuration Service plays an important role as well) all services use the local computer account of the machine that they are currently running on.

68. While it is considered a best practice to keep all Delivery Controllers equally configured, Site services are the exception to the rule, so to speak.

69. Each FMA service can query the configuration service to look up other services using the listing mentioned earlier. In short, service registration and communication

are both reliant on the configuration service. It will also store configuration metadata for all services, relieving Active Directory.

70. If you would like to refresh the cache of one of the FMA services (remember the five minutes), all you have to do is restart the accompanying Windows Service. The cache (services listing) is retreived during service startup.

71. If you do not configure a Host Connection within Studio, when creating a new Device Catalog, the option to use MCS as a provisioning mechanism will not be available (greyed out). Restarting the Citrix Desktop service on the VDA triggers the registration process and can be used to force re-registration when needed.

72. As opposed to the Desktop VDA, which has been around for a couple of years now, there is no PortICA service within a Server VDA, it simply does not exist.

73. Each Terminal Server protocol (like Citrix's ICA) will have a protocol stack instance loaded (a listener stack awaiting a connection request). When installed, the Server VDA basically extends Microsoft's RDS protocol with the ICA/HDX feature set / protocol.

74. Each service group has a unique identifier, which can be queried using the PowerShell SDK if and when needed.

75. The ICA protocol originated with Citrix Multiuser, around 1990 / 1991, meaning that the ICA protocol is actually over 25 years of age already.

76. By default, the ICA protocol uses TCP port 1494. If Session Reliability is enabled a.k.a. the Common Gateway Protocol, or CGP then ICA traffic will be encapsulated through TCP port 2598. Note that any network traces that you might run will also show 2598 instead of 1494.

77. As a (security) best practice Citrix recommends disabling any virtual channels that are not in use.

78. As mentioned, there are 32 virtual channels in total; however, Citrix reserves 17 of those. Third-party companies and customers who want to design and implement their own virtual channels are free to use the other ones. These are also referred to as dynamic virtual channels or DVCs.

79. Other ways to accelerate ICA traffic would include Citrix policies, which can then be applied either per user or per server, or to the whole Site. Implementing a physical accelerator like the Citrix CloudBridge, formerly known as Branch Repeater, is always optional as well.

80. When not using a CloudBridge appliance, formerly known as Branch Repeater, Session Reliability must be enabled for Multi-Stream ICA to function.

81. When Session Reliability is enabled users will be automatically reconnected as soon as the network connection is reinstated, and they will do so without needing to reauthenticate. Configuring the 'Auto client reconnect authentication' policy to prompt users to reauthenticate can change this behaviour.

82. Remember, Citrix HDX isn't a replacement for the ICA protocol. HDX technologies are meant as an extension and as such operate on top of the ICA protocol.

83. Make sure you check out the HDX policy templates in Studio. There are 6 in total.

84. If you go to YouTube and search for Citrix Framehawk you will find multiple comparison clips of Framehawk vs. other technologies. Guess who comes out on top?

85. Note how I say 'true' application virtualisation. This is because solutions like XenApp are also often referred to

as application virtualisation solutions, so it is really a matter of perspective.

86. Published App-V applications can be configured to be launched from the Start menu, through Citrix Receiver, using the locally installed (image) App-V client or from the StoreFront web interface.

87. AppDisks will be available with all XenDesktop / XenDesktop editions, Advanced, Enterprise and Platinum. Note that AppDNA will be for Platinum-licensed customers only.

88. Citrix AppDisks is available as of XenDesktop / XenApp version 7.8

89. Knowing the architecture, the components, the way traffic flows throughout and expected behaviour is the only way to successfully troubleshoot your FMA-based infrastructure.

90. *If you don't enable authentication on the NetScaler's login page the NetScaler will contact StoreFront and the user will be presented (through the NetScaler) with the StoreFront login page (Receiver for Web sites). The user fills in his or her credentials and authentication will be handled by StoreFront.

91. The STA is only used when traffic traverses a NetScaler, so you don't have to worry about the STA service and its tickets when authentication takes place internally. The STA ticket gets generated and sent back after a user launches an application/desktop, and not during the resource enumeration process. It also includes information on the resource to be launched, including the server to launch the application on (load balance).

92. Make sure that the Broker (XML/STA) service on the NetScaler and the StoreFront server is configured

identically. The same applies to the load balance/fail over order in which you configure them.

93. When a Delivery Group gets created, two access rules are created and added by default, one for direct connections and one for connections through NetScaler. Using PowerShell we can look at and change these access rules, as we see fit.

94. With XPS, the earlier mentioned print output is already in an XML format and will be sent over to the print spooler service right away. See image on the next page for an overview.

95. Perhaps you are better off using None and Shared mode in production and use Isolated for troubleshooting purposes only, which of course could apply to production as well, only temporarily.

96. As a side note, most thin client devices are based on Linux, as a result they will not be able to locally handle and process the earlier mentioned print jobs. As a result of this, the client printing pathway will only work with Windows-based (fat) client devices.

97. So you see that it's not just one thing, it is everything combined that makes or breaks your print architecture: the type of end points you use, policies configured, including the physical placement of your machines, including printers.

98. If for whatever reason the Citrix (XenApp) server and the print server are unable to communicate with each other, again the client printing pathway will be used (forced) instead.

99. Proper testing will be necessary to ensure that (enough) compression takes place.

100. Once enabled you might want to have a look at the 'Universal print driver usage and preference' policies. You have a bunch of options to select from.

101. Is printing slow? Remember that it isn't just about the bandwidth exclusively. Make sure to check for congestion and latency.

102. When thought through beforehand this phase wil probably take you somewhere between 30 to 60 minutes, depending on the number of users and user groups, including the number and the type of applications involved.

103. A high number of IOPS is useless unless latency is low! Even with SSDs which are capable of providing a huge number of IOPS compared to traditional HDDs, latency matters. Latency tells us how long it takes to process a single read or write I/O request.

104. Latency is king: the less you have, the faster your infrastructure will be! Also, there is no standard when it comes to measuring IOPS! There are too many factors influencing overall performance and thus the number of IOPS.

105. Although the average amount of IOPS, or the Steady State, does tell us something, it isn't sufficient. We also need to focus on the peak activity measured between the boot and the Steady State phases and size accordingly.

106. Storage throughput isn't the same as IOPS. When we need to be able to process large amounts of data, bandwidth becomes important: the number of GB/sec that can be processed. Although they do have an overlap, there is a clear difference between the two.

107. If IOPS are limited, try (pre-)booting your machines at night. Also, make sure your users can't reboot the machines themselves.

108. Launching applications will generate high read I/O peaks and initial low writes. Chances are that after users log on they will start, either automatically or manually, their main applications. Again, this is something to take into account, as this will probably cause an application launch storm, although it's usually not recognised as such.

109. By leveraging RAM for writes, a.k.a. RAM Cache with Overflow to Disk in terms of Citrix PVS write cache, we can significantly reduce the number of IOPS needed. In fact, Citrix claims to only need 1 to 2 IOPS per user on a XenApp environment without any complex configurations or hardware replacement.

110. CWC supports both MCS as well as PVS for machine provisioning.

111. Because of Microsoft's licensing restriction with regard to desktop Operating Systems, it is very hard to come up with a true DaaS solution based on an actual desktop OS while keeping costs acceptable. With CWC you can host all of your infrastructural components up in the cloud and leverage your own on-premises VDAs, which can be VDI and 100% desktop OS-based deployments. While not exactly the same, it comes close to a desktop OS-based DaaS (private cloud) offering.

112. The Cloud Connector is what your VDAs will point to and use as a broker, instead of a Delivery Controller when compared to an on-premises deployment.

113. You will need to set up at least two Cloud Connectors per Resource Location to achieve HA. You won't have to configure load balancing in any way for these two Cloud Connectors. CWC will send requests and data to one of the two Connectors, and if it gets too busy or

stops responding, the data will be sent over to the idle Connector, or the load will be spread amongst the two.

114. The customer's metadata will always be stored separately for each tenant, and secured with unique credentials.

115. Citrix offers out-of-the-box blueprints for XenDesktop, XenApp, XenMobile, NetScaler and the Workspace Suite.

116. As I mentioned earlier, E2E relies heavily on sponsors: they are the ones who make it all possible. The E2EVC team doesn't make any money from the event: everything that comes in is invested right back into the event itself.

Appendix B – Key takeaways

Is this all still relevant?

- When talking about cloud computing remember that there are multiple cloud services to choose from: it is not a one-size-fits-all solution.
- Even when moving your entire on-premises infrastructure (or the biggest part) might be beneficial in the long run, it will still take careful planning and execution to get there.
- Start small and take it from there. Hybrid solutions are the way forward, think CWC, for example.
- A lot of companies benefit by leveraging the cloud for Burst Capacity and backup.
- Don't forget about printing and scanning when hosting your RDSH / VDI-based infrastructure in the cloud (bandwidth limitations).
- True VDI (or DaaS) from the cloud, and with this I mean virtual machines with a desktop Operating System installed, assigned on a one-to-one basis, are still hard to achieve. This is mainly because of Microsoft's licensing restrictions.
- Most DaaS solutions are based on RDSH / XenApp in the back-end, meaning you will share your 'desktop' with multiple users.
- The cloud will no doubt have a major impact on how we configure and manage our future infrastructures going forward. However, on-premises RDSH and VDI infrastructures are here to stay for at least another five to ten years, if not longer (my guess is longer).

The evolution of the FMA

- Both XenApp and XenDesktop are built and based on the FlexCast Management Architecture (FMA). And I am pretty sure it will stay like this for many more years to come.

- The FMA was first introduced with XenDesktop version 5.0 back in December 2010. Before that, XenDesktop was also based on the Independent Management Architecture (IMA).

- XenApp became part of the FMA on June 26 2013, which was the official GA date of XenDesktop 7.0.

- The FMA was initially built with VDI in mind.

- This also meant that XenApp was no longer available as a separate product and that they (Citrix) also decided to stop any further development regarding 6.5.

- Luckily, Citrix listened and reintroduced XenApp and XenDesktop as separate products with the release of version 7.5. I don't think they will make a mistake like that again.

- With the addition of XenApp to the FMA, a new (server) VDA was needed.

- The FMA was always meant to be the next generation architecture, providing enhanced scalability, robustness, flexibility and manageability over the IMA.

The FMA, its foundation

- The FlexCast Management Architecture is a Microsoft dot-net-based architecture built upon the WCF (Windows Communication Foundation) framework.

- The WCF framework itself is built using the Microsoft .NET framework

- Dot-net-based applications are executed in a software environment known as the Common Language Runtime, or CRL.
- The .NET Framework supports the following programming languages: Visual Basic, Visual C#, Visual F# and Visual C++.
- Citrix offers several SDKs and APIs, plus some additional tools and services to help you build and integrate custom-developed monitoring and management solutions.
- Citrix has its own Citrix Developer Visual Studio Extension free for you to download.
- Google for 'Citrix developer overview' and you are good to go.

Delivery Controller

- As mentioned, your Delivery Controllers have a lot of responsibilities and can therefore be seen as the heart of your FMA deployment.
- Always deploy at least two Delivery Controllers per Site, and if you can per Zone as well. A minimum of one is needed in the case of a WAN link failure.
- Virtualising your Delivery Controller makes them more flexible, especially in bigger environments. Adding extra DCs or compute resources will be a breeze.
- Almost all Site traffic goes directly through your Delivery Controllers over to the Central Site database and vice versa.
- Try to keep your Delivery Controllers physically close to your database server and any Host Connections you might have set up.

- Delivery Controllers are fundamentally different from Data Collectors: remember that. No LHC, direct database communication, no communication between Delivery Controllers, service- and agent (VDA)-based, and so on.
- StoreFront directly communicates with one of your Delivery Controllers during the user authentication, application enumeration and launch process. You can configure your StoreFront server with a NetScaler load balance VIP address, which will load balance the connections to the Delivery Controllers within the NetScaler VIP.

The virtual delivery agent

- VDAs communicate directly with your Delivery Controllers (Desktop service).
- On boot, VDAs register themselves with a Delivery Controller.
- The mechanism used to find a Delivery Controller to register with is referred to as 'auto-update' but can be achieved in other ways as well.
- Registration will be done through port 80 by default; customising your VDA settings through Control Panel can change this.
- VDA registration can be verified by restarting the Citrix Desktop Service on the VDA machine itself. After the restart, look for event 1012 stating it successfully registered with a Delivery Controller.
- A VDA consists of two main services, the Citrix Desktop Service and the Citrix ICA Service. The Desktop Service communicates with the Broker service on the Delivery Controller it registers with.

- The Delivery Controller will also power-manage the VDA, meaning it will (re)boot it when needed (works for desktop VDAs only). It will also tell it to listen for new connections when users login to their VDI environment to ensure a successful connection.
- With the addition of XenApp to the FMA, Citrix created a new Server VDA. This will be discussed in more detail later on.
- Use the VDA in HA mode as a last resort. Hopefully it will never come to this.
- VDAs can be managed through policy.
- Different versions of VDAs can be mixed within the same environment (you can select the VDA used from Studio during configuration and install). Make sure to always check with Citrix to find out which configurations are supported.
- Using mixed versions of VDAs can lead to limited feature support. This includes management and monitoring features through Studio and Director.
- Always try to deinstall the old VDA and install the new VDA.
- Before installing the latest VDA available, make sure to check with Citrix for any known issues that might have surfaced during testing (E-docs).
- Sometimes manually updating to the latest VDA (after reimaging) is recommended.
- For lab set-up purposes you can install the Delivery Controller software, the database, StoreFront, licensing etc. all on one server.

StoreFront

- You basically have two points of authentication within a XenDesktop / XenApp Site: StoreFront and NetScaler.

- When working with Zones always make sure to deploy at least one StoreFront server per Zone. Needed in the case of a WAN link failure.

- Users may need to subscribe themselves to resources they are allowed to start. These user subscriptions are synchronised between all StoreFront servers within the same StoreFront server group.

- The above is also referred to as the 'Self Service Store' setup, which is enabled by default. A bit more on this in the 'The Citrix Receiver' chapter.

- The 'Self Service Store' can be disabled, leaving you with the 'Mandatory Store' configuration. Using this setup all resources for which a user has proper permissions will be displayed by default, no subscriptions needed.

- Combined with the 'Self Service Store' approach you can configure Keywords in Citrix Studio to automatically subscribe your users to certain resources, like a standard desktop, for example. When a user logs in, the resources will be directly displayed on his or her welcome screen.

- If email based discovery is enabled and configured, you have the option to either advertise the Store or to hide the Store. When advertised the Store is presented as an option for your users to add. When you hide it, the user will need configure the Citrix Receiver him or her self using a setup URL or provisioning file, for example.

- When configuring and modifying your StoreFront deployment, especially when editing the web.conf file, make sure you are doing this only using one StoreFront server at the same time. Preferably the one you installed and configured first.

- You can manually propagate any changes you have made to StoreFront to your other StoreFront servers within the same server group.
- When dealing with multi-site deployments, you can configure specific user groups to be mapped to a preferred site.
- StoreFront multi-site configurations let us configure a Recovery site. This site will sit idle until all other StoreFront deployments stop accepting connections, whatever the reason may be.
- When using a Citrix NetScaler think about using it to load balance all external incoming traffic to your StoreFront servers.
- If you only publish a single desktop to a user, StoreFront will automatically launch it directly after the user successfully logs in to StoreFront. This behaviour can be changed by manually editing web.conf file. Have a look at the following CTX document: CTX139058.
- StoreFront plays an important part in configuring Citrix Receiver pass-through authentication a.k.a. Single Sign-on. Look for the support document CTX200157.

The Central Site database

- As of XenDesktop 7.x, only SQL is supported for the Central Site database.
- It contains all static as well as dynamic Site-wide information.
- Make sure you understand the differences between the IMA and FMA when it comes to your Controllers and the Central Site database.

- If your Site is spread over multiple geographically separated locations, or you have multiple Zones configured, your Central Site database should always be in the Primary Zone, or the main datacentre.

- So even with multiple Zones configured it is still one central database.

- Make sure to implement some form of HA solution for your Site databases, since Connection Leasing is only meant as a supplement.

- Your Delivery Controllers and the Site database are constantly communicating: for this, Windows authentication is required between the Delivery Controller and the database.

- When the database fails (even without Connection Leasing) existing connections will continue to work. New sessions cannot be established and Site-wide configuration changes are also not possible.

- It is not recommended to install SQL on the same machine as a Delivery Controller.

- Try to keep your database server physically close to your Delivery Controllers in the data centre.

- SQL software, server or Express, must be installed and configured before creating a XenDesktop Site after its initial installation.

- While SQL Express is primarily used for PoC and testing purposes it could be used for smaller production environments as well. No HA capabilities though. It's up to you.

- You must be a local administrator and a domain user to create and initialise the databases (or change the database location).

- To be able to create an empty database, to add Delivery Controllers to it, create and apply schema updates and so on, you will need to have the following server and database roles: dbcreator, securityadmin and db_owner.
- When using Citrix Studio to perform these operations, the user account must be a member of the sysadmin server role.

The Citrix Receiver

- No matter how you decide to deploy and configure Citrix Receiver, make sure to instruct your users.
- Don't forget to inform your helpdesk employees when planning configuration changes to Receiver.
- I briefly introduced you to the Web Access and Self Service modes. Remember, it does not have to be one or the other. They can be configured and used side-by-side.
- A couple of years ago the Self Service mode was released as a separate plugin; it is now built into Receiver.
- In fact, some of the most important modules that make up Receiver today are the ICA Client software, the Self Service plugin, and the Single Sign-on module for ICA.
- It all started with the ICA Client software back in 2009. Since then it has gone through a lot of name changes and of course the underlying technology also matured over time.
- The upcoming Receiver X1 is probably a great example of its evolution during the last decade.
- When upgrading to a newer version of Receiver, make sure to follow the step-by-step procedure as outlined by Citrix; have a look this CTX article: CTX135933.

- As it stands today, the Citrix Receiver version 4.4 should be able to upgrade from any of the older Receiver versions that might be installed without any issues.
- When upgrading to a version older than 4.4 and you run into any issues, have a look at CTX137494, the Receiver Clean-Up utility.
- Do not forget about the ICA handshake and the earlier mentioned virtual channels.
- The Citrix Receiver can be managed and configured using various methods, for example: using the command-line, registry settings, StoreFront account settings, or on a per application basis using Studio and Group Policy Objects.
- When viewing the Citrix Receiver Feature Matrix, remember that not all features are on there.
- By default, the HTML5-based and built-in (StoreFront) Receiver is not enabled: this needs to be done manually.

Studio / Zones

- Citrix Studio is THE management console that allows us to administrate, configure and manage our XenDesktop and/or XenApp Sites from a single pane of glass. It also provides us with access to real-time data collected through the Broker service running on the Delivery Controller.
- Studio also provides us with a range of basic troubleshooting tools and options.
- While Zones are not a new concept, you need to be aware that Zones within a 7.x deployment are not the same as with XenApp 6.5 – not yet anyway. There are some distinct differences between the two, as we have clearly seen in this chapter.

- Citrix is working on a phased approach with regard to the reintroduction of Zones; needless to say, this is phase one.
- Zones in the FMA still depend on the Central Site database: there is no LHC.
- The main focus of this first releases is to simplify overall management and keep traffic local.
- Make sure to keep an eye on the RTT between Zones; it needs to be below 250 milliseconds; less is more in this case. Consult the table for recommended values.

Director

- Director is a real-time monitoring and troubleshooting web-based tool.
- Citrix EdgeSight technology has been built into Director (primarily used for historical data reporting, trends and analyses). The EdgeSight software will no longer be available as a separate product. The latest version of EdgeSight was 5.4, which is still supported until 31-Dec-17 if you have a valid software maintenance and/or Subscription Advantage.
- To be able to make use of the built-in historical reporting fucntionality Platinum XenDesktop / XenApp licenses will be needed.
- To make use of the network analysis functionality you will need to have at least a NetScaler Enterprise or Platinum license.
- Depending on your XenDesktop / XenApp / NetScaler licenses, you will be able to store historical data for a certain period of time. See the overview.

- Director offers different views for administration and troubleshooting purposes, including the ability to configure delegated administration on a per role basis.
- Alerts and notifications are directly visible and accessible from the main dashboard.
- The main XenDesktop / XenApp infrastructural services are also being monitored by Director, these are visible from the main dashboard view. It uses PowerShell for this.
- SCOM alerts and notification can be configured and viewed from Director as well. Just recently, Citrix acquired the SCOM Comtrade management packs for Citrix environments.
- Insight Services can now be accessed directly from Director. It is fuelled with analytics data from Scout, as well as Citrix Call Home.
- Insight services can also be accessed directly by going to www.cis.citrix.com.
- Director can also be used with older IMA, XenApp 6.5 environments. It also supports older VDAs.

Citrix License Server and licensing

- Citrix Licensing relies on Flexera software, as do many other product vendors, by the way.
- The license server is a relatively light role and can easily be shared with other roles on a single virtual of physical server. A single license server is able to handle over 10,000 continuous connections.
- XenDesktop and XenApp licenses come in different forms. There are per user, per device and concurrent licenses available.

- A user license gives a single user the right to start sessions on an unlimited number of devices. The license is bound to the user and is device-independent.

- A device license works the other way around. A session can be started from a single device, but it does not matter by whom. It is user-independent.

- If a user/device license is issued, it is applied to a license token for both a XenDesktop and a XenApp license token, even if you only connect to just one or the other. They are always issued in pairs.

- Concurrent licenses are not bound to a user or device: you can use them for both. However, these are more expensive to purchase.

- If the license server becomes unavailable for some reason it will make use of a built-in grace period of 30 days. Everything will continue to function as before. This basically means you will have 30 days to get the license server up and running again.

- While products like XenDesktop and XenApp are both licensed through a central license server, a product like NetScaler, will need its license installed directly on the device itself.

- Citrix offers various forms of support and maintenance. Subscription Advantage allows you to upgrade to the latest versions, Feature Packs and so on. Software Maintenance, on the other hand, offers you 24x7x365 support. When purchasing either XenDesktop and/or XenApp you will need to also purchase at least one year of Subscription Advantage and/or Software Maintenance, which isn't that uncommon.

- Recently they released their Current Release (CR) and Long Term Service Release (LTSR) product support options. For each Long Term Service Release, the clock restarts, giving you 5 years of mainstream support and 5 years of extended support, plus more. Current Releases will provide access to the latest security, productivity and collaboration features to help keep your workforce competitive, plus extras.

- The 'new' CR release isn't really new; it is basically the way it has always been before they introduced the LTSR option.

Host Connection

- While in earlier releases of XenDesktop / XenApp 7.x Host Connections were limited to Hypervisor platforms, cloud environments are now supported as well.

- As it stands today, MCS can be used in combination with Azure, AWS and/or the Citrix CloudPlatform. However, PVS is not supported: it simply does not work. It also works for, or with all Hypervisors mentioned. The Nutanix Acropolis Hypervisor will be added to the list shortly.

- MCS only works with virtual machines.

- You can add multiple Host Connections if you want, also combining cloud and on-premises Hypervisors.

- When adding Hypervisor Host Connections you will have to use the addresses of your System Center Virtual Machine Manager, Virtual Center or XenCenter.

- When using Zones make sure that the Host Connection configured for a Zone is close to, or actually physically located within, that Zone.

NetScaler

- The NetScaler can do more than 'just' provide secure remote access to XenDesktop and/or XenApp environments.

- All NetScalers are (almost) equal with regard to the functionality and features that they can deliver. Depending on the type of license you upload, certain functionalities and/or features will become available. Pay as you Grow.

- The main differences between the physical appliances can be found in the compute resources and the type of Cavium SSL accelerator card that they hold. This card is used to decrypt and encrypt SSL traffic. The more powerful the card, the more SSL transactions it will be able to handle.

- NetScalers can be physical (MPX and SDX), virtual (VPX), virtual on physical (VPX on SDX) and containerised (CPX).

- While not mentioned earlier (except for the license type) there is also a NetScaler Express edtion. It is free of charge and a potential great resource for smaller deployments, PoC's and test environments. The VPX Express edition offers the same features as the VPX standard edition. However, there are a few limitations to keep in mind like: no SSL Offload capabilities, max 5 Mbps throughput, licensed per year. Other than that it is definitely worth having a look at.

- There are three main ADC platform licenses available: Standard, Enterprise and Platinum. There is also a separate NetScaler Gateway license and a universal license.

- If you need to temporarily increase your network bandwidth think about purchasing and applying a Burst Pack.

- Remember the one is none rule? Well, it applies to NetScalers as well.

- NetScaler HA (2 nodes) is always set up as active-passive, with one NetScaler being the primary node of the two, and thus the active one. The secondary node(s) will send a continuous stream of heartbeat messages (interval is configurable), checking to see if the primary device is active and accepting connections. If it fails to respond, and after multiple retries, a secondary node will take over, which is referred to as a failover. NetScaler clustering, which is Active / Active using ECMO, can grow up to 32 nodes in total.

- When applying NetScaler HA be aware that different NetScaler models cannot be paired: the model and make of both NetScaler appliances must be equal and both NetScalers must run the same software version, licenses included.

- The NetScaler can also provide secure remote access to XenMobile web, SaaS and mobile applications. The latter is referred to as Micro VPNs. In fact, you need a NetScaler for this.

- Always start small and contact your Citrix sales representative when in doubt. Remember the Pay as you Grow model: you can't go wrong.

- When dealing with larger and more complex environments, consider having a look at the NetScaler Unified Gateway set-up.

- Make sure to apply SSL certificates to secure your in- and outbound connections.

- It is thought of as a best practice to use third-party certificates when dealing with external, inbound connections, and to use internal CA certificates for all internal SSL traffic, from your StoreFront Server to your Delivery Controllers, for example.
- When setting up a test lab or PoC environment, self-signed certificates can be helpful.
- NetScaler can secure remote access for both StoreFront as well as Web Interface.
- When implementing a Citrix NetScaler certain firewall ports will need to be opened. Always check the Citrix product documentation before implementing.

Provisioning Services

- Provisioning Services streams a base image over the network down to either virtual or physical machines.
- It works for both desktop as well as server Operating Systems.
- A device using a vDisk is also referred to as a Target Device.
- The machine used to create and maintain the vDisk is referred to as the Master Target Device.
- Target Devices are managed using Device Collections.
- Dozens, hundreds or thousands of Target Devices can share a single vDisk.
- The life cycle of a vDisk consists of creation, deployment, maintenance and finally retirement. For this we can leverage the built-in PVS Versioning mechanism.
- Give your write cache sizing and location some consideration: you will be glad that you did.

- Although PVS vDisks can also be streamed in Private Mode, where any changes made to the vDisk will be saved, this isn't a very popular approach.
- Provisioning Services can seem complicated and challenging at first. Take your time and take it step by step, you will be fine. There are many excellent resources out there to help you on your way.
- Make sure to make your PVS infrastructure highly available.
- While PvDs have their use, apply them wisely: it's not for everyone. And while this may be somewhat off topic, in many cases where VDI is being considered, RDSH might make more sense.
- Make sure to check out CTX117372 for some best practices around PVS networking.
- While in the past it was always considered a best practice to use physical machines for your Provisioning Servers, today virtual machines are almost always recommend by Citrix. This has a lot to do with the enhancements around standard networking.
- The same applies to isolating your PVS traffic, again mainly due to the advancements that have been made on the networking and virtualisation side of things during the last couple of years. Keep it simple. One of the main reasons why isolation might still make sense is because of security considerations.
- CTX131611 lists a bunch of Known Hardware Related Provisioning Services Issues.
- Check out CTX124185 for best practices around antivirus on PVS vDisks.

Machine Creation Services

- MCS is considered to be easy. It is managed and configured directly from Studio and you do not need any additional infrastructural components as you do with PVS.

- MCS is based on differencing disks technology.

- Your base or golden image will be copied over to all datastores, which are part of the virtual machine deployment. Take this into account when thinking about your storage needs.

- When application virtualisation is not an option, often forcing you to install applications into your base image, think about using application layering as an alternative.

- When using MCS, rollbacks are treated the same way as a new or updated base image: they will again need to be copied over to all datastores involved. Note that in some cases the previous image might still be in use by some machines. If so, than no full copy will be needed.

- Give your Idle and Disconnect session policies some thought. This will make it easier to reboot your machines during night-time, depending on company policy, of course.

- Go over the earlier mentioned list of storage implications a couple of times: there is a lot to consider.

The FMA core services

- FMA stands for FlexCast Management Architecture and, as of XenDesktop version 7, includes a Desktop as well as a Server VDA.

- It is the next generation architecture for XenDesktop and XenApp VDI and/or RDSH-based deployments.

- Over the years it has evolved from six up to eleven main services in total.

- Internal communication takes place over port 80 using Windows Communication Foundation end points.

- Each service runs complete separated from the other services, as a result each service also has its own separate database connection string: if one service fails it will not directly affect any of the other services.

- There is a distinct difference in architecture when compared to the IMA. All of the HDX / ICA bits and bytes are installed as part of the VDA on the Session Host and VDI based VMs while the Delivery Controllers primarily concerns itself with brokering, maintaining and optimizing existing sessions.

- All services run under the NT AUTHORITY \ Network account and use the local computer account for database authentication purposes. One of the benefits this brings is that password are automatically changed every 30 days. This is a big deal, as service accounts are usually very dangerous.

- The Broker service includes the XML as well as the STA service.

- There are 18 active (sub) site services in total, all running within the Broker services, taking care of various Site housekeeping tasks.

- There needs to be a way that VDAs can track and contact the various Delivery Controllers within a Site to be able to register themselves. Citrix uses the auto-update feature for this.

- As we have seen, the PortICA, or picaSvc2.exe, service is an important one during the VDA launch and user login process.

- The PortICA a.k.a. PicaSvc2.exe and the Citrix Desktop Service a.k.a. BrokerAgent.exe services are the two main FMA services within the Desktop VDA.
- The Connection Brokering Protocol (CPB) plays an important role in the VDA registration process. It is basically a collection of WCF end points.
- The Server VDA does not have the PortICA service; however, it does have a Broker service.
- It basically uses the same ICA stack as with XenApp 6.5, but with a different management interface to make it compatible with the 7.x Delivery Controllers.
- Service groups make FMA services highly available.

The ICA / HDX protocol

- Edward Lacobucci founded Citrix in 1989.
- Initially they started developing a multi-user platform for Microsoft's OS/2.
- Citrix actually started out as Citrus.
- They licensed the OS/2 source code from Microsoft and started developing Multiuser, which would later become their first major release.
- ICA was introduced when Citrix Multiuser was launched, which was around 1990 / 1991.
- Shortly after Citrix launched Multiuser, Microsoft announced that they would drop OS/2 and move to Windows.
- With some help of other companies, Microsoft included, Citrix managed to stay in business.
- In the meantime Citrix patented ICA and they started working on a new and improved version of ICA.

- Eventually a new agreement was signed giving Microsoft access to the ICA source code. This is how the Microsoft RDP protocol came to exist.
- ICA supports most, if not all, standard protocols today.
- It uses TCI/IP port 1494 by default, and is tunnelled through port Nr. 2598 when Session Reliability is enabled.
- The ICA protocol consists of 32 virtual channels in total, 17 of which are reserved by Citrix.
- The client capabilities are negotiated at session launch time, also referred to as the handshake.
- Virtual channels consist of, and communicate through, virtual drivers at the client side and server-side applications on the server side.
- Customers and other third parties have the ability to develop their own virtual channels.
- Each virtual channel has a default priority assigned to it, ranging from 0 to 3, with 0 being the highest, or most important. A higher priority means more bandwidth.
- By editing the registry you can manually change priorities. Be careful with this, giving more priority to one VC means you also take away priority (bandwidth) somewhere else.
- Multi-Stream ICA works by assigning separate TCP/IP ports to groups of priorities, or streams, establishing true QoS.
- Session Reliability ensures that the user session is not disconnected and that the user's session freezes, while in the background the ICA traffic is buffered.
- All buffered ICA traffic will be flushed out to the user's device once the user session reconnects.

- Session Reliability can leverage the Auto client reconnect feature to enforce users to reauthenticate when a session is reconnected.
- HDX is an extension to the ICA protocol and is in no way intended to replace ICA. It works on top of the ICA protocol.
- The Citrix ThinWire technology has multiple names: it is known as ThinWire Plus, ThinWire Advanced, Legacy ThinWire and ThinWire compatibility mode. They all have one thing in common: ThinWire is all about compressing data and enhancing the overall user experience.
- ThinWire has a small CPU and memory footprint and doesn't need much bandwidth.
- Framehawk is all about packet loss and high latency connections, delivering a more than acceptable user experience under challenging circumstances.
- In general, Framehawk needs more CPU and bandwidth than ThinWire, although this has been greatly enhanced with the latest 7.8 release.

Application delivery

- Although I narrowed it down to three ways of application delivery, there are of course a lot more flavours to choose from, especially when talking virtualisation, layering and containerisation. Search for the Application Virtualization Smackdown whitepaper, or visit rorymon.com. You will be amazed by the options you have.
- AppDisks is Citrix's approach to application layering. But again, make sure to give the others some thought as

well. Although with AppDisks you will be able to manage everything directly from Studio.

- AppDisks will be available for all licenses. AppDNA integration with AppDisks will be for Platinum customers only. When used in conjunction with AppDisks, AppDNA will automatically check your AppDisks, or any other applications you might have for that matter. It will tell you if they are good to go in combination (compatible) with the platform you want to deploy them on.

- Application layering is not meant as a direct replacement for application virtualisation: they go hand-in-hand. In practice you will probably use all three, base image-installed applications, virtualised and layered apps.

- Application layering does not isolate applications.

- Think of it as just another tool in the toolbox to make life a little easier.

- Remember that, although a single master image is great to have, it is also a utopia in most cases. Just don't go nuts: keep the number of images to manage to a minimum. Less is more.

The user login process

- There are two main authentication points within a Flex Management-based Architecture: NetScaler (optional) and StoreFront.

- Knowing the difference between the IMA and the FMA, how traffic flows throughout each component, and the way they are supposed to interact is or can be vital to successfully troubleshooting the FMA.

- As of version 3.0, StoreFront can also use the XML service for authenticating users.

- Note that there is a distinct difference between authentication and verification. Authentication is to make sure that somebody is who he or she claims to be. Verification is done to find out which resources are assigned (permissions) to the user, which will then be displayed in the user's store, ready for subscription.

- User authentication and resource enumeration basically go hand-in-hand.

- The STA only applies when connections are coming in externally through NetScaler.

- The STA service is part of the Broker server, and so is the perhaps better-known XML service.

- The HTML5-based Citrix Receiver, as part of your Internet browser, can offer the exact same functionality and features as a natively installed Receiver.

- The Windows authentication process is also involved when launching a Citrix published resource.

- Site policies allow us to exclude certain users or to apply certain policies when specific conditions are met. PowerShell can be used to manage and configure Site policies.

A deeper look into Citrix printing

- There are two main (Microsoft) print file formats, EMF and XPS.

- EMF print output is first rendered by the GDI – Graphics Device Interface – before being handed over to the spooler service.

- XPS was introduced as of Windows Vista. EMF development ended with Windows XP and Server 2003.

- EMF data is not compressed. XPS data does get compressed.

- With EMF, each image needs to be redrawn over and over again, even if the same image is used multiple times. XPS can reference a single image multiple times: think company logos, watermarks etc.

- To be able to use XPS, both your print device and the print driver need to support the XPS print file format. If not, it will fall back to EMF.

- High-level Print Spooling: Print output is received by the spooler service, print driver renders Metafile into raw data readable by print device (the actual print job), spooler service sends print job to physical print device.

- When spooled locally, local resources (CPU, memory) are leveraged. No network traffic is generated.

- When spooled remotely (print server) remote resources are leveraged. This will also produce additional network traffic between the XenApp and print server. Might be something to consider depending on your print architecture.

- Most print issues can be led back to badly written drivers. Not tested and/or optimised for multi-user environments.

- Main problems used to be (or still are): Spooler service crashes, CTX print manager service crashes, blue screens, auto-print creation failures, high CPU loads.

- Do NOT make use of kernel mode (version 2) print drivers.

- Use user mode (version 3 and 4) print drivers exclusively.

- Consider isolating your print drivers a.k.a. Print Driver Isolation introduced with Windows Server 2008 R2. But... only apply Print Driver Isolation where it makes sense.

- Version 4 modes print drivers: Designed for Metro-style applications (XPS), enhanced printer sharing, easier to install, maintain, manage etc.

- When a Citrix session starts, after the user logs in, it will, by default, try to map all printers known to the client device within the session.

- Change this behaviour to: map the client's default printer only. Configure the 'Auto-create client printers' policy for this. Of course you have multiple options to choose from.

- Tthe XenApp server will try to match the print driver (s) found on the client device. If the print driver cannot be found, the system attempts to install the driver from the Windows operating system. If the driver is not available in Windows it will (try and) use the Citrix Universal Print Driver (it will need to be enabled for this to work).

- Configure the 'Automatic installation of inbox printer drivers' to change this behaviour.

- Think about implementing 'printer driver mapping compatibility'. Print driver mapping is useful in situations where the print driver on the client is named differently than the print driver on the server (these need to match), but offer the exact same functionality. It can also be configured to create a whitelist: this way you can tell the XenApp server that it is ok to auto-install print drivers when not found on the system, but only if those drivers are on the (white) list.

- Use 'signed' drivers exclusively and always thoroughly test your print architecture set-up, no matter how convinced you may be that it will work.

- Limit the number of print drivers installed: less is more!

- Avoid upgrading print drivers. Always uninstall the old driver and install the new one.
- Always match the print server OS to that of the XenApp server OS.
- The Citrix Print Management Service communicates with the spooler service and the local ICA Client, it compresses print data before sending it over the ICA channel, and also manages the ICA virtual channel for client print mapping.
- Printing preferences (user) and properties will be stored on the client device by default. If this is not supported, they will be stored in the user profile within the server Operating System.
- Configure the 'Printer properties retention' policy to change this. Again, you have multiple options.
- A printing pathway defines how print traffic can or will be routed throughout your environment. It also tells us where a job gets processed, spooled, rendered etc.
- There are two Citrix printing pathways: the client printing pathway and the network printing pathway.
- Besides these pathways there is also a set-up named 'Server local printers', which is basically a physical print device directly attached to a XenApp server.
- When using the client printing pathway, application print output is spooled / rendered on the XenApp server (local from a client perspective) before it is sent back to the client device.
- With the client printing pathway the traffic between the XenApp server and the client device is sent through the ICA protocol, meaning it can be managed / compressed.

- When a (fat) client device has a local printer attached, the client printing pathway will always be used.
- When TCP/IP direct printers are added manually or by using / applying Group Policy Preferences, the printer is seen and treated as a locally attached printer. As such, print traffic will flow through the client printing pathway.
- Thin client devices (Linux-based) do not support the client printing pathway. They lack local printing capabilities. The network printing pathway (session printers) will need to be used instead.
- The network printing pathway will send the application print output from the XenApp server to the print server where it will be spooled / rendered. Spooling takes place remotely. From there it will send the print job to the physical print device.
- Using the network printing pathway all traffic sent between the XenApp server and the print server will be uncompressed / unmanaged, non-ICA.
- The Universal Print Server can help compress / manage traffic sent between the XenApp server and the print server.
- When a client device has a network-provisioned (print server) printer, Citrix will always try and route print traffic over the network printing pathway.
- I say 'try', because if the print server and the XenApp server are in different domains and they are unable to communicate, the client printing pathway will be used instead. The same applies when both machines are unable to communicate for other reasons.
- By disabling the 'Direct connection to print servers' policy, we can force the client printing pathway to be

used, even when network-provisioned printers are leveraged.

- There is no 'one size fits all', period!

- Keeping the XenApp and print server close together isn't always the best solution.

- All this applies to XenApp as well as XenDesktop, and isn't IMA- or FMA-specific.

- The Universal Print Driver (UPD) is disabled by default.

- The UPD is installed as part of the VDA.

- There is an EMF as well as an XPS print file format UPD.

- The EMF UPD will be used by default. This can be changed through policy.

- Both the Universal Print Server and the Universal Printer use the Universal Print Driver by default.

- The Universal Printer is a logical / generic object created at the beginning of a session. It will be mapped to the client's default printer but this can be changed to any printer known to the client device.

- When using the Universal Printer, no print mapping / enumeration takes place, speeding up the logon / login process.

- The Universal Printer only works for Windows devices.

- It is potentially useful when the 'Wait for printer to be created' policy is used or when you need access to multiple printers, local & network.

- The Universal Print Server (UPS) consists of a client (UPClient) and server (UPServer) component.

- It uses the UPD by default but can be paired with Windows Native print drivers, again, for more enhanced printing capabilities.

- It's optimised for network printers and offers additional compression and QoS options.
- It supports both EMF and XPS-based print drivers.
- It also works for thin client devices and tablets, based on network (session) printers.
- The UPS does not support client side rendering / spooling, meaning that all application print output will be sent over to the print server (which has the UPServer component installed) right away.
- All traffic sent between the XenApp (UPClient component) and print server (UPServer component) can be managed / compressed when enabling the UPS.
- Network printers will leverage the UPS automatically through a process called auto-discovery.
- It can handle up to 50 print jobs per minute.
- Recommended for remote office scenarios. Please note that testing will be necessary to see if adequate compression ratios are achieved.
- Helps in managing a large number of network printers.
- Can be used for proximity printing. The UPS is a prerequisite.
- Use session (network) printers on fast(er) networks.
- Session printers are network printers that can be assigned and mapped to a specific user or user groups.
- With proximity printing, sessions are filtered based on IP addresses or subnets (there are some more options). This way a user will always connect to the closest printer (UPS is needed).
- When dealing with slow printing remember that it's not all about network bandwidth. Also check for congestion and latency.

- The 'simpler' the print driver, the less traffic will be generated. Use vendor drivers only when specific functionality is needed.

- Last-minute addition from the E-docs pages: XenApp and XenDesktop 7.6 FP3 include an Always-On logging feature for the print server and printing subsystem on the VDA. In order to collate the logs as a ZIP for emailing, or to automatically upload to Citrix Insight Services, use the PowerShell cmdlet (Start-TelemetryUpload) supplied with the VDA installer in 7.6 FP3.

- Citrix Printing Tool 3.1 helps configuring and troubleshooting the Citrix Printing subsystem on XenApp, XenApp Online Plug-in and XenDesktop.

- Print Detective is an information-gathering utility that can be used for troubleshooting problems related to print drivers. It enumerates all printer drivers from the specified Windows machine, including driver-specific information. It can also be used to delete specified print drivers. It allows for log file capabilities and provides a command-line interface as well.

- All-purpose troubleshooting tool – Run Citrix Scout from a single XenDesktop controller (DDC) or XenApp server to capture key data points and CDF traces for selected computers followed by a secure and reliable upload of the data package to Citrix Technical Support.

- The Citrix UPS Print Driver Certification Tool can be used to test the compatibility of a print driver with the Citrix Universal Print Server.

- Not sure? Test your print drivers thoroughly using StressPrinters.

- Check out Microsoft's (MSDN) web page to find out more about Print Driver Isolation.
- Release data: February 2012, primarily focused on XenApp 6.5: XenApp Printer Driver Manager. Manage your XenApp print drivers. Update the Automatic Printer Replication List with a GUI.
- A collection of Citrix troubleshooting and diagnostic tools: CtxAdmTools.

Troubleshooting the FMA

- Successful troubleshooting starts with understanding the environment, architecture and components you're working with.
- In times of 'peace' make sure you spend some time getting to know the various troubleshooting tools and methodologies out there. Assemble your own tool kit and/or come up with your own troubleshooting methodology /approach.
- Make sure to go over some of the tips I gave you at the beginning of this chapter: there are some useful pointers in there. Not much use in repeating them all here, the same applies to all the tool listed.

Sizing and storage considerations

- When it comes to sizing your XenDesktop / XenApp infrastructures: there is no 'one size fits all'.
- You need to understand the workloads you have to deal with and size accordingly.
- There is more to it than 'just' compute resources: don't forget about your underlying storage platform.
- While sizing is important, try not to overdo it. Real-world testing will always be needed.

- Ask peers for help and/or advice, consult the Citrix XenDesktop Handbook, use Project Accelerator and test, test and test some more.

- Load testing can give us an indication of what might be possible, but remember that your users can be (very) unpredictable.

- When conducting load tests, always try to incorporate any exotic applications that you might have. These are the ones you should be most curious about.

- IOPS fundamentals help you in understanding what is going on under the hood. It will also help in understanding what other IT folks might be talking about in other articles / blogs.

- A random IOPS number on its own doesn't mean anything. What type of IOPS are we talking about: reads, writes, random, sequential, rereads and/or writes, single or multiple threads, block sizes and so on. And even more importantly, what is the latency number in MS?

- Storage providers should be able to provide you with at least the latency in MS, the reads vs. writes ratio, and the data block sizes used during testing.

- Remember that there is a big difference between steady state, boot logon, application launch and logoff storms.

- Storage throughput is not the same as IOPS. When dealing with large amounts of data that need to be processed and transmitted, storage throughput becomes more important.

- Reads are less intensive than writes. Also, today we have a lot of options when it comes to caching reads.

- While IOPS are important when it comes to sizing and forming a potential bottleneck, do not forget about

CPU, memory and storage controllers. They can only handle so much..

The Citrix Workspace Cloud

- CWC offers customers the ultimate hybrid model and an easy way to get used to and migrate to the cloud.
- All the latest and greatest FMA features will first be made available to CWC before being built into the on-premises XenApp and XenDesktop products. And this also applies to both ShareFile as well as XenMobile.
- They use a unique, but very simple updating and testing mechanism for this, which unfortunately is still under NDA at the time of writing.
- Although when using the life cycle management service, you will still need to maintain and manage your VDAs, StoreFront and NetScalers to some extent, it will make life a lot easier. Take it for a test-drive.
- Resource Locations include: on-premises / your own datacentres, Azure, AWS and/or the Citrix CloudPlatform, and more will follow I'm sure.
- Ongoing management and monitoring are done from the CWC consoles; they have the exact same look and feel as the on-premises Studio and Director consoles.

7537978R00295

Printed in Germany
by Amazon Distribution
GmbH, Leipzig